The Wilmington & Raleigh
Rail Road Company, 1833–1854

The Wilmington & Raleigh Rail Road Company, 1833–1854

James C. Burke

McFarland & Company, Inc., Publishers
Jefferson, North Carolina, and London

Unless otherwise stated the photographs and maps are by the author.

Library of Congress Cataloguing-in-Publication Data

Burke, James C., 1958–
 The Wilmington & Raleigh Rail Road Company, 1833–1854 / James C. Burke.
  p.   cm.
 Includes bibliographical references and index.

 ISBN 978-0-7864-6505-7
 softcover : 50# alkaline paper ∞

 1. Wilmington and Raleigh Rail Road Company—History—19th century. 2. Railroads—North Carolina—History—19th century. 3. North Carolina—Economic conditions—19th century. I. Title.
 HE2791.W7523B87   2011
 385.09756'09034—dc23   2011026228

British Library cataloguing data are available

© 2011 James C. Burke. All rights reserved

No part of this book may be reproduced or transmitted in any form or by any means, electronic or mechanical, including photocopying or recording, or by any information storage and retrieval system, without permission in writing from the publisher.

On the cover: *inset* the locomotive *S.D. Wallace* (New Hanover Public Library, Robert M. Fales Collection); background © 2011 Shutterstock

Manufactured in the United States of America

McFarland & Company, Inc., Publishers
 Box 611, Jefferson, North Carolina 28640
  www.mcfarlandpub.com

In memory of
Anne Rhodes Burke

Acknowledgments

The section of Chapter IV concerned with railroad iron was originally published under the title "British Iron on American Railroad" in the Spring–Summer 2008 issue of *Railroad History,* the journal of the Railway and Locomotive Historical Society, and is reprinted through their permission. Portions of Chapter III previously appeared as "The Journal of Frances Anne Kemble and the Stagecoach Line of the Wilmington and Raleigh Rail Road — Enfield to Stantonsburg" published in Volume 13 of *The North Carolina Geographer,* and are reprinted through their permission. Archival maps and photographs in this work were provided courtesy of the New Hanover Public Library, Robert M. Fales Collection.

During the preparation of the manuscript, I received valuable feedback and suggestions from Donna Kelly of the Historic Publications Section of the North Carolina Office of Archives and History. I am grateful for the help that I received from Debra J. Justin and Almira Johnson in deciphering the handwriting of Charles F. Osborne, president of the Petersburg Rail Road Company, in his letters to Edward B. Dudley, president of the Wilmington & Raleigh Rail Road Company. Beverly Tetterton and Joseph Sheppard of the New Hanover Public Library provided copies of useful maps, and most of the stockholder reports of the Wilmington & Weldon Rail Road Company referenced in this study. Mark Koenig and the staff of the Wilmington Railroad Museum provided access to their archives and collection of artifacts. Through their assistance, I gained insight into the early railroad technology and the day-to-day operation of the Wilmington & Raleigh Rail Road. I appreciate the assistance of Traci Thompson of the Braswell Library, Elaine Sandberg of the South Carolina State Library, Molley French of the Charleston County Public Library, Rhonda Koenig of the Wayne County Public Library, and the staff of the Richmond Public Library.

F. Donald Hickman applied his skills to the grueling task of proofing multiple drafts of this work, along with offering valuable editorial criticism, encouragement, and sound advice in dealing with the less pleasant moments of this endeavor. I appreciate his tireless work, often proofing different versions of the same chapter many times over. Dr. Cyn Johnson assisted me with field study since the early days of the project.

I would like to express my thanks to Dr. Maureen Basedow for suggesting the Wilmington & Raleigh Rail Road as a research topic when I was a graduate student at the University of North Carolina at Wilmington in 2000, and the late Dr. John L. Zintsmaster for foreseeing the potential for continued research on the early railroads of North Carolina. At the University of North Carolina at Greensboro, Dr. Jeffery Patton served as chairman of my dissertation committee, and I greatly appreciate the many enlightening four-hour meetings he set aside to discuss the many drafts of my work, and provide sound advice from the preparation of my research design to the completion of the dissertation. Dr. Elizabeth Nelson devoted a considerable portion of her time to reviewing the maps in my dissertation and offering her editorial skills to its final preparation. Dr. Zhi-Jun Liu encouraged me to apply GIS programming and spatial analysis to some of the geographic problems the research presented. Dr. Phillip Royall encouraged me to expand my inquiry into the realm of physical geography, a direction that had a profound influence upon the changing of my original research design. The late Dr. W. Frank Ainsley of the Earth Sciences department at the University of North Carolina at Wilmington maintained an unflagging interest in my research from the beginning and encouraged me to enter the field of geography. He was the epitome of the great teacher, not only learned, but inspiring and committed to the advancement of knowledge. I was honored that he chose to serve on my dissertation committee.

I feel fortunate to have had the benefit of support and encouragement from friends and family during the preparing of the book manuscript, particularly John E. Best, Edmund E. Burke, Ernesto Ferreri, Victor Galloway, F. Donald Hickman, Dr. Cyn Johnson, and Clyde Rollins Jr.

Table of Contents

Acknowledgments vii

Preface 1

Introduction 5

    I. Weldon, Tollgate of North Carolina 11

    II. Early Plans for Railroads in North Carolina 32

    III. The Building of a Railroad 60

    IV. The Technology: Its Origins and History 79

    V. Conflict and Crisis 109

    VI. Rail Transportation and Economic Growth 141

Appendix A: The Railroad Land in Wilmington 169

Appendix B: The Depot Site at Wilmington 178

Chapter Notes 189

Bibliography 209

Index 217

Preface

The impetus for assembling this work was the need to establish the significance of the Wilmington & Raleigh Rail Road within the context of American railroad history and the role civil engineering played in it. Only a few scholarly works exist that address the subject, and they do so merely in passing: concentrating mainly on the political aspects and notable individuals, these sources provide little more than an overview of the company and its operations. As a result, the practitioners of applied history — architectural historians, preservationists, archaeologists, geographers, and historical economists — must immerse themselves in extensive archival research to accomplish the simplest task, say to determine the period of construction, to date an artifact and place it within a context, or to interpret the spatial patterns of economic development in the antebellum railroad corridor. Most important to all these tasks is answering the question, "What makes this significant?"

In any inquiry, historic or scientific, to establish the significance of your findings is extremely difficult, especially if the object of the inquiry is ill-defined and fragmentary. Further, if the very nature of the object is poorly understood by most people, as is the case with practically everything related to early railroad technology, many readers can draw erroneous conclusions from facts about the objects that are well documented. For this reason, the scope of this work is limited to the history of the corporation known as the Wilmington & Raleigh Rail Road Company, including details concerning its formation, construction, operation, and economic impact.

This is the appropriate starting point for establishing significance. The period covered in this work includes the events leading up to incorporation in 1833, to the years immediately following the change of the corporate name to the Wilmington & Weldon Railroad Company in 1855: the formative period of a railroad that would dominate the economic history of eastern North Carolina for a hundred years to follow. The history of the Wilmington & Weldon Railroad is not that of a different corporate entity, but the era in which it existed places it within the context of a different North Carolina. For this reason, it should be addressed separately in another work.

There are two overarching themes to this history of the Wilmington & Raleigh Rail Road Company: countering the disruptive interference of the railroads of Virginia and conflicting sectional agendas; and weathering a daunting array of setbacks during the financially unstable era of the 1840s. Among the accomplishments of the company before the change of its corporate name in 1855 was the rebuilding of the entire railroad in heavy iron. With connections to the Wilmington & Manchester Railroad and the North Carolina Railroad accomplished in the early 1850s, the Wilmington & Raleigh became profitable and it fostered economic growth in eastern North Carolina.

The significance of the Wilmington & Raleigh Rail Road rests on three concepts that are responsible for its success: it was a well-planned and remarkable accomplishment of civil engineering, testing the limits of what could be accomplished with early railroad technology; the organization and financing of the railroad was structured around an arrangement that would later be termed a "public-private partnership"; and with the use of a company-owned steamboat packet making scheduled connections between Wilmington and Charleston, and its use of a stagecoach line during construction, the Wilmington & Raleigh Rail Road provides an early successful example of multimodal transportation.

At the time of its completion in 1840, it was the longest railroad in the world and the most ambitious internal improvements project ever undertaken in the state of North Carolina. It would prove to be a test of the transportation policy for state government, and lead to refinements when the state took on more expansive works such as the North Carolina Railroad.

The author chose to organize this volume into six topics including a narrative that describes how the plan to build a railroad from Wilmington to Weldon evolved; a chapter devoted to early internal improvements in Virginia and North Carolina that influenced the course of railroad development in both states; a chapter devoted to the building of the railroad and its components, railroad, steamboats, and stagecoach line; a chapter that describes the technology and its origins with specific references to records of the company; a chapter that explains the causes of the financial condition of the company during the 1840s, and the conflict between two Virginia railroads that threatened the interests of the Wilmington & Raleigh; and an analysis of the data derived from period documents that illustrates the patterns of transportation and economic development occurring in the rail corridor between 1840 and 1860. The introduction includes an overview of the history of the Wilmington & Raleigh Rail Road. Two appendices are included on the special topics of the landholdings and facilities of the railroad at Wilmington.

Introduction

The Wilmington & Raleigh Rail Road was unique in that the company provided continuous transportation from the town of Weldon on the Roanoke River to Wilmington by railroad and thence to Charleston, South Carolina, by steamboat from 1837 through 1854. Originally intended to connect the port of Wilmington to Raleigh, its route was changed in 1835 to create a connection between Wilmington and Weldon. Service began while the railroad was under construction with a company that owned a stagecoach line with a route that was adjusted as construction advanced on the southern and northern divisions of the line. Thus, it was multimodal in concept. In 1838, the railroad was awarded the contract to take the "Southern Great Mail" by the Post Office Department over a long established interior stage route, thus validating this railroad as the most direct means to access the Deep South through North Carolina.[1] When completed in 1840, at 161½ miles, it was the longest railroad in the world. By the standards of the day, the construction of this railroad constituted an achievement in civil engineering; in the state of North Carolina, it amounted to an undertaking of visionary scale that was at once both exhilarating and terrifying, risking the fortunes of individuals and the credit of the state to a degree that would have not been contemplated a few years earlier. It was born as a suggestion, nurtured in an atmosphere of economic and political conflict, and it matured under the weight of overwhelming adversity.

Hitherto, this *tour de force* of organization, finance, and political will has not received the attention it deserves. As a result, to answer any questions concerning its significance within the context of American railroad history has been difficult. Further, to fathom the ultimate impact it had on subsequent railroad development in North Carolina without being fully knowledgeable of its complex origins was nearly impossible. Unfortunately, the body of scholarly work on this railroad is limited, and to a great extent, dated and lacking in detail. By contrast, the most commonly cited local histories are anecdotal, regionally chauvinistic, and often poorly documented in primary sources.[2] As a result, the importance of the Wilmington & Raleigh Rail Road within the evolving network of rail corridors on the Atlantic seaboard could not be addressed adequately, and a multitude of overlapping historical connections reaching beyond North Carolina were never contemplated.

The purpose of this study is to present a historical narrative of the Wilmington & Raleigh Rail Road progressing chronologically from the first mention of building a railroad in North Carolina during the 1820s to the establishment of the company in its final phase of development as the Wilmington & Weldon Railroad prior to the Civil War in 1855; and to follow with a detailed examination of all the principal topics that aid the interpretation of the project.[3]

Clearly, this railroad did not come into existence within the framework of well crafted public policy; the historical record gives testimony that policy lagged behind the general willingness to embrace this promising, yet still experimental, technology. At the federal level, legislation proposed early in the century that would support the development of a national system of roads and canals met with opposition from the states. However, technical support from the United States Engineers was readily accepted for internal improvement projects.

In North Carolina, early efforts to devise a state system of internal improvements produced limited results. The prevailing political position asserted the notion that works of internal improvements were best executed by private corporations, and the state could lend its support by investing in the stock of these companies.[4] In practice, this policy encouraged small scale projects of regional interest, some of which proved to be poorly executed or wasteful. For example, the commonwealth of Virginia took a similar approach but backed it with a two-fifths investment on the part of the state to the companies. After failed attempts to secure private capital for early large scale railroad projects, internal improvements conventions attended by delegates representing many counties throughout North Carolina met twice at Raleigh in 1833. The memorial to the General Assembly recommended the two-fifths investment policy. It was finally adopted in 1837.[5] The Wilmington & Raleigh Rail Road was the only railroad of that period selected for the state's investment that would be built. While it is doubtful that railroad development in North Carolina and Virginia would have progressed without state investment, the practice contributed to regional ambitions to monopolize trade at the expense of creating a transportation network that would benefit the citizens of those states across regions, and facilitate interstate communication and commerce as well.

Only after the most egregious affronts to the integrity of the system of railroads had been committed in the early 1840s did the two states intervene on behalf of the right of the traveling public. Escalating trade competition between the Virginia commercial centers of Petersburg and Norfolk influenced railroad planning in North Carolina. A sequence of navigational improvements on the Roanoke River caused the regional shares of agricultural resources from the vast river basin to be shifted between these Virginia markets unevenly, thus triggering railroad building as a countermeasure. The main purpose behind this was intercepting river commerce — a type of economic "stream piracy." This is the overarching theme of the early years of the Wilmington & Raleigh Rail Road.

As the Wilmington & Raleigh emerged from its uncertain beginnings and weathered the national economic crisis that followed the Panic of 1837, the railroad faced a more tangible threat: the strap-iron wooden rails of its original construction were deteriorating. The railroad needed to be rebuilt with heavy T-iron. As a result, the company had to take out a mortgage to purchase the new iron from England, and it called upon the shareholders to help pay the duties. However, by the early 1850s the fortunes of the company began to improve. In 1854, the Wilmington & Manchester Railroad established a rail connection to South Carolina, replacing the steamboat line; and the North Carolina Railroad intersected the Wilmington & Raleigh at Goldsboro. The General Assembly of North Carolina ratified an act that allowed the Wilmington & Raleigh Rail Road Company to change its corporate name to the Wilmington & Weldon Railroad Company in 1855. Governor Edward B. Dudley, the first president of the railroad and its most steadfast champion, died on October 30, 1855, a little more than a week before the annual meeting of the stockholders acting for the first time under their new corporate name.

The history of the Wilmington & Raleigh Rail Road ended where the Wilmington & Weldon Railroad began, not merely because of the change of its name or the death of Gov. Dudley. The age of the Whig governors of North Carolina ended in 1851. William Shepperd Ashe, the "fire eating" Democratic congressman that would eventually assume a position managing transportation for the Confederacy early in the Civil War, became president of the railroad. The old leadership of the company during the years of struggle, such as the man Ashe replaced, Alexander MacRae, had played their roles, and receded into the background.

Overview

Routes are spatial manifestations, and properly rest within the realm of geographic inquiry; and their origins can be connected to specific political and socioeconomic problems. Once established, a useful route tends to remain a fixture on the landscape long after the original set of problems that brought it into existence are resolved. Early planning decisions therefore continue to have lasting geopolitical consequences. The primary trunk lines of the present-day rail network in North Carolina, and the major highways that parallel these corridors, trace the path of railroads planned and or commenced, or both, during the Jacksonian Era — a period of political and economic upheaval. Conceived at a time when railroad technology was primitive and no example of length existed anywhere, two substantial railroads were completed in North Carolina by 1840 — the Raleigh & Gaston Rail Road and the Wilmington & Raleigh Rail Road. Another great railroad conceived in the late 1820s, the Central Rail Road, would be completed as the North Carolina Railroad before the 1850s. A review of the history of internal improvements in North Carolina exposes several questions about the routes selected for these railroads. What was the cause of the paradigm shift from canal projects to railroads? Who proposed the early railroad routes, and how were these routes different? Why were the earliest railroads in North Carolina built to obscure places on the Roanoke River rather than between the state's commercial towns or connecting with those in South Carolina? A simple summary of events does not explain the larger context in which railroad development advanced in North Carolina or anywhere else.

Railroad planning began in North Carolina in the 1820s with two concepts: experimental railroads of short length, such as those used by English collieries at the time, had been recommended for special projects and local transportation problems; and vast visionary plans such as the Central Rail Road that would stretch from the coast to the mountains. The experimental railroads were the progenitors of the earliest railroads that were built. Even before the experimental Fayetteville Rail Road was built, promoters were recommending that it be extended first to the Yadkin River, and then to Morganton. Likewise, promoters in Raleigh recommended that the experimental railroad used in rebuilding the State House be extended towards Waynesborough and then to New Bern, to Wilmington, or to both places.

The Wilmington & Raleigh Rail Road was the offshoot of this idea.

The delegates to the Internal Improvements Conventions of 1833 recommended to the General Assembly of North Carolina a north-to-south railroad traversing the state from the Roanoke River to the South Carolina line and an east-to-west railroad from Beaufort, North Carolina, to the Tennessee line. These railroad systems could be any combination of railroads, canals, and river routes. In all the plans, pragmatic or grand, obviously none of the promoters had a full understanding of the nature of railroads. They were working with a limited body of information derived from the railroads that already existed, none of which formed part of a true network, and grafted this to what they were familiar with, namely canals and turnpikes.

The Wilmington & Raleigh Rail Road belongs to the first generation of railroads, not only in America, but in the world. It was not merely an application of railroad technology as a substitute for building a canal or turnpike to a river landing as exemplified by the Fayetteville Rail Road, the Petersburg Rail Road, or the Portsmouth & Roanoke Rail Road. Rather, it was a successful effort to establish a transportation corridor through one state and to another. This is the concept the promoters of the Raleigh & Gaston and Raleigh & Columbia aspired to achieve. Yet it failed despite the most encouraging support of the experts that touted the superior advantages of the "Metropolitan Route." That the financial downturn of the late 1830s doomed this enterprise is obvious.

However, the awarding of the contract for the "Southern Great Mail" to the Wilmington & Raleigh in 1838 can be taken as an indication that the corridor had already been established. The steamboat line of the Wilmington & Raleigh completed the route to Charleston; there transportation south could continue on the Charleston & Hamburg Rail Road. The bridge forming a connection north already existed, and the only section of railroad that needed to be built was that between Weldon and Wilmington. After the completion of the Raleigh & Gaston in 1840, there remained a considerable distance of rails to be put down before realizing the goal of connecting to Columbia, South Carolina.

As the antebellum period drew to a close, the existence of the Wilmington & Raleigh Rail Road corridor drove the economy of eastern North Carolina. It induced a qualitative change in the region, not only in galvanizing its political position, but also in binding it to a larger political economy and material culture. The agriculture of the region, opened to new markets, expanded beyond the subsistence crops to cotton, and an increased need for slave labor followed. After the old order was swept aside by the Civil War, the corridor endured to exercise its influence upon the state in ways unimagined by its creators.

Chapter I

Weldon, Tollgate of North Carolina

The charter of the Wilmington & Raleigh Rail Road Company was amended in 1835 to allow the company to change the route of the railroad: rather than connecting towns of Wilmington and Raleigh, the route would begin at the port of Wilmington and end at Weldon on the Roanoke River. In the same year, the Raleigh & Gaston Rail Road Company was incorporated to construct a railroad that would connect Raleigh to the Roanoke River a few miles west of Weldon. Both railroads were completed in 1840. The Petersburg Rail Road was built to Blakeley on the Roanoke River opposite Weldon in 1833, and the Portsmouth & Roanoke Rail Road to the Weldon Toll Bridge in 1837. In the history of early railroad development in North Carolina and Virginia, Weldon is the *omphalos;* the idea of building a railroad to connect the coast with the interior was deferred while every exertion was directed towards a meager slice of territory in North Carolina on the Roanoke in Halifax and Northampton counties.

In the 1836 issue of Edmund Ruffin's *Farmers' Register,* the letter writer P.Q. asks, "What magic is there in the name of Weldon, that it should be constituted the toll-gate of North Carolina?" This supporter of the Raleigh & Gaston Rail Road was of the opinion that the citizens of Wilmington would do better to build their railroad to Raleigh rather than to Halifax. The Raleigh & Gaston would intercept all river trade from the interior; the Wilmington & Raleigh Rail Road, when the competing route was established, was bound to fail.[1]

He was wrong. Four railroads connected at Weldon by the end of the antebellum period, including the Raleigh & Gaston. It was the Raleigh & Gaston that failed, unable to pay its debts; the state of North Carolina took possession of it, reorganizing it under a new charter in 1850. While the Wilmington & Raleigh experienced hard times early in its history, it would survive and eventually prosper in the years before the Civil War. Weldon did indeed prove to be the tollgate of North Carolina, as the early trunk lines connecting north and south evolved on the eastern seaboard. If we are to understand the origins of the Wilmington & Raleigh Rail Road, the reasons for its change in route, the atmosphere of conflict in which it came into being, and the reasons why it survived the protracted national financial crisis that began in the late 1830s, this inquiry must begin with an understanding of the logistical factors that shaped Weldon into this "toll-gate."

First, the geographic significance of this obscure town on the Roanoke River is intimately linked to the earlier internal improvements in North Carolina and Virginia. Its history as an attractor of commercial interest dates back to the construction of the Roanoke Canal: downstream of the Great Falls of the Roanoke at the lower entrance of the canal, its location was both ideal for the exploitation of the vast agricultural trade of the upper Roanoke Basin and for its navigability by the commercial vessels of the lower basin. Lacking adequate systems of roads, river transportation of produce to market was the most practical option for the farmers in the interior of North Carolina and other mid–Atlantic states. In turn, any place along these rivers that offered a convenient landing to break bulk, afford access to the main roads leading to commercial centers, and that was situated at the head of navigation would exercise an influence on route selection during the early period of railroad construction.

Second, the history of Weldon as a place of commercial interest can be traced back to a specific natural event that altered the economic balance between North Carolina and Virginia, and proved to be a central element in the first state program of internal improvements undertaken in North Carolina. Along with navigational improvements on the state's rivers, including a system of canals to bypass the falls inhibiting navigation from the interior to the coast, the Board of Public Improvements of North Carolina advanced a plan to reopen Roanoke Inlet in the late 1810s. The inlet had closed completely during the mid–1790s, and thus deprived the ports of Albemarle Sound of a convenient outlet to the ocean. With the opening of the Dismal Swamp Canal in 1805, the trade of the lower Roanoke River Basin entering Albemarle was diverted to the port of Norfolk. Although plans were prepared and contemplated, undertakings received considerable attention throughout the antebellum period, and numerous surveys were done by civil engineers in the employment of North Carolina and the

United States, nothing of consequence was achieved towards reopening the inlet; and with the potential of railroads having been realized by the 1850s, reopening Roanoke Inlet became less important.

The logistical significance of the Roanoke Canal was firmly established by the 1830s. It had less to do with creating an appropriate rail corridor through North Carolina than with prior plans of internal improvements in both Virginia and North Carolina concerned with inland navigation, the physical geography of the state, the way the political boundary divided the Roanoke River Basin between Virginia and North Carolina, and competing sectional interests in both states. The canal was the place to intersect river commerce on the Roanoke.

There remained the question of where to bridge the Roanoke River, above the canal at Gaston or below it at Weldon. The Petersburg Rail Road had constructed a branch line, the Greensville & Roanoke Rail Road, to the Roanoke opposite the western entrance to the canal in anticipation of connecting south through Raleigh and Columbia. The main line of the railroad terminated opposite the eastern end of the canal at Blakeley. However, the Portsmouth & Roanoke Rail Road was nearing completion, and would cross the river by way of the Weldon Toll Bridge. That railroad anticipated connections to Halifax and eventually Wilmington. The primacy of one crossing of the Roanoke, Gaston or Weldon, would depend upon the success of projected plans to establish a rail connection through North Carolina to South Carolina.

Edmund Ruffin's *Farmers' Register* became the arena for a debate on this topic when two writers that identified themselves only as P.Q., mentioned above, and G.L.C. began a discussion of railroad routes in February 1836. Their literary joust, replete with classical references, antiquated wit, and chivalrous concessions, is both amusing and somewhat annoying to the current reader; yet, when all the gentlemanly conceit is set aside, the letters detail the merits and defects of the planned rail routes that were being discussed in North Carolina. Writer P.Q. signs his letters from Raleigh, and favors the Raleigh to Gaston route as well as its extension to the Pee Dee and beyond. G.L.C., signing his initial letter from Camden, South Carolina, prefers a route from Weldon to Waynesborough, and defends the Wilmington to Halifax route. G.L.C. begins the contest with a critique that expresses regret that the Petersburg Rail Road had constructed two branch lines to the Roanoke rather than applying the funds to building a railroad from Raleigh to Fayetteville. The writer sees Petersburg's redundant routes to the Roanoke as a waste. He is critical of the opinions of writer "Raleigh" in the *Raleigh Register* who had proclaimed that the Raleigh & Gaston would attract the produce of the western portion of the state, while the east would continue to ship produce from its coast.[2] P.Q. responds from Raleigh with an accusation that his rival is trying to envision the whole system of internal improvements for much of the Union without full consideration of the landscapes of these different states, or desires of communities that have long supported a "favorite scheme." He asserts that "every rail road is an invention, so far that one was never tried before, under the same circumstance," and he does not believe the Wilmington to Halifax route would work. In general, he believes the state should carefully consider when granting charters whether a new railroad would weaken one that already existed. He is also sure that the west would support the Raleigh & Gaston, and that Wilmington would have been better off had they built their railroad to Raleigh.[3]

In his response, writer G.L.C. expresses his doubts about the effectiveness of legislatures to manage railroads and notes that the North Carolina Legislature refused to grant funds to build the experimental railroad to Swift Creek that was recommended by Hamilton Fulton. He does not think legislatures should be entrusted with the authority to protect railroads from competition, and he lectures P.Q. on "odious" monopolies. He also refers to a report by Lt. Col. S.H. Long of the United States Topographical Engineers entitled "Railroads — Atlantic to the Mississippi" that supported a Darlington to Halifax route. The report had been transmitted by Lewis Cass, the Secretary of War.[4] The text of this document describes a central trunk line.

> Among the numerous opportunities presented for connecting the contemplated railroad with important points on the Atlantic seaboard, by means of lateral branches, there is one of no less moment than that relating to the main stem, as already described. We allude to a route which is to be regarded as a part or prolongation of the main road itself rather than a branch leading from it, and which is as follows: Commencing at the crossing of the Oconee at the point designated, the route may be extended in a northeasterly direction, through the broad and flat diluvial region bordering upon the Atlantic coast of Georgia, South Carolina, North Carolina, and Virginia, and passing the vicinity of Swainsborough, in Georgia; Barnwell, Sumterville, Darlington, Harleesville, South Carolina; Fayetteville, Waynesborough, Tarboro,' and Halifax, North Carolina; and then by the Portsmouth and Roanoke railroad, to Norfolk, in Virginia, or by the Petersburg railroad to Richmond, and thence, by the Richmond and Fredericksburg railroad, to Fredericksburg; and thence, by some route situated more or less remote from the Potomac river, passing perhaps through Falmouth and Stafford, and in rear of Dumfries and Alexandria, in a direction to meet the Washington and Baltimore railroad at Washington City.[5]

P.Q. responds again on 25 May 1836. After lengthy formalities, he asserts that the Halifax to Fayetteville via Waynesborough route would not secure travel unless it were to be connected through Raleigh; and if both the other coastal route and in inland route from Raleigh south were completed, the Raleigh route would prove superior. He supposes, since the Raleigh & Gaston Rail Road was on its way to being realized, that Col. Long's opinion could be adapted to the new situation; and disagrees that Weldon should be the only place on the Roanoke to terminate a railroad from Raleigh.

The last letter written by G.L.C. on the subject appears in the October 1836 issue of the *Farmers' Register*. He reiterates his support for the Halifax to Darlington line, and adds that it could be constructed more cheaply than the interior route. Also, he pointed out the military advantages of this route. He briefly mentions the dangers of monopolies and joint stock companies, and recommends a two-fifths investment on the part of the federal government in exchange for the mails and the transport of troops. The editor of the *Farmers' Register* recommended in a closing note that should P.Q. and G.L.C. wish to continue their discussion they should begin a new series that sets forth their view on the subject of the two important routes,[6] but the letters ended at this point.

The writers are correct in assuming that a rail connection through North Carolina would have to cross near the Roanoke Canal. The canal not only constituted a division between the upper and lower basin, it also was built across the physiographic boundary between the Piedmont and Coastal Plain. The Petersburg Rail Road, with its branch line, the Greensville & Roanoke Rail Road, presented the opportunity for a crossing of the Roanoke above and below the canal: both opportunities led to Petersburg.

Weldon would assume the advantage when the Portsmouth & Roanoke Rail Road was completed in 1837, thus offering access to southeastern Virginia. From the Roanoke northward, destiny depended upon where the river would be bridged first. As for proposed railroads south of the Roanoke, the writers could place their rulers upon the maps and run lines from the fixed points where the Virginia railroads terminated and create equally valid, in a theoretical sense, corridors through the Piedmont or Coastal Plain on North Carolina to corresponding towns in South Carolina, but there was not a railroad being built northward from these places to establish the fixed point(s), merely Col. Long's idea of a rail corridor. The determining factor was the entirety of internal improvements that had taken place in southern Virginia up to the building of its railroads.

The first significant public works project in Virginia, the Dismal Swamp

Canal, would affect the economy of North Carolina and influence the development of the state's first plans for a system of internal improvements. It would also spark the trade competition between the commercial centers of southern Virginia. The canal connected the Elizabeth River at Portsmouth, Virginia, to the Pasquotank River in Camden County, North Carolina. Completed in 1805 and subsequently improved to handle more traffic, it diverted the commerce from northeastern North Carolina to Norfolk. The federal government required an increase in depth to facilitate the passage of larger craft from the North Carolina sounds.

This change in the Dismal Swamp Canal had a twofold impact. Opposition to federal funding by central Virginia thwarted the subscription

This photograph of the Dismal Swamp Canal was taken in 2006 at Mile 28 near the North Carolina-Virginia line. This great work of civil engineering, completed in 1805, allowed the commercial towns of southeastern Virginia to access navigation on the lower Roanoke River by way of Albemarle Sound. Early advocates of internal improvements in North Carolina, most notably Judge Archibald D. Murphey, realized that the canal promoted the transport of agricultural output of the lower Roanoke from North Carolina to the Virginia market.

to the company stock by the United States, so there would be several lotteries held to aid the canal. Notices for the Virginia State Lottery (Fifth Class — For the benefit of the Dismal Swamp Canal Co.) appear in North Carolina newspapers. Congress eventually subscribed to shares in the company stock[7]; and the new depth of the canal eventually made it possible to ship produce from the upper Roanoke Valley via the Roanoke Canal to Portsmouth and Norfolk, thus contributing to a trade imbalance between Petersburg and the Hampton Roads region.[8] The lack of a national plan for internal improvements[9] placed the full burden of financing state projects on citizens that resisted taxation for improvements that would benefit another region of the state. The jealousy between towns and regions in North Carolina cannot be overstated. This is the central theme of early railroad development in North Carolina. Different sections of the state, with their respective commercial towns, would align their interests with commercial centers in Virginia.

In Virginia, corporations were set up to receive the investment of both private shareholders and the state. By 1838, Virginia had amassed $6,662,180 in debt for its support of canals, railroads, turnpikes, and miscellaneous improvements. It had created a fund for internal improvement and the Board of Public Works, in 1816, to administer it. The board could authorize the subscription on the part of the commonwealth to two-fifths of stock of companies engaged in improvement projects when private investors subscribed to three-fifths of the stock. The investors had to pay for at least one-fifth of the stock subscriptions. The state deemed this method appropriate for small scale projects; but great works, such as navigation improvements to the James River by the James River Company, were beyond the means of private capital. The commonwealth bought up interests in the company and contracted its officials to carry through the work.

By 1823, the management of the company was transferred to state officials. This pattern continued with other large-scale canal and turnpike projects, and the railroad companies received aid in the form of state funded stock subscription. Virginia borrowed funds on the credit of the state. By 1837, Virginia had incurred debts of $1,324,500 for the James River Company and $780,000 for the James River & Kanawha Company. Examples of state debts for several projects include $250,000 to the Portsmouth & Roanoke Railroad Company, $206,800 to the Richmond, Fredericksburg & Potomac Railroad Company, and $80,000 to the Petersburg Railroad Company. The Winchester & Potomac Railroad Company received $120,000 in aid from the state. The remaining companies that the state aided received amounts below $64,200.[10]

Judge Archibald Murphey, a visionary North Carolina state senator, labored to create the state's first policy on internal improvements. In 1815, he chaired a committee on inland navigation. The *Report of the Committee on Inland Navigation* concluded that river improvements would lead to the growth of commercial towns on the state's major rivers. His report to the legislature of the following year notes that trade from the Roanoke was entering the Norfolk market via Albemarle Sound, thus drawing off potential revenue.[11] The *Memoir on the Internal Improvements Contemplated by the Legislature of North Carolina and on the Resources and Finances of the State* was a comprehensive plan of improvements that would transform the state's rivers into a transportation network. It recommended a system of canals to bypass the falls on the major rivers and proposed a connection between at least two of them.[12]

The state made a step forward towards this goal when it hired its first professional civil engineer. Hamilton Fulton arrived in North Carolina to begin his employment in 1819. Fulton examined the work of the Roanoke Navigation Company at the Great Falls, and noticed problems with the work on the Roanoke Canal; and in the course of developing plans for similar works, he consulted the observations of civil engineer and architect Benjamin H. Latrobe on the physical geography of coastal states. In the area of commerce, he noted that Franklin, Granville, Warren, and Halifax counties in North Carolina sent tobacco and wheat by wagon to the Virginia markets, likely destined for the Petersburg market.[13]

The *Annual Report of the Board of Public Improvements* for 1820 included examinations of the progress of the Clubfoot and Harlowe Creek Canal, the Fayetteville Canal, a joint report on the Roanoke Canal by the state engineer for Virginia, Thomas Moore, and Hamilton Fulton, and Mr. Fulton's report on the practicality of reopening Roanoke Inlet. There are also reports concerning other projects on coastal navigation, the Cape Fear, the Broad, the Yadkin and the Catawba rivers.[14] The following year, *The Annual Report of the Board of Public Improvements* for 1821 included a report by the United States engineers on the practicality of reopening Roanoke Inlet, as well as Mr. Fulton's reports on the progress of the Roanoke Canal — including his plans for the aqueduct over Chockoyotte Creek. He also mentions the possible useful application of a timber railroad in connection with improvements on the Neuse River. His report on the Clubfoot and Harlowe Canal indicates that the design for a lock constructed for that canal was defective. This document also contains a report from Denison Olmsted, professor of chemistry and mineralogy at the University of North Carolina, on the mineral resources of the state.

While much of Mr. Fulton's report is fascinating, the 1821 *Annual Report* is significant because it defines the objects of a system for internal improvements in North Carolina: to provide all the citizens of the state with a way of getting the "productions of their industry" to market; and to "fix that market within our own limits." The suggested means of paying for this system involved the state taking out a loan of $500,000 at an annual rate not exceeding six per cent, and the Treasurer issuing certificates of stock. The state would subscribe to $225,000 in shares of the canal and navigation companies.[15] Murphey's plan for internal improvements received the attention of the national press for its comprehensive approach and scope.[16]

Very little came of these plans; that they established a dialogue on internal improvement policy, however, is significant. Hamilton Fulton's plan to reopen Roanoke Inlet is particularly interesting since access to the

The Clubfoot & Harlowe Creek Canal is in Craven and Carteret counties and can be accessed from NC 101. It connects the Neuse River with the Newport River. Its promoters hoped to improve commerce by creating a channel between New Bern and Beaufort.

oceans would prevent all the trade on the lower Roanoke from entering Virginia via the Dismal Swamp Canal. The port towns of Albemarle Sound had enjoyed access to the Atlantic via Roanoke Inlet during colonial times; however the inlet closed in the mid–1790s. Reopening the inlet became an important element of North Carolina's internal improvement policy during the antebellum period. Several plans recommended by engineers for the state and the United States Topographical Bureau received consideration, but the project never advanced far beyond the planning stage.[17] The great disappointment of public works undertaken in North Carolina during the nineteenth century was the Clubfoot and Harlowe Creek Canal. The project conceived before the Revolution and finally completed in 1827 never proved very useful. Its purpose was to facilitate navigation between the Neuse River and Beaufort harbor. The canal had consumed tens of thousands of dollars of public funds over many decades; yet, when opened the tolls were merely a fraction of the investment required to build it, and revenue continued to diminish year after year. The anticipated traffic on the canal never materialized, and the canal fell into disrepair. The state was unable to sell the canal until 1872.[18] The first attempt at a state system of internal improvements was underfunded and mismanaged. Its defects included the lack of engineering expertise to oversee the various projects, the absence of a sufficient labor force, and a waste of funds.[19] Some of the more profound defects were intrinsic and would have an impact on the development of railroads.

There was a widely held belief that private corporations could carry through internal improvement projects more effectively; and the power block of the eastern counties opposed plans that they perceived to suggest taxation for improvements that would benefit the west at their expense. There were those that shared the ideology of North Carolina's veteran United States senator and unshakeable conservative, Nathaniel Macon, who was opposed to soliciting aid from the general government for internal improvements. He also believed that the state had little commercial potential, and tax revenues would be better applied to education.[20] Yet, when all factors are considered, it appears that Archibald Murphey's plan for a state system was beneficial, insomuch as it focused attention towards the need for transportation policy in North Carolina, and identified the causes of the degradation of its economy. The Roanoke Canal, constructed by the Roanoke Navigation Company and jointly supported by North Carolina and Virginia, was the principal work completed during this period; and, as it came into operation, its existence would exert attraction for the early railroads built in both states.

The remains of the upper locks of the Roanoke Canal are at the Roanoke Canal Museum in Roanoke Rapids, North Carolina. The narrow width of the locks was designed for the bateau, a shallow-draft boat of about eight feet in beam. The bateau could carry ten to twelve hogsheads.

The Roanoke River crosses the political boundary between North Carolina and Virginia. Through its tributaries, the Staunton and Dan, its basin extends deeply into the interior of both states. The river courses southward through the coastal plan North Carolina, and empties into Albemarle Sound. In 1663, the Lord Proprietors had set the boundary between Virginia and Carolina at 36 degrees north. In 1728, the line was surveyed to thirty miles east of the Blue Ridge where it has remained since.[21] The earlier line would have placed most of the basin within Virginia. However, for the early railroads, the river served as a *de facto* economic boundary. The Petersburg Company completed their railroad to the north side of the Roanoke in 1833, and the Portsmouth & Roanoke Rail Road followed in 1837. The latter used the toll bridge to carry its trains to Weldon on the south side of the river. Each railroad was an extension of a commercial center in Virginia, and both were competing for the agricultural output throughout the entire basin; thus, the rivalry between Norfolk and Petersburg had its origin in previous internal improvement projects.

The Roanoke Canal was thirty feet wide at the bottom with slopes of one and a half feet to one foot, and three feet deep. The total length at the water's surface was thirty-nine feet and it had a towpath that was ten feet wide.[22] The Clubfoot & Harlowe Creek Canal was four feet deep and fourteen feet wide at its bottom. Its slopes were one and half feet to one foot, and the total width at the surface of the water was twenty-six feet. Its towpath was eight feet wide.[23] The Roanoke Canal extended approximately eight miles, of which a little more than seven miles remain. The stone culverts, massive aqueduct, and locks remain. The upper sections of the canal are dry. The Clubfoot & Harlowe Creek Canal also remains, and water still flows in it. Though slightly larger when completed and now silted to half its original depth, it is apparent to the observer that small shallow-draft bateaux navigated these canals. The Roanoke Navigation Company continued its improvements of the Dan and Staunton rivers after the Roanoke Canal was in operation.[24]

By 1831, the Virginia & North Carolina Transportation Company was operating eight boats of sixty tons burthen between Norfolk and Weldon. The trip took between eight and thirteen days. The monthly average loads on these boats included 400 hogsheads of tobacco, 1,200 barrels of flour, and 800 bales of cotton. The company put two steamboats in service on the lower river for towing boats to Norfolk. The steamboats carried their own loads of freight.[25] In the same year, the State of North Carolina received the sum of $875 as dividends on its 500 shares of stock in the Roanoke Navigation Company.[26]

In 1821, the Board of Public Improvements of North Carolina proposed a plan for borrowing $500,000 on the credit of the state to help pay for transportation improvements. The board recommended that the state invest nearly half of this amount in the stock of the Roanoke Navigation Company, the Yadkin Navigation Company, the Cape Fear Navigation Company, the Tar Navigation Company, the Neuse Navigation Company, the Catawba Navigation Company, and the Clubfoot & Harlowe Creek Canal Company. The remainder was committed to a number of coastal navigation projects and road projects in the western part of the state.

The citizens of the state were averse to paying for improvements with high taxes, so the board recommended that the treasurer of the state issue certificates on the debt payable at six percent interest annually. The board also noted that some projects, such as improving access to the port of Beaufort, have commercial advantages over other projects. They were of the opinion that the jealousy between commercial towns interfered with developing a general plan of internal improvements. Each town supported the projects that would direct commerce to their neighborhood.[27]

The Roanoke Navigation Company proved a successful investment, but it benefited Norfolk more than the other commercial towns in North Carolina and Virginia. As South Carolina and Virginia secured more capital for public works, North Carolina made plans and invested in the stock of the several navigation companies. Weldon, at the lower end of the Roanoke Canal, became the focus of plans for early railroad construction. At the time when Petersburg was contemplating a railroad to the Roanoke, the Roanoke Navigation Company anticipated the transport of 4,800 hogsheads of tobacco, 14,400 barrels of flour, and 9,600 bales of cotton on the Roanoke River annually. They estimated that the actual annual agricultural output of the Roanoke Valley included 15,000 hogsheads of tobacco and 20,000 bales of cotton.[28]

Construction of the Petersburg Rail Road commenced in January of 1831, and by August 1833, the railroad was completed to Blakeley, opposite and a short distance downriver from Weldon. The citizens of Petersburg anticipated an extension of the railroad northward that would connect to the projected railroad between Richmond and Fredricksburg.[29] It seems obvious that the corridor could continue only to Baltimore and Washington; so the idea of a continuous line connecting the metropolitan markets of the Atlantic states was a consideration even as the railroad was completed.

The immediate benefits of connecting to the Roanoke were appearing in the Petersburg market. The editor of the *Norfolk Herald* printed a letter from a friend in Petersburg dated August 22, 1833, that an inclined plane was being constructed from Blakeley down to the Roanoke. He witnessed sacks of wheat and corn, as well as some cotton and tobacco, brought in on the railroad. Also worthy of note, the letter writer observed that staves, produced by a newly formed local company "ten to twenty miles from the Rail Road" that had purchased timber lands in Southampton County, North Carolina, were being introduced into the Petersburg market.[30] Not only was the railroad intercepting produce at the Roanoke, it was also facilitating the development of new industries along the line.

The response to the success of the Petersburg Rail Road in North Carolina, as seen from the perspective of the Northern press, appears as an immediate willingness to see the connections formed on the Roanoke that would continue the trunk into the state and establish branch lines. For example, *The Newport Mercury* (Newport, Rhode Island) reported that the legislature of North Carolina was considering bills in December of 1833 that would allow the Petersburg Rail Road to be extended to Raleigh, and for the incorporation of the Roanoke and Yadkin Rail Road, a further expansion of the trunk into the interior.[31] Earlier, in August, the *New-Hampshire Gazette* (Portsmouth, New Hampshire) had noted that the citizens of Johnston County, North Carolina, had subscribed $20,000 to the railroad from Raleigh to Wilmington by way of Waynesborough.[32] Raleigh intuitively appeared to be the ultimate objective in the continuation of the line; however, crossing the Roanoke had become a problem. But a letter dated August 1834 from the president of the Petersburg Rail Road Company (D. Mackenzie) to Governor David L. Swain of North Carolina that included both references to the act passed by the North Carolina Legislature on January 3, 1831, that allowed the Petersburg Rail Road to continue from the Virginia line to the Roanoke River, as well as a statement of the cost of construction on the North Carolina section of the railroad suggested the railroad was stalled at the Roanoke. Most notable of the items listed were "Inclined Plane & fixtures to shift in and out of Bends" and "foot of Plane." The statement also includes the cost for warehouses and a hotel at Blakeley.[33] The debates in the Virginia House of Delegates surrounding state subscription to the Portsmouth & Roanoke Rail Road early that year explain why the inclined plane was constructed. Originally, the Petersburg Rail Road had anticipated a joint arrangement with another company like the Portsmouth & Roanoke Rail Road for a bridge to cross the Roanoke to Weldon. This didn't materialize, so the terminus of the railroad was placed two miles downriver at a more navigable place on the north bank. Here, bateaux passing through the Roanoke Canal could have their loads lifted by machinery onto the train.[34]

The Portsmouth & Roanoke Rail Road entered into a contract with the company building the bridge at Weldon (the Weldon Toll Bridge Company) to widen it to permit putting down rails.[35] In early 1834, this presented the possibility of another trunk running from Weldon to Halifax to Waynesborough and continuing to Fayetteville. With the Halifax & Weldon Rail Road and the Wilmington & Raleigh Rail Road having been recently chartered by the North Carolina General Assembly, this possibility of connecting the segments of an eastern trunk line through the state seemed equally valid, if not more so since the Portsmouth & Roanoke had solved the problem of bridging the Roanoke River. The bridge made Weldon the tollgate of North Carolina.

Fayetteville, the Unattainable Alternative

While the north-to-south corridor was evolving in the pivotal year of 1834, an earlier plan of great potential was, in spite of the exertions of its long-standing supporters, entering the realm of remote ideals. This was the plan to build a railroad from Fayetteville westward. In the fall of 1829, prompted by reading of a gentleman from Salisbury, North Carolina, supporting the building of a railroad from Fayetteville to Salisbury, a writer to the *Richmond Enquirer* foresaw the potential of a north to south corridor that would extend from Petersburg to Salisbury, passing through Raleigh. From Salisbury, a spur would extend east to the Yadkin River. He anticipated that this railroad would attract cotton shipments from the region embracing the North Carolina–South Carolina line and promote the development of an iron industry in the region that could supplant the British product.[36]

While this idea is no less fanciful than those that P.Q. and G.L.C. recommended, the realization that a railroad in this region of North Carolina could provide the foundation for industrial scale production of iron was visionary. The single-minded desire to attract agricultural commodities to particular markets, and the prevailing notion that a railroad was merely an improved version of a turnpike, distracted the promoters of the grand scheme from the most daunting handicap to their construction: while there was an abundance of timber throughout the eastern states, iron had to be imported from abroad until a domestic industry was established. A railroad from Fayetteville to Salisbury, a variant of one of the earlier proposed plans in North Carolina, appeared to offer the greatest long-term benefit per mile of rail constructed. The approximate distance between Salisbury and the Egypt coalfields (near Gulf, North Carolina) is seventy miles, and an additional fifty to Fayetteville, less than the distance of the Wilmington & Raleigh. Fayetteville and Raleigh could be connected by another sixty miles of rail. Could it be done?

It might seem appropriate to dismiss the construction of a railroad from Fayetteville to the Yadkin, or Wilmington to Morganton, as financial and technically impractical for the early 1830s; but it also seemed incomprehensible two decades later, when Wilmington had commenced work on the Wilmington, Charlotte, & Rutherford Railroad, a railroad that would pass due south of Fayetteville at Lumberton and not include a branch line to that town and its railroad. In the late nineteenth century, North Carolina historian James Sprunt briefly described the early efforts to build a railroad from Fayetteville to the west. On the eve of the Civil

War, the Western Railroad (chartered in 1852) extended from Fayetteville to the Chatham County coal fields at Egypt and was isolated from the state's other railroads. Fayetteville's connection to the west was by way of plank roads. Sprunt expressed his puzzlement as to why it took so long to build a railroad to the Yadkin Valley when its vast resources had been widely known, and were considered vital to the state's interests.[37] Throughout the antebellum period, Fayetteville was a receiving point for the produce of the southwestern counties, and its plank road system extended west to Charlotte, south to Cheraw, and north to Winston-Salem.[38] Stagecoach lines operated between Raleigh and Fayetteville. The town had been a commercial center since the colonial era and had enjoyed the advantages of its location: it was situated at the head of the navigation of the Cape Fear, and was also well positioned on an evolving road network extending south and west. Yet it had no other option but to rely on river transport for its exports, for north to south rail traffic was deflected from the direct line a considerable distance to Wilmington.

By the early 1850s, several problems having their origin in past and current conditions complicated transportation to and from Fayetteville, both for travelers and commerce. The first, a result of the Raleigh & Gaston Rail Road not having a spur to Weldon, was a failure of the railroad to coordinate its schedule with the railroads converging at Weldon. The second problem, the absence of a rail connection between Raleigh and Fayetteville,[39] or even as far as the Cape Fear River, proved to be a significant disadvantage for travelers and local farmers. The third problem involved heavy investment by Fayetteville and its region in plank roads and less effective navigational improvements on the Cape Fear rather than in railroads.[40]

The first two of these problems were directly related to the financial failure of the Raleigh & Gaston, and can be traced back the Petersburg Rail Road not being able to cross the Roanoke at Weldon. The third was a less costly means of attracting agricultural commodities from a larger geographic area to Fayetteville than building a railroad. It might be safe to conjecture that Fayetteville's far-flung network of plank roads sufficed to bring in produce from the western regions, but it was merely an improvement upon what had existed before; and it could easily be thwarted when railroads were built through any of its extent. Its chief disadvantage was being a deterrent to the development of heavy industry. The railroads being built in the regions around it during the late antebellum period, such as the North Carolina Railroad in the Piedmont, and the Wilmington, Charlotte, and Rutherford Railroad to the south, threatened to cut this off from south central North Carolina. Thus, the produce from the mountains would be closer to railheads at Charlotte, Salisbury, and Greensboro; and the produce of the Yadkin and upper Pee Dee would be intercepted south of Fayetteville. The travelers going south from Raleigh would have to make their way by Charlotte or Wilmington, or endure the painful, inefficient stagecoach ride such as Olmsted experienced. The most serious drawback to Fayetteville's plank road network then was its limiting effect upon industrial development.

During the Civil War, and for a period starting during the 1870s, the Endor Iron Works operated a successful smelting operation. It was ideally located near the Egypt coalfields (Cumnock). The Fayetteville & Western Railroad serviced the coalfields at this time. The coal and iron industry could have been established in the region earlier, had its potential been recognized earlier, and had the railroad connections existed. While the navigation of the Cape Fear River from Fayetteville to Wilmington appears to have been both adequate and appropriate for transporting bulk such as iron and coal, a rail connection between the two towns was the subject of much discussion in Wilmington during the summer of 1854.[41] Unlike the Cape Fear River, with its course set by nature, a railroad from Chatham County through Fayetteville to Wilmington would offer the possibility of additional connections. The author of one article to the *Wilmington Journal* recognized the potential of carrying the railroad to Salisbury, where it would intersect the North Carolina Railroad, and he recommended branch lines into Robeson, Anson, Richmond, Union and Mecklenburg counties.[42]

But *The Report of the Committee on Int. Improvements on the Cape Fear and Deep River Navigation Company* which was presented to the North Carolina General Assembly during their 1854–55 session discouraged the further use of railroads to exploit the coal and iron resources of the Deep River, while continuing to support funding of the ongoing navigational improvements to the Cape Fear and the Deep River drainage network. River transport, unfortunately, was linked to the existing operations at the coalfields.[43] The report indicates that seventeen of twenty-two locks and fourteen of seventeen dams planned by an engineer named Douglass, who had worked on the Lehigh Canal in Pennsylvania, had been completed. The works at Jones' Falls, eight miles above Fayetteville, and Smiley's Falls, near Erwin, are mentioned favorably in allowing free navigation from Fayetteville to Haywood in Chatham County. A canal, one mile in length, needed to be cut around Pullen's Falls, and the canal at Buckhorn Falls required additional excavation to make it wider and deeper. The existing locks and dams needed improvements as well. The committee presented some information on the coal and iron deposits of the Deep River, noting that the quality of the iron ore was suitable for the manufacturing of rails; and two companies manufacturing iron — one in Petersburg, Virginia and the other in Pottsville, Pennsylvania — had subscribed to $10,000 of stock in a proposed company that would be set up to smelt iron in the area.[44] A correspondence to the *New York Times* dated December 10, 1860, described the activities and facilities of the Deep River Coal and Iron Company and the Cape Fear Coal and Iron Company. In addition to smelting iron, the Deep River Coal and Iron Company had the capacity of producing 10,000 barrels of coal oil daily.[45]

The history of the effort to improve navigation on the upper Cape Fear had always been problematic. The duration of construction for the multiple canals around the several falls appears to have been protracted. For example, Hamilton Fulton, in his 1821 report to the Board of Public Improvements, noted that the dams above Branson's Mill were so low that the canal needed to be excavated a foot from Buckhorn Falls to Haywood. However, he recommended that the dams be raised in spite of Mr. Branson's objections, and he referred the board to Branson for an explanation of these objections. He estimated $3,348 for cutting and lockage for the new canal and $3,554 for improving Parker's Creek.[46] In a letter to Governor Edward B. Dudley dated February 16, 1837, George McNeill, agent for the Cape Fear Navigation Company, reports that the company had achieved, in part, a bateau navigation from Haywood to Buckhorn Falls. However, Mr. James Wyche of the Board of Internal Improvements, under the direction of Mr. Kerr, determined without consulting that company that Buckhorn Falls could be circumvented by sluicing, and that the locks should be abandoned. The company had by that time spent $40,000 on the canal and locks.[47]

Plank roads and canals, in spite of the confidence expressed by antebellum officials, were less efficient forms of transportation for developing an iron industry in North Carolina. That they were cheaper in the end is questionable, and they certainly were not permanent. The Cape Fear and Deep rivers were rich in the raw materials of iron production, and this had been known since the early nineteenth century; and so the building of a railroad west from Fayetteville offered the potential for early industrial development. A connection between Wilmington and Salisbury during the 1850s would have provided a distribution network for iron production, and allowed for the emergence of manufacturing of finished iron products such as iron rails, boilers and hardware, and consumer products such as stoves at the commercial towns along the way. Frederick Law Olmsted's description of the arrival of wagons in Fayetteville and the subsequent intercourse between the merchants of that town and the drivers on the purchase of the goods was a far different economic culture from the relentless flow of arrivals that had to be contracted for in advance. The turnpike and river were open to all at their pleasure, whereas the railroad operated on a schedule. A train of cars functioned as a mobile warehouse, a natural domain for agents and brokers that could receive goods from all places on the route. Thus, the merchants of a town such as Fayetteville might have been relieved of bargaining in the street with their suppliers; rather the task would be reserved to a network of agents working in concert over a large area. They could keep the price of commodities uniform, and the warehouses of the commercial town would be adequately stocked to support permanent local industry. That the merchant could make the transition to industrialist is possible, but it is perhaps a vision too far removed from an economy based on agriculture and wood products to project a coherent system of production and consumption where tasks are fragmented over space with the whole process dependent on the timely delivery of raw materials. This is exactly what the letter writer from Petersburg to the *Norfolk Herald* was describing in 1833 concerning new industries such as stave manufacturing and lumber production emerging as a result of the railroad.

The incorporation of Fayetteville's experimental railroad in 1831, with consideration of its proposed extension to the Yadkin, reflected the most frequently observed pattern of railroad development found in an underdeveloped country; that is, building from the coast to the interior.[48] Insomuch as Weldon was the tollgate of North Carolina, the Narrows of the Yadkin was the tollgate of western North Carolina. Fayetteville's connection to Wilmington by the Cape Fear River was less problematic than navigation from Weldon to Norfolk. A connection from Fayetteville to the Yadkin by rail would be the counterpart of the Petersburg Rail Road, the essential first link, with some place like Weldon on the Yadkin drawing river trade from the interior of both Carolinas. A rail connection to Raleigh would seem a likely next step, and finally to Wilmington.

It is often an inconsequential intellectual exercise to ponder counterfactual histories, but counterfactual geographies tend to shed light on the nature of actual geographic phenomena attributed to human agency, particularly in the area of transportation. Simply put, transportation networks are landscape objects that can be modeled, empirically or conceptually. For what they were originally intended, the Petersburg Rail Road model and the Fayetteville &

Yadkin Rail Road model function similarly to divert river commerce to an interior commercial center. They differ in direction, south for the Petersburg Rail Road and west for the proposed Fayetteville & Yadkin. However, potential in history is unattainable. That the mineral resources of the upper Cape Fear basin and their early exploitation presented the possibility of developing an iron industry in this region does not account for the lack of capital and misplaced capital. The British advantage was not only their ability to offer railroads iron in quantity: they also could satisfy the credit needs of railroad companies. The geographic insight of the promoters of early railroad schemes did not rest upon the foundation of experience. Each railroad that was attempted would be for some time an experiment that exposed the potential and limitations of the new technology.

The Two-Fifths Investment

The General Assembly of North Carolina did not establish a policy of two-fifths investment on the part of the state in certain railroad companies until their 1836–37 session. The Wilmington & Raleigh Rail Road, the Fayetteville & Western Rail Road and North Carolina Central Rail Road were designated as eligible for the state subscription if the companies were able to secure three-fifths subscriptions to the stock from private investors. The Wilmington & Raleigh was the only company to achieve this goal, and the subscription on the part of the state proved to be its saving grace during the economic downturn that began in the late 1830s and lasted into the early 1840s. Virginia had instituted its two-fifths policy for state support for internal improvements long before North Carolina. Aside from long standing support for turnpikes and canals, the state provided two-fifths subscription ($160,000) to the Petersburg Rail Road in 1831; and in the coming years, it would aid several of the state's railroads.[49] The Petersburg Rail Road was both the first interstate railroad and the first railroad in North Carolina. Built to secure Petersburg's share of commerce on the Roanoke, it was the vanguard of the north to south drive to construct railroads through North Carolina. While unable to effect a crossing of the Roanoke at Weldon, its rival, the Portsmouth & Roanoke, achieved this goal in 1837 though its contract with the Weldon Toll Bridge Company. This was the culminating event that established Weldon as the prime attractor for a rail corridor through North Carolina. Its history can be traced back to internal improvements undertaken in Virginia beginning with the Dismal Swamp Canal.

The purely geographical advantage of Weldon being situated on the boundary of the Piedmont and Coastal Plain of North Carolina, as well as the convenient location of the vast Roanoke basin that included regions of North Carolina and Virginia, was not its key advantage. The Fayetteville to the Yadkin route presented attractive geographical advantages as previously discussed. What makes Weldon more significant as an attractor for rail construction is location in the context of prior internal improvements, including the Petersburg Rail Road and the Portsmouth & Roanoke Rail Road. Virginia was early to institute a policy for state investment in internal improvements; thus North Carolina's first railroads would necessarily form a continuation of what was in place.

The Wilmington & Raleigh Rail Road changed the direction of its route to Weldon in its amended charter of 1835. This change should be viewed as the most rational continuation of internal improvements for both states, given the limits of available capital, the existing technology, and the mismatch between Virginia and North Carolina concerning public investment policy in infrastructure. The great interior route proposed by professional civil engineers and insightful amateurs represents an ideal more remote than they could have imagined. For the time being, the toll gate of North Carolina would open to a nearly direct corridor to the toll gate of South Carolina, the port of Wilmington.

CHAPTER II

Early Plans for Railroads in North Carolina

British mechanical engineer Richard Trevithick is credited with the invention of the steam locomotive in 1804. It would take twenty years of experimentation before the first permanent steam railroad, George Stephenson's Stockton & Darlington Railway, was put into operation in 1825. The first intercity passenger railroad, the Liverpool & Manchester Railway, would open in 1830. It is safe to assert, regardless of the success of early British railways and railroad experiments in the United States, that the construction of large-scale railroads was still theoretical at the time. While the Charleston & Hamburg Rail Road and the Baltimore & Ohio Rail Road, both chartered in 1827, would be the test model for the concept, these railroads would not be put into regular use along a substantial length of their extent for a number of years. Even then, deficiencies in early railroad technology, the consequences of selecting different track gauges, and the long term cost effectiveness of various routes would not become evident until much later. The early plans for railroads in North Carolina fall into two distinct categories, large-scale, essentially theoretical railroads, and small-scale experimental railroads intended to fulfill a specific purpose. The Wilmington & Raleigh Rail Road was a large-scale railroad with experimental roots that emerged through the curtain of visionary proposals to become a reality.

Joseph Caldwell, the first president of the University of North Carolina, proposed a central railroad spanning the state from Beaufort to the mountains in *The Numbers of Carlton* in 1828. Caldwell, a mathematician, provided in his text a route for this road that can be determined indirectly from a table of places in the state and their distance from the line. Its western terminus can be located approximately as north of Asheville. In addition, the work includes useful statistics on the cost of transporting crops to market by the prevailing means.[1] For the time, the plan was both visionary and impractical. However, the idea of Caldwell's Central Rail Road took hold of the public mind, particularly in the Piedmont. On August 1, 1828, a meeting was held at the home of William Albright in Chatham County to discuss the Central Rail Road. Two hundred people attended the meeting, and listened to an address by Dr. Caldwell. The address and resolutions of that meeting were thereafter published.[2] By the early 1830s, the plan was at the core of the state's policy on projected internal improvements. In theory, the projected railroad would be accessible to many farmers of the interior.

James Iredell Jr., governor of North Carolina from 1827 through 1828, recommended building an experimental railroad from Fayetteville to Campbellton, a distance of approximately two miles; this plan was supported by his successor, John Owen. Owen went further by recommending that the Cape Fear River should be connected to the Yadkin in North Carolina or to the Great Pee Dee in South Carolina by a turnpike or railroad.[3]

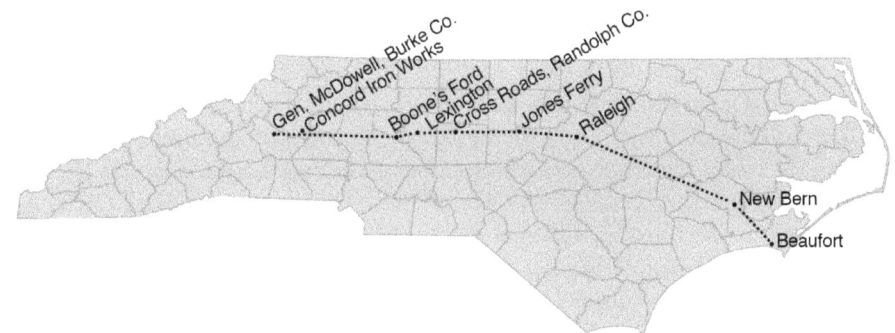

This is the Central Rail Road as Joseph Caldwell described it in his 1828 *The Numbers of Carlton.* The locations illustrated on the line of the route appear in a table provided in the text. The route is mapped on the present counties for reference. It is unclear how it would extend to the Tennessee line as later promoters suggested. By 1831, the Central Rail Road plan was a route from Salisbury to Beaufort. The Central Rail Road concept matured into the North Carolina Railroad in 1849. The route extended north through Greensboro and Hillsboro, and then to Raleigh. *See* Joseph Caldwell, *Numbers of Carlton* (New York: G. Long, 1828); W.P. Cumming, *North Carolina in Maps* (Raleigh: State Department of Archives and History, 1966), Plate XI.

In January of 1830, a steam locomotive demonstration was set up at the Court House in Fayetteville for citizens to take a ride on a circular track. The General Assembly of North Carolina passed *An Act to Incorporate a Company Styled the Fayetteville Rail Road Company* during their 1830–1831 Session. This "experimental railroad" was to be built from Fayetteville to Campbellton on the Cape Fear River. The two-mile steam railroad was to be capitalized at $20,000 with a single share costing $100. Though the distance of this railroad seems insignificant, the use of a steam locomotive is its remarkable feature. To put this into perspective, the Charleston & Hamburg Rail Road, the only commercial railroad in the United States using steam power exclusively at that time, was only in operation over five miles of its length. The cost of Fayetteville's railroad was estimated to be $16,000 for two miles of railroad at $8,000, an engine at the river, costing $4,000; a locomotive engine, costing $3,000; and other fixtures, costing $1,000. When the books were opened to subscribers in March of 1831, the citizens of Fayetteville subscribed liberally to the stock of the company. When the books were closed, subscriptions amounting to $52,300 had been taken. This was $32,000 in excess of what was required to capitalize the company, and all but $1,000 was subscribed to by citizens of Fayetteville. However, it would be three years before work would commence on this project.[4]

About noon on Sunday May 29, 1831, the citizens of Fayetteville emerged from church to find their town in flames. The fire that had started at the kitchen of James Kyle on the Market Square quickly consumed much of the town, including businesses, public buildings, hotels, churches, and the Academy. A detailed account of the terrific property losses can be found in the *Carolina Observer* published the same day. In short order, another instance of fire transformed Fayetteville's loss into a political opportunity. The North Carolina Capitol building caught fire less than a month later, on Tuesday June 21, 1831. John M. Mason, John Bell, and William Adams, workers employed to apply zinc to the building's roof, were blamed for accidentally causing the conflagration that reduced the structure to the point that its walls fell in. David L. Swain, future governor, would give a firsthand account of the fire in the 1860s.[5]

The destruction of the State House in Raleigh roused slumbering ambitions in Fayetteville and the Cape Fear region. Following the Revolution, Fayetteville had anticipated being the seat of government for the state, and had commenced the building of a gracefully designed brick State House in 1787, only to be disappointed when the General Assembly chose to locate the capital in Wake County the following year.[6] That Fayetteville could no longer offer the use of this facility to the homeless legislature following the burning of the Capitol, for the State House in Fayetteville had been one of the structures destroyed in that town's great fire, is perhaps a cruel irony. However, the ensuing debate concerning the relocation of the capital to Fayetteville would have far-reaching consequences: it exposed the need to resolve by convention problems with the state's constitution; it magnified the political frictions between the State's regions; and it prompted further discourse on internal improvements. The Cape Fear political faction, with its economic interests in the southwest, would do anything — even force a constitutional convention — to remove the political center of gravity to its domain.[7] The Piedmont and port towns of the extreme East, though very different from each other, could not possibly benefit from having the state's capital so closely located to the favorable port of Wilmington. At the same time, two plans for east-west railroads were evolving that mirrored the geopolitical divisions.

Railroad legislation and the debate over relocating the capital also brought back to the Legislature one of the state's greatest minds — Judge William Gaston. In May 1831 at New Bern, he had expressed his support for a railroad from Beaufort to New Bern and thence to Raleigh to be known as the *North Carolina Central Rail Road* to be built with the aid of the state. About the same time, J. S. Smith, P. H. Winston, and Walker Anderson of Orange County were drafting a memorial to the legislature concerning a variant of the *Central Rail Road* that would extend from Beaufort to Salisbury with the potential for connecting spurs to the Cape Fear and the Roanoke.[8]

On the day that the particulars of the burning of the capitol building appeared in the *Carolina Observer,* another article in the same issue suggested that the building of a railroad from Fayetteville to the interior of the state would aid the town's recovery. The plan received the immediate support of Charles Fisher, Speaker of the North Carolina House of Commons. However, his open support of a competing plan for the Central Rail Road from Salisbury to Beaufort led the *Carolina Observer* to remark that he had abandoned Fayetteville's plan, his first love. However, another prominent supporter, John Pearson, introduced a resolution at a meeting at Salisbury for the preparation of a memorial to the legislature to commission a survey of a route from Fayetteville to the Yadkin River above the Narrows. In December, a resolution was introduced in the North Carolina Senate to incorporate a Cape Fear to Yadkin railroad, owned by individual stockholders, to connect Haywood, at the confluence of the Cape Fear and the Haw in Chatham County, to Louisburg in Franklin County

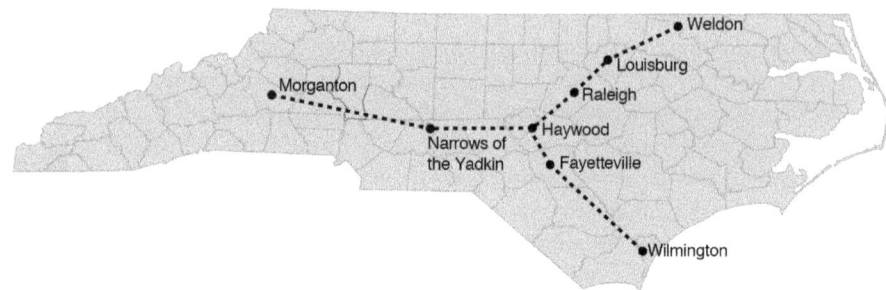

The 1832 route of the Cape Fear & Yadkin Rail Road extended from Wilmington to Morganton. North Carolina State Senate member Williams introduced a resolution to connect the Cape Fear and Yadkin to the Petersburg Rail Road from Haywood via Louisburg. This branch line would have passed through Raleigh. The Petersburg Rail Road, completed in 1833, ended at Blakeley on the Roanoke near to Weldon's Orchard (Weldon).

where it could connect with the Petersburg Rail Road. Senator Williams introduced a resolution to inquire into a Haywood to Louisburg to Halifax route. At the same time, a committee in Wilmington was preparing another memorial for the upcoming meeting of the General Assembly, proposing a railroad that would run from Wilmington, to Fayetteville, to the Yadkin and thence to Morganton. On December 19, 1831, this memorial was presented to the General Assembly; and several days later in the session, Judge Gaston introduced a bill for surveying the route of the *Cape Fear and Yadkin Rail Road* from the ocean to the mountains at the state's expense.

The bill passed, and the railroad moved towards a beginning. The Cape Fear & Yadkin Rail Road was incorporated during the 1831–32 session of the General Assembly and the capital stock of the company was to be $2,000,000. The state paid the cost of the survey. The books were opened for subscription on May 8, 1832. A notice in the Wilmington newspaper, *The People's Press,* a year later marks the demise of this plan to connect the mountains with the coast. The subscribers were informed that their money would be returned.[9] The company had failed to meet the subscriptions required to maintain its charter, and now the disappointed investors looked to assign blame. Some blamed the engineer employed by the state to survey the route. The claim was that the engineer ignored the council of locals who said a route could be devised that would be less expensive if the physical obstacles that might be encountered by terminating the road at Flat Swamp Creek where it joins the Yadkin on the Davidson and Rowan county line were avoided. Wilmingtonians tended to blame the citizens of Fayetteville, citing local rivalries for the cause of the failure. Others suggested that the original plan to connect Wilmington to the mountains would have been the preferred route, but the commissioners of Fayetteville caused the route from Fayetteville to the mountains to be surveyed first without allowing Wilmingtonians to have a say in the matter. The editor of the *Carolina Observer* refuted accusations that the citizens of Fayetteville did not fully support the project. Though he implied that the impetus for obtaining the charter started with Wilmington, he clearly stated that the citizens of Fayetteville had subscribed liberally; however, the western counties received blame for not subscribing.[10]

An examination of articles from the Raleigh newspaper provides further insight into the failure of the *Cape Fear & Yadkin Rail Road*. The May 7, 1833, issue of the weekly *Raleigh Register* reported that Dr. William P. Hort was prepared to return money to the investors, and added that the western counties "failed to subscribe a cent towards affecting the proposed object." The failure of the proposed Central Railroad effort is mentioned in the same article. Nearly a week later, *The Raleigh Register* included an excerpt from a letter by James Wyche, the Superintendent of Internal Improvements for North Carolina, and a citation from the estimate of the cost of one mile of track (single and double) prepared by engineer Francis William Rawle. Mr. Rawle, a civil engineer from Pennsylvania, had been hired to survey both the Cape Fear and Yadkin Valley route and the Central Rail Road route. Mr. Wyche stated that the estimate was based on building a permanent way that was designed for double track on well-made embankments executed by experienced contractors and varying types of labor; the figures place cost per mile for single track at $2,278.64, and $4,557.28 for double track. In the same issue, the *Raleigh Register* cites statements by the editor of the *Carolina Observer* that a railroad could be built to the Narrows of the Yadkin, but the conditions set forth by the charter would require too much capital; and that amendments to the charter would be addressed at the next session of the General Assembly. The commissioners at Fayetteville persisted in making it known that they had not abandoned the project. The most obvious problem for the project was the failure by the company to secure the necessary funds. Alan D. Watson, in his book *Wilmington, North Carolina, to 1861,* notes that even though subscriptions amounting to more than $100,000 in stock had been secured in the Cape Fear region (two-thirds of it by Wilmingtonians), the conditions of the charter required $300,000 in subscriptions to secure the existence of the company. The disappointment that resulted from the failure of the Cape Fear & Yadkin Rail Road Company to meet the $300,000 in subscriptions required by its charter led the citizens of Wilmington to consider a plan to build a railroad between Wilmington and Raleigh.[11]

Forty-eight of North Carolina's then sixty-four counties were represented at the internal improvements convention held in Raleigh on November 25, 1833. Early in the convention, a committee under the chairmanship of Duncan Cameron was formed, consisting of one member of each of the state's Congressional districts. The primary objectives of the committee were to determine what plans embraced the interests of the state's different regions and to recommend a plan of internal improvements to the General Assembly for state patronage. First, they defined five sections of the state having different needs for addressing their respective markets. Of the many plans the committee considered, they excluded those that were of only local benefit and those that were beyond the resources of the state. The general plan of the committee recommended a rail from Edenton to the Portsmouth & Roanoke Rail Road, or a canal to the Dismal Swamp Canal for the northern counties and those below Halifax. The remainder of their general plan recommended any combinations of roads, railroads, river routes, and canals to serve the other regions of the state.

> They propose further a communication, by rail road, river, or canal, or any two of them, or all *united*, from some point on the seaboard of the State, to the Tennessee line; and another communication of the same kind from some point on the Roanoke river, running southwardly, to the South Carolina line. These two latter works, it is believed, will fully answer the purposes of the other remaining portions of the State; while the whole combined will, it is hoped, meet the wants of the State at large, and all, and every part, readily fall in with, and form a part of, any internal communication which it may be hereafter thought necessary to form between the eastern, western, northern and southern portions of the Union.[12]

The committee further recommended that any company incorporated in the state for improving transportation should be allowed to intersect with, or cross, any other project completed or planned by another such company. The companies could, when three-fifths of their capital stock was subscribed to, request the General Assembly consider a subscription by the state to the remaining two-fifths of the shares. The *Memorial* continued with an estimate for a general plan that involved building thirty-five miles of railroad, at a cost of $280,000, for the northern counties, 150 miles of a north-to-south railroad costing $1,200,000, an east-to-west railroad costing $2,920,000, and a ship channel from New Bern to Beaufort that would cost $600,000. The estimate for the railroads was $8,000 per mile. The total cost of this plan was given at $5,000,000; and the committee recommended that this amount could be borrowed in Europe for a rate of four or five per cent. The financial resources of the state were listed as $1,067,000 in actual property, and $706,000 in uncertain items. The actual property included $500,000 in bank stock, and shares in the Roanoke Navigation Company, the Cape Fear Navigation Company, the Pungo and Plymouth Road, and the Buncombe Turnpike; loans to the Clubfoot and Harlowe Canal Company, the Tennessee Turnpike Company, and the Swannanoa Turnpike Company. Included in the state's assets were land bonds amounting to $440,000. The state's claim for military expenditures during the War of 1812, and the proportion of western lands were the uncertain items. The annual interest on the actual property at four per cent was given as $42,680, and other regular sources of income amounted to $8,375.[13]

The North Carolina Legislature responded to the *Memorial of the Convention upon the Subject of Internal Improvements* by assembling the Joint Select Committee on Internal Improvements to prepare a report. While the committee concurred with the memorialists on the necessity of a general program of internal improvements, they did not recommend any immediate action. They did recommend that further surveys and estimates should be made before the state should commit to a plan.[14] Their position was understandable, considering both the multitude of projects being considered and the dismal performance of past programs of internal improvements. The 1833 *Report of the Board of Internal Improvements* identified the cause of past failures as too many projects undertaken at one time. The survey of the Central Rail Road and the Cape Fear & Yadkin Rail Road cost the state $7,022.46, and both railroads had failed to raise the capital required by their charter. The board considered two important objectives as part of a general plan: there must be a good outlet to the ocean, and a railroad should be connected to that outlet. A railroad from the Roanoke to South Carolina was also considered important, with a connection between Raleigh and Wilmington.[15] A rail connection through the state anticipated a multi-state interior corridor to be known as the "Metropolitan Route."

The *Report of the Committee on Internal Improvements* expanded on the report of the board, recommended changes to its membership with one member acting as superintendent of public works, and pointed out that the citizens of North Carolina were quick to realize the potential of the steam locomotive; and they supported the convention's proposal

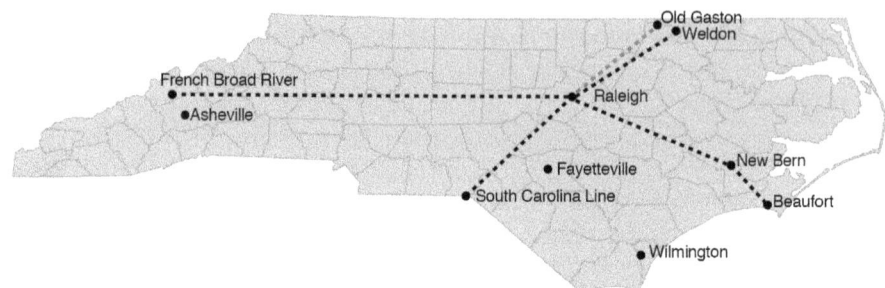

The *Memorial of the Convention upon the Subject of Internal Improvements held in Raleigh, November 1833,* recommended to the General Assembly two railroads that would cross the state. The north-to-south railroad would span 150 miles, and the east-to-west railroad would extend 365 miles to the mountains. In this map, the east-to-west route begins at Beaufort and ends at the French Broad River near present-day Marshall. The point on the South Carolina line is placed north on a line to Cheraw, South Carolina. A continuation of this line would extend to Columbia, South Carolina. The dark line extending to Weldon represents a connection with the Virginia railroads. The gray line represents an extension from Raleigh to Old Gaston (Wilkes' Ferry) where the Raleigh & Gaston did connect to Petersburg Rail Road via the Greensville & Roanoke Rail Road. The Greensville & Roanoke was incorporated in North Carolina after the Memorial in 1834. *See* North Carolina, *Memorial of the Convention upon the Subject of Internal Improvements held in Raleigh, November 1833, to the General Assembly of North Carolina* (Raleigh: Lawrence and Lemay, 1833), 9.

for a policy of two-fifths investment on the part of the state.[16] In addition, the committee recommended that the state should employ a topographical engineer, perhaps from the topographical bureau of the United States government, to make estimates and surveys of the proposed routes.[17]

During the 1833–1834 session of the General Assembly, an act to incorporate the Halifax and Weldon Rail Road Company passed, and an act to incorporate the Halifax Rail Road Bridge Company passed. The General Assembly was busy with other acts and acts to amend acts concerning railroads during that session. These included the Lumber River and Cape Fear Canal and Rail Road Company, the Greensville & Roanoke Rail Road Company, the Roanoke & Raleigh Rail Road Company, the Roanoke & Yadkin Rail Road Company, and the Fayetteville & Campbellton Rail Road Company. In the same session of the General

Assembly, the representatives from New Hanover County inexplicably voted against an appropriation for railroad surveys against the wishes of their own constituents. There was a bill presented to amend the charter of the Petersburg Rail Road so that it could continue from the Roanoke to Raleigh.[18]

Some of the most interesting amendments presented during that session pertain to the charter for the Weldon Toll Bridge. During the 1832–1833 session of the General Assembly, an act to incorporate the Portsmouth & Roanoke Rail Road Company, passed by the Virginia Legislature on March 8, 1832, was read. Mr. Mathews, the same senator that introduced the Halifax & Weldon Rail Road bill in 1833, moved that the words "at any point on the Roanoke below Weldon" be changed to the words "opposite Weldon." The bill was then sent on to the House of Commons for approval. On the bill's return to the Senate, the words "opposite" and "or below" had not been agreed upon. The Weldon Toll Bridge was incorporated during the same session. A year later, the company presented amendments to its charter. A motion was presented to amend the bill by adding to the third section a paragraph that would set the annual tolls at fifteen per cent of the cost of the bridge and its railroad until the project had paid for itself. Thereafter, the tolls would be regulated by the legislature. The president and directors of the company were required to submit an annual report. This amendment was rejected. The fifth section of the bill was amended with a paragraph that made the company and its agents liable for the loss of service due to disrepair of the bridge and railroad, and prescribed a penalty for overcharging or undercharging the toll. This change was accepted, and the bill was sent on to the House of Commons.[19] It is clear from this bill that the Weldon Toll Bridge Company originally had control of the bridge and the railroad track that crossed it.

Of the many railroads incorporated during the 1833–1834 session of the General Assembly, the most significant included the Wilmington & Raleigh Rail Road, the Roanoke & Raleigh, and the Greensville & Roanoke.[20] The Halifax & Weldon Rail Road and the Weldon Toll Bridge are significant because they constituted a crossing of the Roanoke in anticipation of the connection to the Portsmouth & Roanoke, with the Halifax & Weldon constituting its extension. The projected network of railroads at the end of 1833 connected the ports of Beaufort and Wilmington to Raleigh and the Roanoke. The Fayetteville to the Yadkin River route was revived. The Roanoke & Raleigh Rail Road was a separate effort to connect Raleigh to the Roanoke River, which was different from the Raleigh & Gaston

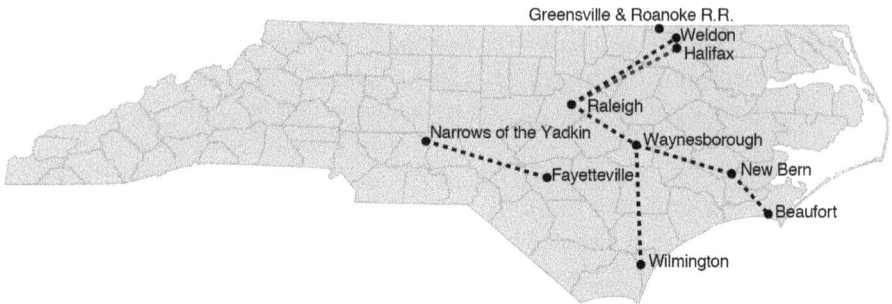

The network of the proposed railroad incorporated at the end of 1833 included the Roanoke & Raleigh connecting the capital to Weldon or Halifax; the Halifax & Weldon; the Wilmington & Raleigh connecting through Waynesborough; the North Carolina Centre & Seaport connecting Beaufort to Raleigh or the Wilmington & Raleigh; and the revived Cape Fear to Yadkin River route. The Greensville & Roanoke was an extension of the Petersburg Rail Road that terminated on the north side of the Roanoke River west of Weldon. *See* Cecil K. Brown, *A State Movement in Railroad Development* (Chapel Hill: University of North Carolina Press, 1928), 26–27.

that would be incorporated in 1835. That all of these railroads were incorporated as private entities without any investment on the part of the state is important to remember.

A tradition that has often been cited by various local historians in Wilmington since the late 1890s, but never substantiated by primary sources, was that the Wilmington & Raleigh Rail Road was the brainchild of a Wilmington businessman named P. K. Dickinson, who was inspired by witnessing the operation of an experimental railroad in New England. Supposedly, he took every opportunity to promote the idea for building a railroad to the business community of Wilmington. Finally, an informal meeting was held at a Wilmington residence, and those in attendance resolved to build a railroad. It is likely that something of the sort happened, but its significance is diminished by the fact that the first railroad scheme that the citizens of Wilmington embraced was that which had been spearheaded by the citizens of Fayetteville, and a suggestion by the editor of the *Raleigh Register* to build a railroad between Wilmington and Raleigh rather than a turnpike appears in the June 11, 1833, issue shortly after the failure of the Fayetteville scheme. The focus of the origin of the Wilmington & Raleigh Rail Road is at Raleigh.

The Experimental Rail Road Company was incorporated during

the 1832–1833 session of the General Assembly; and in addition to carrying stone from the quarry for use in building the new State House, the company's charter set the price for hauling stone of any future public building.[21] It was the first railroad in the state built by North Carolinians. Gov. David Swain later reported that one of Raleigh's most respected and enlightened women originally suggested it, Mrs. Sarah Polk.[22] During the Internal Improvement Convention held in Raleigh during November of 1833, Edmund Ruffin's monthly publication, the *Farmers' Register,* published an article entitled "Memoranda and Scraps from a Traveler's Note Book" that provides an outsider's perspective on the proceedings. During his stay in Raleigh, the writer had an opportunity to examine the Experimental Railroad.

> A rail-way of 1¼ miles was made from the quarry to the statehouse, solely to bring the stone, and has yielded profitable dividends to the proprietors, and at the same time enabled the transportation of the stone to be effected at one-third of the expense (as I heard,) that it would have otherwise cost. This facility also induces a much larger use of granite for new houses which are erecting on Fayette[ville] street, and will ultimately cause the town of Raleigh to show more beauty than many others of thrice its wealth and population ... of the 2200 yards of the whole road, 1304 required either excavation or embankment, the greatest depth being apparently four feet, and the greatest height eight, judging by my eye. The length of the places excavated and embanked, was counted by sills. The total cost of the rail-way, 2200 yards, including every material, and every source of expense, amounted to only $2,700, or $2,160 the mile. It is true that the sills are not of as large, nor of as good timer, as a work intended for permanent use would require, and that the iron strips are not more than one-sixth of an inch in thickness. But if the timber and iron had been such as were used on the Petersburg and Roanoke rail-way, it would have scarcely have made this cost $3,000 the mile; and yet this work, from the far greater unevenness of surface, must be more costly for its extent, than would be a rail-way from Roanoke, by Fayetteville, to South Carolina, exclusive of the viaducts over rivers.[23]

Following the disappointment of the Cape Fear & Yadkin Rail Road project's failure, the citizens of Wilmington proposed a plan to the citizens of Raleigh to connect their cities by means of a turnpike via Clinton.[24] In their response, the *Raleigh Register* advanced an idea that some had suggested (the article does not mention who they were) of extending the Experimental Rail Road in Raleigh to the town of South Washington on the Northeast Cape Fear. In the same article was a plan submitted by individuals in New Bern for a railroad connecting Raleigh to some point on the Neuse that could support navigation.

The proposition from Wilmington, is to connect Raleigh with that town by means of a Turnpike, on a simple and cheap plan. This plan, we fear, though preferable on the score of cheapness would not answer the purpose intended, to say nothing of the constant repairs required on a road so constructed. The main idea of connecting the two places is however, so obviously important, that it must not be lost sight of. A plan [which] we have heard mentioned, and with general approbation is this: By a *bona fide* Rail Road. From the termination of our Experimental Rail-Road, to connect this City with South-Washington, in New Hanover county, making that place the head of Navigation. We understand from a most respectable source, that the distance between Raleigh and that point is *only* 75 miles in a direct line, and that from thence, boats, drawing three or four feet of water, can at any season of the year ascend and descend the river. Such are the great advantages of location and convenience of timber, on this route, that it is believed a Road could be constructed for about $2,000 per mile.[25]

Prior to the Internal Improvements Convention held in Raleigh on July 4, 1833, the delegates from Wilmington, New Hanover County, and the surrounding area assembled at a public meeting at the courthouse in Wilmington. Their committee instructed them to cooperate with the citizens of Raleigh and others in the construction of a railroad between Raleigh and Wilmington, and to protest plans that would carry resources out of the state.[26] At the July Internal Improvements Convention, the survey and estimates from the Cape Fear were referred to the general committee, and a number of railroad projects were discussed. These included a railroad from the Roanoke running west, a railroad from the Cape Fear running west, a railroad from Raleigh to the Roanoke, and a railroad from Raleigh to Fayetteville.

John D. Jones of Wilmington introduced a proposal for a railroad from Wilmington to Raleigh. Jones was a lawyer by trade, but was also an agriculturalist, a member of the House of Commons, and president of the Bank of the Cape Fear; and was associated with a deed of land to the Wilmington & Raleigh Rail Road on the northern outskirts of Wilmington.[27] Judge William Gaston, a statesman of great reputation both in the state and nationally, had come out of retirement after the State House fire for the sole purpose of preserving the capital at Raleigh and championing the plan for the Central Rail Road. In the legislature, he was active in supporting railroad projects. At the convention, he presented a resolution to build a railroad from Raleigh to Waynesborough with branch lines to Wilmington and/or New Bern. The Raleigh to New Bern branch would be a significant section of the Central Rail Road. On the same day that the minutes of the convention were printed in the *Raleigh Register*, an appeal commenced to build a railroad from Raleigh to Waynesborough.

> Rail-Road to Waynesborough — It has been determined to make a vigorous and united effort to raise subscriptions to effect the construction of a Rail Road from this City to some point on the Neuse River, at or very near Waynesborough, to be continued from thence to Newbern, or to Wilmington, or to both places. We have been requested to publish the annexed form of a caption, to be used in securing a pledge of subscription to the stock of a Company to be incorporated for this purpose: "The Subscribers bind and oblige themselves severally, to take the number of Shares attached to their names, in a Company to be formed and incorporated for the erection of a Rail Road from Raleigh to or near to Waynesborough. The said Shares at the prices of 100 Dollars each, and the Subscribers respectfully ask the General Assembly to grant a charter of Incorporation, and they hereby submit to have themselves charged by enactments in said charter with the amount of Stock herein subscribed.[28]

The notice concluded with a statement for committees who wanted to open a subscription to continue the railroad to New Bern or Wilmington. When the books were opened at Waynesborough, $25,000 in stock was subscribed to immediately by an unnamed gentleman from Wilmington.

In August, a meeting was held at Roles Store in the northern part of Wake County. The purpose of this meeting was to determine the amount of subscriptions that could be expected from the area. Col. Allen Rogers was appointed chairman, and Joseph Fowler served as secretary. Governor Swain and William H. Haywood addressed the assembly. Wilmington had at this point subscribed to $100,000 in stock, and the promoters hoped Wake County would subscribe to enough stock to carry the proposed railroad from Raleigh to some point on the Neuse. The resolutions adopted at this meeting included instructions to be given to the representatives from Wake County to the next General Assembly, urging the representatives to support a system of internal improvements and seek state funds to aid in their realization. During September, eight subscribers from Pittsboro subscribed to $15,000 in stock, and the railroad was first referred to as the Raleigh & Wilmington Rail Road. When the General Assembly met in 1833, the engrossed bill from the House of Commons to incorporate the Wilmington & Raleigh Rail-road Company was read the first time and passed on December 23, 1833.[29]

During the year 1834, the Wilmington Committee would have a long running battle of words over statements presented in the *Address of the*

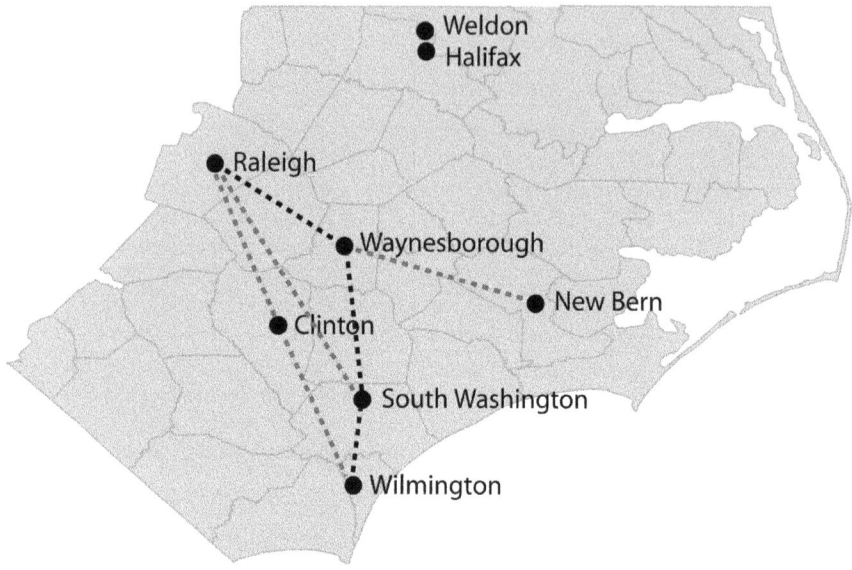

This map of eastern North Carolina illustrates the evolution of the Wilmington & Raleigh Rail Road concept through the year 1833. It began with a proposal from citizens in Wilmington to the citizens of Raleigh to build a turnpike between Wilmington and Raleigh via Clinton. The editor of the *Raleigh Register* suggested extending the Experimental Rail Road in Raleigh to the head of navigation on the Northeast Cape Fear at South Washington. During the Internal Improvements Convention held in Raleigh in early July, the promoters of the scheme began an effort to secure subscription for a railroad between Raleigh and Waynesborough with branch lines to Wilmington and New Bern, or both. The Wilmington & Raleigh Rail Road was chartered at the 1833–1834 session of the North Carolina General Assembly. The Halifax & Weldon Rail Road, later to merge with the Wilmington & Raleigh, was chartered the same year. See *The Peoples Press and Wilmington Advertiser,* June 26, 1833; *Raleigh Register,* June 25, 1833, July 16, 1833, July 30, 1833, August 13, 1833, September 3, 1833, September 17, 1833, December 31, 1833, January 7, 1834; *Richmond Enquirer,* August 16, 1833.

Internal Improvement Central Committee. Gavin Hogg, one of the original commissioners at Raleigh listed in the charter of the Wilmington & Raleigh Rail Road, authored it. At the heart of this dispute was the proposal set forth in the statements in the *Address* that the first railroad in the state should be built from the South Carolina line, through the Piedmont, to the Roanoke.

We object to the proposition to construct the *first* rail road, from the southern boundary to form a connection with those from Petersburg and Norfolk. Such a road would be intersected by every road, river and canal conveying produce from the interior; and this produce would consequently go to Petersburg or Norfolk. The current of trade, thus firmly established could never be diverted, and the interior of the State would become tributary to Virginia, and the whole sea-board abandoned to utter ruin. Under such circumstances, what rational hope could the people of the sea-board entertain from constructing a road to intersect the great transverse route, what would the citizens in the interior care about such a route to our own seaboard, possessing already one of primary importance to Norfolk! If the object to the Committee be to divert the trade of North Carolina from South Carolina and Virginia, the *first* rail road constructed should be from the interior of the State to Beaufort, or some other port in North Carolina. No connection should be formed with those of Norfolk and Petersburg, until the current of trade is firmly established in its proper channel. This being accomplished, the people in this quarter would not wish to interfere, to retard the general plan of internal transportation, that our Legislature or the citizens of the State may think proper to adopt.[30]

Gavin Hogg responded to the New Hanover Committee in July. He accused the town leaders of having a leaning toward commerce, not agriculture; they inclined to condemn any plan that did not bring the resources of the state into their commercial sphere. The Wilmington committee responded with a rebuttal stating that the entire trade of the seaboard would be ruined by building a railroad from Fayetteville, or the South Carolina line, to meet the Virginia railroads at the Roanoke. Interests in Halifax were also critical of the Central Committee's *Address:* the adoption of the plan would carry commerce out of the state to Virginia and South Carolina.[31]

The *Report of the Board of Internal Improvements of North Carolina, transmitted by the Governor to the General Assembly, December 10, 1834* stated that of all the railroad companies incorporated during the last session of the General Assembly, only a part of the Cape Fear and Yadkin Rail Road from Fayetteville to Campbellton was under way. The board was of the opinion "that no general system of improvement can be effected in North Carolina by incorporated companies," and that each of the companies needed one principal engineer with assistants. A resolution was introduced to the General Assembly whereby two-fifths of the stock of any chartered railroad in the state should be supported by the state. During the same session, Edward B. Dudley, representing New Hanover County, attempted to introduce a bill in the House of Commons to amend the charter of the Wilmington & Raleigh Rail Road. Samuel Smallwood, the representative of Beaufort County, moved that the bill be laid on the table until November 3, 1835, during the next session of the General Assembly. The motion passed seventy-one to thirty.[32]

The major railroads chartered in 1833 include the Wilmington & Raleigh Rail Road, the Roanoke & Raleigh Rail Road, the Greensville & Roanoke Rail Road, and the Halifax & Weldon Rail Road. Of these, the Roanoke & Raleigh, a plan to connect Raleigh with Halifax or Weldon, failed to progress beyond its incorporation. Brown has suggested that the change of route of the Wilmington & Raleigh was a practical decision based upon the commercial potential afforded by connecting to the Virginia railroads and, noting Sprunt, that Raleigh may have been indifferent to the project.[33] Sprunt, however, also mentions that at the time the railroad was chartered in 1833, the company had not considered the advantages of building to the Roanoke.[34] A response to a letter from a writer "Petersburg" by writer "Roanoke" concerning the bridge at Weldon, printed in the *Wilmington Chronicle* in November of 1840, yields clues to the nature of the outside forces acting upon railroad planning in North Carolina. Writer "Roanoke" clearly states that both the Petersburg Rail Road and Raleigh were displeased by the Wilmington & Raleigh Rail Road's change of route.

> He says, first, "that when the Wilmington Rail Road was first commenced, the Petersburg Company was of course very anxious to see it carried to Raleigh—but when they found the Company intended to run it to the Roanoke, they were equally as anxious to have a good connexion with it there." He does not say, but I shall say it for him, that as soon as it was mentioned that the Wilmington Road would not go to Raleigh, but would go to the Roanoke River, his Company made the most imperious threats of opposition, which threats were energetically carried out, by the united influence of Petersburg and Raleigh, and even the lobbies of the Legislature Halls of North Carolina were besieged by this Petersburg Company, urging the defeat of the Wilmington Road—and I call on "Petersburg" if he denies this, to show forth the correspondence which then took place between Messrs. Osborne and Dudley, Presidents of these respective Companies, upon this very subject. Nor was this opposition of short duration, but continued unrelentingly, until it was seen the Wilmington Company would succeed in despite of their efforts ... and then was expressed this great anxiety to connect with the Wilmington Company at the Roanoke. This was a wonderful exhibition of good feeling towards the Wilmington Road, truly, and worthy of all consideration by your community. And here we want it to be borne in mind, that during all this conflict, the much abused Portsmouth Company was lending its feeble aid to the Wilmington Company, and has never ceased to continue this friendly feeling, because it is its interest to do so.[35]

II. Early Plans for Railroads in North Carolina 49

There are two letters written by Charles F. Osborne, president of the Petersburg Rail Road, in the Edward B. Dudley papers housed in the North Carolina State Archives. The first, dated Petersburg, January 21, 1836, begins with Mr. Osborne's explanation of why his opposition to a railroad from Wilmington to Weldon via Waynesborough was rooted in the mutual interests of the Petersburg Rail Road and the Wilmington & Raleigh Rail Road rather than their differences. He continues by stating that Petersburg had made a large subscription to the Raleigh & Gaston, and in short order, a survey would commence, the work force would be assembled, and stone masons would be employed building a bridge over the Roanoke at Gaston. He did not think that enough capital could be raised to build two railroads from the Roanoke southward, and expressed no interest in connection to a railroad that terminated at Halifax or Weldon. However, anticipating great railroad that would extend from Gaston to the north, he mentions that Wilmington could eventually connect to New York if the Wilmington & Raleigh was built to Raleigh. Finally, he noted that the projected bridge over the Roanoke at Gaston would cost half as much as the bridge at Weldon. Work on the bridge had been underway for a year already; two more years of work would be required before it would be completed, and it might not be able to withstand the heavy freshets at that point on the Roanoke. The proposed bridge at Gaston was in a better position on the river.[36]

The second letter to Edward B. Dudley from Charles F. Osborne is dated Petersburg, March 1, 1836. Here, Mr. Osborne appears supportive of a connection between a new route of the Wilmington & Raleigh Rail Road and the Petersburg Rail Road, but not likely at Weldon. He admits that the new route of the Wilmington & Raleigh might contribute to an increase the business on the Petersburg Rail Road, and he thinks his company should purchase shares in Dudley's company. However, he remarks that a continuation of the Raleigh & Gaston would inevitably extend to Fayetteville.[37]

It would seem that the promoters of railroads in North Carolina had fallen under the influence of two opposing factions. The interests in Raleigh had aligned themselves with the Petersburg Rail Road. The Wilmington & Raleigh Rail Road, through its change of route to Halifax, would open the entire market of eastern North Carolina to the Portsmouth & Roanoke Rail Road, as well as creating the opportunity for a through ticket to the south. When the Petersburg Rail Road sought to establish a connection to the Roanoke by way of the Greensville & Roanoke Rail Road in 1833, the continuation of service through Raleigh and Wilmington would have given the Petersburg market the advantage. The Greensville & Roanoke Rail Road could only realize its potential if railroads extended from its terminus on the Roanoke at (Old) Gaston to Raleigh, then Fayetteville, and eventually to Columbia, South Carolina. This arrangement would constitute an interior through route that could compete with the coastal through route.

As early as August of 1833, the residents of the Cape Fear had voiced concerns about the Petersburg Rail Road's plans to extend their railroad south to Fayetteville, and hoped the delegates to the Internal Improvements Convention would support plans that encouraged commerce within the state. By year's end, the Petersburg Rail Road Company had moved to have their charter amended to extend the railroad from the Roanoke to Raleigh. Bills to incorporate the Halifax & Weldon Rail Road Company, the Weldon Toll Bridge Company, and the Halifax Rail Road Bridge Company were presented to the North Carolina General Assembly in 1833. These separate private corporations in total were intended to be used by the Portsmouth & Roanoke Rail Road.[38]

This was a very practical arrangement. The Halifax & Weldon Company did not have to acquire locomotives and rolling stock. The company would construct what amounted to an extension of the Portsmouth & Roanoke Rail Road while remaining an independent entity. Walter Gwynn, acting as chief engineer for the Portsmouth & Roanoke Rail Road, reported in his 1833 survey for that company that an extension of the railroad past the Roanoke by "enterprizing citizens of North Carolina" was favorable.[39] The *New York Farmer,* reprinting an article from the *Farmers' Register* published on December 1, 1836, explains why the Petersburg Rail Road, in essence, created the Greensville & Roanoke Rail Road. Not long after reaching Blakeley, the Portsmouth & Roanoke Rail Road was projected to terminate four miles upriver at Weldon. Petersburg responded by planning a railroad that would extend from Hicksford (Emporia) to Wilkes' Ferry (Gaston). The bridge over the Roanoke at that point was to be built by the Raleigh & Gaston Rail Road.[40]

The Wilmington & Raleigh Rail Road managed to overcome opposition to the changes in its charter by the time the General Assembly met in late 1835. There are several notable compromises in the plan, some of which would be rendered moot by subsequent developments. In early December, the company came to agreement with interests in New Bern that the route should pass as closely as possible to Waynesborough, the head of navigation of the Neuse. Branch lines were projected to be built to Raleigh and New Bern after the completion of the main line, and the project would proceed without any provisions for the state to take stock in the company.[41]

Building the railroad through Waynesborough was logical. It had been part of the original plan, and it was not too far removed west of a direct line from Wilmington to Halifax. The state would later become the railroad's largest shareholder, and its branches to Raleigh and New Bern would not be built by the company. The Raleigh & Gaston Rail Road was also incorporated during this session of the General Assembly.

During the 1834–1835 session of the North Carolina General Assembly, legislators considered a bill to amend the charter of the Raleigh & Roanoke Rail Road and a bill to construct a railroad from Gaston, at the termination of the Greensville & Roanoke Rail Road, to Raleigh — the Raleigh & Gaston Rail Road. The bill to incorporate the Raleigh & Gaston excited interest because it had not been before any committee. The incorporators had observed that the legislature had been liberal about granting charters to railroads if they were not seeking state aid; thus, the railroad was chartered as a private undertaking.[42]

Three months after the company was incorporated, an article from a writer identified as "Petersburg," reprinted from the *Petersburg Intelligencer,* appeared in the *Farmers' Register.*

> We have been going on very quietly with the subscription to the Raleigh and Gaston Rail Road Company — little has been said and much done. But so much may be said in favor of the scheme that I think it would be proper to publish in your paper some of the reasons on which the friends of the work rely to recommend it to the public.[43]

There was a strong connection between the officers of the Raleigh & Gaston Rail Road and Petersburg interests. Charles F. Osborne, president of the Petersburg Rail Road, was a business associate in cotton and textile manufacturing in Petersburg with investor Samuel Mordecai, an officer in the Petersburg Rail Road Company. George W. Mordecai, the half-brother of Samuel, was the first president of the Raleigh & Gaston Rail Road. Osborne also served on the board of the Raleigh & Gaston Rail Road, and his name appears conspicuously in the company's second annual report.[44] The Greensville & Roanoke Rail Road, the Raleigh & Gaston Rail Road, and the proposed Raleigh & Columbia were to serve as a *de facto* extension of the Petersburg's market influence. The 1836 "Proceedings of the Petersburg Rail Road Company" printed in the *Farmers' Register* states this goal outright. The company projected an extension of their market to the Yadkin.

> On the south within the short space of a year, we have grafted on our road the Greensville and Roanoke Rail Road; and proposals will soon be submitted for a bridge across the Roanoke at Gaston, connecting that improvement

with the Raleigh and Gaston Rail Road — and satisfactory assurances are given us that before the present year rolls away, the connexion will be complete, and part of the road on the other side of the Roanoke so far made, that it may be used for travel and transportation ... at no distant day a connexion with the Yadkin country, (perhaps the finest in the south,) either at Raleigh or at Oxford, we are insured a continued and increased value to our investment: nor is it too much to anticipate, that the period is almost at hand when from the profit on travel alone, we shall declare such dividends to our stockholders, as will amply satisfy them, and consequently have it in our power to reduce the rates of transportation of produce, to the mere expense of its receipt and delivery.[45]

The assumed destiny of Virginia's railroads was perceived before these railroads were built. An article in the *Richmond Enquirer* published not long after the Fayetteville Rail Road was incorporated suggests that Petersburg would eventually extend their railroad to Fayetteville, and Norfolk would build a railroad to Raleigh via Halifax.[46]

The Raleigh & Gaston Rail Road had commenced work with several built-in handicaps: it was a private corporation owned by individual stockholders; work on the railroad had to begin at the Roanoke River, not Raleigh; and the company had to build a bridge over the Roanoke. The Wilmington & Raleigh Rail Road was incorporated under a public act, had benefited from having merged with the Halifax & Weldon Rail Road, and had received the two-fifths investment on the part of the state. The latter was possible only because of the distribution of the federal surplus to the states, an element of Jacksonian monetary policy. The same policy would trigger the Panic of 1837, and the subsequent depression. This subject was touched on briefly in the discussion of railroad iron. Its impact on the Raleigh & Gaston was crippling, setting it on a path to insolvency.

In the months before the Panic of 1837, the *Raleigh Register* celebrated a burgeoning new era of internal improvements beginning with Gov. Edward B. Dudley's inaugural speech, and William Graham's speech on the application of public moneys for railroads and canals. Work on the Raleigh & Gaston Rail Road had commenced, though by February there were reports of an outbreak of smallpox along the line. The first meeting of the Raleigh & Columbia Rail Road had taken place, and the first annual meeting of the company was scheduled for that month. The Raleigh and Gaston was constructing its bridge over the Roanoke: three piers and one abutment of the bridge at Gaston had been constructed, and iron for the rails had been ordered from Maury, Latham and Company of Liverpool and A & G Ralston of Philadelphia.[47]

On May 2, 1837, eight days before the onset of the Panic, the *Raleigh Register* reported that the Warren County Superior Court was considering the constitutionality of the condemnation of land for use by the Raleigh & Gaston Rail Road. It was unclear that the charter of the company provided for it. The company had 1,200 laborers employed on the line by late July, and the five stone piers — 160 feet apart — and the abutments of the bridge at Gaston were finished. The total length of the bridge was 1,000 feet. The sixth installment on the stock of the Raleigh & Gaston was announced in September, and installments came due in the next month. As the year was drawing to a close, the Weldon Toll Bridge was nearly finished and several cars were taken across by horses; the Wilmington & Raleigh Rail Road had finished work on the bridge across the Northeast Cape Fear ten miles from Wilmington.[48]

The second annual meeting of the stockholders of the Raleigh & Gaston Rail Road was held on January 22, 1838, at the state bank in Raleigh. The railroad clearly was experiencing some problems, even though the tone of the text appears to be optimistic. Thirty-eight miles of the road had been graded, a shipment of iron had been received, and they expected forty-eight miles of the railroad to be in operation by June. Sills had not been laid on the roadbed due to the frost. The company had expended considerable time and capital building on their bridge over the Roanoke; however, it had yet to be completed. Deliveries of timber had been delayed by low water levels on the Roanoke. The company admitted it did not have the capital to finish the project, offered its remaining shares for subscription, and also contemplated pursuing a loan in England.[49] George Mordecai failed in his attempt to secure money in Europe; however, he managed to purchase 800 tons of iron at a low rate. The North Carolina General Assembly in their 1838–1839 session passed "An Act for the relief of the Raleigh and Gaston Rail Road Company" wherein the state endorsed the bonds of the company in the amount of $500,000, and required the railroad to mortgage their property to secure the state from any loss. The General Assembly would later foreclose on the mortgage when the company became insolvent.[50]

In an obvious way, the Raleigh & Gaston Rail Road needed to be connected south or east. The projected Raleigh & Columbia Rail Road failed to meet sufficient subscriptions to its stock as required by its charter. By the time of their annual meeting in 1839, the company reported that there were five bridges on the route of the railroad and that their total estimated cost was $155,000. The cost of the railroad, including the bridges, was $14,378 per mile. The report mentioned that travelers were deterred

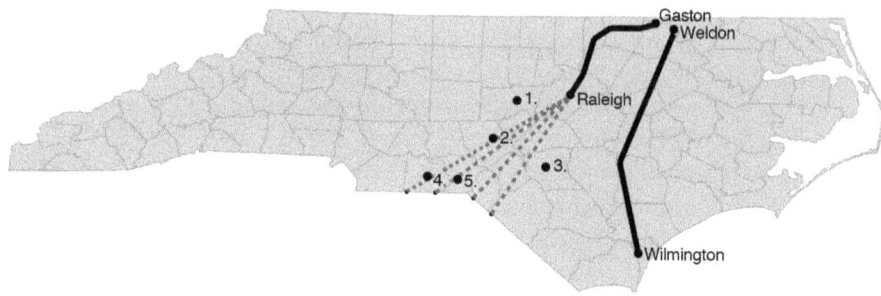

This map illustrates the routes of the Raleigh & Gaston Rail Road and the Wilmington & Raleigh Rail Road. By its charter, the projected Raleigh & Columbia Rail Road could extend from the Raleigh & Gaston to any point on the South Carolina line within thirty miles of Rockingham (5). The gray dotted lines indicate possible routes that end fifteen miles apart at the state line. The numbered points are towns where subscriptions were taken for the Raleigh & Columbia: Pittsboro (1), Carthage (2), Fayetteville (3), Wadesboro (4). The second line west of Fayetteville is the shortest. However, the line passing through Rockingham is in a direct line to Columbia, South Carolina. *See* North Carolina, *Laws of the State of North Carolina Passed by the General Assembly at the Session of 1836–37* (Raleigh: Thomas J. Lemay, 1837), 207–207.

by the difficult stage ride from Columbia and Augusta to Raleigh, but they still anticipated the eventual benefits of a Raleigh to Columbia railroad. They dismissed the merits of an inland rail connection between Wilmington and Charleston that would replace that company's steamship line.[51] That the officers of the Raleigh & Gaston Rail Road were perpetually enamored with their connections to Petersburg and never abandoned the dream of pushing their railroad south to Columbia is significant. This connection was an element of their plans, despite the proposed building of any railroad link between Wilmington and Raleigh. It was, in essence, the official position presented in Gavin Hogg's *Address of the Internal Improvement Central Committee*. Had the Raleigh & Columbia Rail Road been constructed, it would have diverted north-to-south traffic away from the coast.

The Raleigh & Gaston had anticipated carrying the "Great Mail," through its connection with the Greensville & Roanoke at Gaston, rather than via the junction of the several railroads at Weldon. Others, such as early promoter Judge Duncan Cameron, were of the opinion that the Weldon junction would "command the transportation of the mails." The company suffered the loss of a significant source of income when the contract was awarded to the Wilmington & Raleigh.[52] Cameron's reasoning was fatally correct. If there were a first law of transporting the mails, major junctions on operating networks would be favored over dead-ends on projected networks. Connecting the Raleigh & Gaston Rail Road to Weldon was inevitable, and is evidenced by that the fact the Post Office Department had determined that its First Class — the "Great Atlantic line" from Boston to New Orleans — should connect south via Charleston. Once set, it would be developed from Charleston southward to New Orleans via Augusta and Covington, Georgia, by rail and Mobile to New Orleans by steamboat. The Wilmington to Charleston steamboat connection, albeit the weakest link, was the most direct. The Greensville & Roanoke Rail Road and the Raleigh & Gaston Rail Road were Second Class routes. The difference in the contract was significant. The Wilmington & Raleigh Rail Road received $75,000 annually to carry the mails from Weldon to Charleston seven times a week. The Petersburg Rail Road received $15,200 annually to carry the mails to Weldon seven times a week. The Greensville & Roanoke Rail Road received $2,000 annually to carry the mails to Gaston six times a week, and the Raleigh & Gaston Rail Road received $8,000 annually to carry the mails to Raleigh six times a week. The Norfolk to Weldon route and the Charleston to Savannah steamboat route were Second Class routes.[53] The Petersburg Rail Road and the Wilmington & Raleigh Rail Road, in the view of the Post Office Department, formed a section of the main trunk.

The Weldon to Charleston route had a somewhat controversial beginning. The *Memorial of Many Inhabitants of the City of Charleston Praying that the Southern Mail be Carried by Way of Halifax and Wilmington* dated November 27, 1837, and signed by David Alexander, president of the Charleston Chamber of Commerce, was submitted to Congress and was referred to the Committee on the Post Office and Post Roads on February 14, 1838. The memorial notes that the State of North Carolina had subscribed to two-fifths of the stock of the Wilmington & Raleigh Rail Road, sixty miles of the railroad would be completed by May 1, 1838, and in the interim, four horse coaches would run the line. Two steamboats would complete the connection from Wilmington to Charleston. The memorialists presented a timetable that shows that the change of route would result in a saving of time over the Halifax to Columbia route, via Fayetteville, Cheraw, and Camden. This memorial did not merely suggest the creation of a new route. It recommended the changing of the "Southern Great Mail" route — that is, all the mail dispatched south. This memorial was protested by the citizens of Cheraw in their *Petition of the Citizens of Cheraw*. They challenged Charleston's estimates of the times on the existing route, noting that the Raleigh & Gaston Rail Road would be completed by the following summer and the Raleigh & Columbia Rail Road had recently been incorporated by the North Carolina Legislature. Additionally, an application was made to the South Carolina Legislature for the incorporation of a railroad to run from the South Carolina line to Columbia. The *Petition of the Citizens of Camden* noted that the Wilmington & Raleigh Rail Road route to Charleston was at the extreme east of both North Carolina and South Carolina. The Wilmington to Charleston steamboat connection excluded an extensive area of commercial towns, coastal and interior, from direct distribution of mails. The interior route was geographically situated to distribute the mails east and west. The *Memorial of John Bryce and 212 Others, Inhabitants of Columbia, S.C., and Vicinity, Remonstrating Against the Removal of the Great Southern Mail Route* argued in favor of the superior efficiency of the interior route when the projected Raleigh & Gaston and Raleigh & Columbia would be completed. On July 7, 1838, Congress ratified *An Act to Establish Certain Post Routes and to Discontinue Others*. This piece of legislation is significant in two aspects. "Section Two" of the act makes all railroads in the United States, in existence or thereafter to be built, post routes, and "Section One" establishes a route from Weldon to Charleston via Halifax, Enfield, Waynesborough, South Washington, and Wilmington. The route changes mentioned in the act in "Section Three" were to go into effect on July 1, 1839, or sooner.[54]

The awarding of the Southern Great Mail contract to the Wilmington & Raleigh Rail Road illustrates that there were two great rail networks developing to the north and south that were independent of the influence of Petersburg and Norfolk. The decision on the part of the Petersburg Rail Road to build to Blakeley had determined the subsequent development of the network to the south of the Roanoke. The building of the Greensville & Roanoke was a wasted move, for there was one direction to take after reaching the Roanoke, which was to cross it. The building of the Portsmouth & Roanoke Rail Road, and the subsequent bridging of the Roanoke at Weldon, established a new objective: Halifax. Had the original Roanoke & Raleigh Rail Road scheme proceeded, Raleigh would have connected to Weldon or Halifax.[55] To the north, the railroads being built from New York, to Philadelphia, and to Fredericksburg were trending south. The early construction of the Charleston & Hamburg Rail Road established a westward trending rail network below the Santee River. These networks, even if one considers the transport of Great Mail, needed to be linked. The early construction of the Petersburg Rail Road established a southward trending rail network to intersect the South Carolina railroads. The Petersburg Rail Road thus became aware of this when the 1838 changes brought about a change in the designation of the express mail route.

The *Memorial of The Petersburg Railroad Company, Praying the Payment of a Sum of Money Withheld from Them, Under Their Contract for the Transportation of the Mail*, dated December 27, 1838, and signed by Charles F. Osborne, expresses the company's bewilderment of a loss of $8,000 from their contract for changes brought about in 1838. The changes, issued to the company by S. R. Hobbie of the Contract Office of the Post Office Department, placed the beginning of the express mail route going south at Gaston and the end of express mail service north of Petersburg. In a letter to the company, included in a report to the Committee on the Post Office and Post Roads of the Senate dated January 23, 1839, Postmaster General Kendall explained to the company that Petersburg was the last distributing post office going south and the first going north. The express mail began at Gaston and extended south. The Post Office Department had also given contracts to the railroads operating from Richmond to Philadelphia, thus eliminating a need to provide express service — all the mail from the Roanoke to New York City traveled by rail. The mail separated from the total dispatch at Gaston as express mail, even if it arrived there from New York in a separate express pouch, was not express mail until it left Gaston south. The express mail arriving at Gaston from the south, was part of the great mail traveling north on the Petersburg Rail Road.[56]

This is more than an interesting piece of historical trivia. That the express dispatch had been changed from Blakeley to Gaston — the Petersburg Rail Road had to wait for its scheduled arrival at Gaston — indicates that the Great Mail was dispatched on the Wilmington & Raleigh Rail Road. The express dispatch was not needed at this junction with the Petersburg Rail Road, and the discontinuation of the express service north of Gaston indicates that the railroads north of Petersburg had formed a continuous network. The merger of the Weldon & Halifax and the Wilmington & Raleigh, and the early operation of this road with its mix of rail, stage, and steamboat connections, ensured that it would receive the contract for the Southern Great Mail — the validation that the Wilmington & Raleigh Rail Road was the only trunk line passing through North Carolina.

The "Report of Walter Gwynn, Esq., Engineer, to the President and Directors of the Wilmington and Raleigh Rail Road Company," prepared in 1836, justified the route to Halifax in the conclusion to his survey.

> Routes passing through the interior, with a view to divert travel, must be regarded as experiments, running counter to all experience, and of very doubtful success. And I lay it down as an incontrovertible fact, that those works which will prove most profitable, and conducive to the great and varied interests of the country, may be classified under two heads. Those which connect the commercial cities, and those which lead from commercial towns by the most direct routes to the interior and western portions of our country.... All the improvements which are contemplated from the sea-board to the western part of your state, must cross the line of your railway; and to whatever point destined, will find it to their interest, to some extent, to pursue it, in order to make of the most favorable location. Under this aspect, your rail road presents itself to the state in a peculiarly interesting point of view. It traverses it nearly through its entire length from north to south, and forms the basis upon which the internal improvement scheme of the Raleigh Convention may be most economically carried out.[57]

Gwynn noted three additional significant features of the route that recommended its acceptance. The railroad, through its connections with the Portsmouth & Roanoke and Petersburg railroads to the north and connection to Charleston by steamboat to the south, would be a work of national importance. The railroad could serve a strategic function for the concentration of troops and munitions for the defense of the seaboard. The scope of the project placed it "beyond the reach of competition."[58]

Contrary to the opinions of the critics of the Wilmington to Halifax route, the citizens of Wilmington could not do better by running their railroad to Raleigh. It did not matter that Raleigh interests did or did not support the Wilmington to Raleigh route, nor that the Wilmington & Raleigh Rail Road officials threatened commercial interests in Petersburg—and their Raleigh business partners—by upsetting their plans to create a monopoly on the agricultural output of North Carolina's Piedmont. The benefits of maintaining competition between the Virginia railroads for market share at their junction near Weldon, in addition to opening up the Charleston market to the same, were obviously better for the citizens of the east than supporting the Petersburg monopoly. If Gwynn's assessment of the viability of routes were correct, the Central Rail Road, not the Raleigh & Gaston, would have served the best interests of the city of Raleigh and Piedmont agriculturalists. By 1839, the incorporators of the Raleigh & Gaston Rail Road had joined with some who had served the Wilmington & Raleigh Rail Road to form the Weldon Rail Road Company to connect the Raleigh & Gaston to the Portsmouth & Roanoke at Weldon.[59] During the 1840s, the Petersburg Rail Road built its own bridge over the Roanoke at Blakeley; and by the end of the Civil War, the Raleigh & Gaston opted to use their connection to Weldon rather than rebuild their bridge at Gaston that was destroyed during the war. The Greensville & Roanoke Rail Road, with its connection south severed, would cease to exist.

CHAPTER III

The Building of a Railroad

The Wilmington & Raleigh Rail Road was completed in March of 1840. At 161½ miles long, it was the longest railroad in the world, and it operated another 150 miles of steamboat service. During its construction, the company had used a stagecoach line to bridge the gap in the rails between the northern and southern sections, and its steamboats maintained regular service to Charleston. The railroad had actually been in service since mid–1837, providing a through ticket—"tri-weekly line of communication between Charleston and Weldon."[1] It was a multimodal trunk linking north to south through relatively underdeveloped territory. The Wilmington & Manchester Railroad, through its junction with the South Carolina Railroad, would replace the steamboat connection to Charleston through its junction with the South Carolina Railroad in the 1850s. Another railroad route passing north to south through North Carolina would not exist until the Piedmont Railroad, between Danville and Greensboro, was built during the Civil War.

The unprecedented length of the Wilmington & Raleigh Rail Road, and the interstate concepts behind its design, established the significance of this railroad in the history of transportation planning. It was not merely a railroad for accumulation of agricultural produce for a regional commercial center, or a railroad connecting a port with the interior, or a railroad connecting commercial towns; it actually formed the original north-south trunk through North Carolina that would endure, with some changes, into the twentieth century. It was the product of state and private capital, and was the only railroad of the several recommended for state investment in the mid–1830s that would proceed. There were abundant surveys for vast railroads such as the Charleston & Cincinnati Rail Road, and many companies were chartered to build stupendous railroads. This was the only railroad that had actually proceeded to completion. Hitherto, the early history of the Wilmington & Raleigh Rail Road, from both a technical and economic perspective, has gone unexamined. To appreciate fully this successful route, one must understand from primary sources the details of its planning, construction, and equipment.

Walter Gwynn, who later became the chief engineer of the Wilmington & Raleigh Rail Road, was one of nine West Point graduates on the team of topographical assistants selected by the principal engineers to undertake the survey of the Baltimore & Ohio Rail Road in 1828. During this survey, the engineers marked a 66-foot wide path with stakes. Stations, or places where instrument readings were taken, were numbered in sequence. Benchmarks were marked in red, and places that needed to be cut or filled were marked. The engineers and assistants required a team of men to set up instruments, clear undergrowth, set stakes, prepare meals, and drive the wagons. The survey party usually included fifteen men.[2] Gwynn would work on the survey for the Petersburg Rail Road, and later become the chief engineer for the Portsmouth & Roanoke Rail Road.[3] He was surveying the route for it in early 1836, and by April, he had found three sites for crossing the Northeast Cape Fear River on the outskirts of Wilmington. The company expected the survey to be done in time to lay a cornerstone for the Fourth of July.[4] No doubt he applied the same expertise in North Carolina that he had exhibited in his earlier work. The issues of *The Wilmington Advertiser* between July 1836 and March 1837 are missing, but other North Carolina newspapers contain articles that fill the gap. It appears that the survey took longer than anticipated.

> *Wilmington and Raleigh Rail Road.*—We are gratified to learn, that the Engineers of this road, have completed a survey of one entire line, running between the N. E. River and Long Creek, through Waynesboro to Halifax; and a part of another line from Goshen down on the west side of Long Creek. They are now engaged on a line, on the east side of the N. E. river by Rockfort, on the Neuse, through Tarborough.[5]

Walter Gwynn's report on the survey for the Wilmington & Halifax Railway (an early unofficial name of the Wilmington & Raleigh) appears in the October issue of *Farmers' Register,* a monthly journal published by Edmund Ruffin. Gwynn proposed an eastern and a western route that would begin in the town of Wilmington and junction with the Halifax & Weldon Rail Road. The western route commences in Wilmington at a place known as "Dry Pond" on the southern boundary of Wilmington. The Wilmington terminus would actually be located on the northern boundary. Crossing Smith Creek, the railroad continued to the site of the old bridge over the Northeast Cape Fear River. The route crossed Rockfish Creek and Stewart Creek to Bear Swamp in a direct line of forty-five miles. It then turned toward Waynesborough at Goshen Swamp, crossed Brooks Branch and Yellow Marsh, and entered Waynesborough near the site of the bridge that carries the stage road between that town and Fayetteville over the Neuse River. The route continued to Enfield and Halifax. Walter Gwynn included a variant to the Western Route beginning at the "timber pens" presumably that existed at Point Peter opposite Wilmington on the

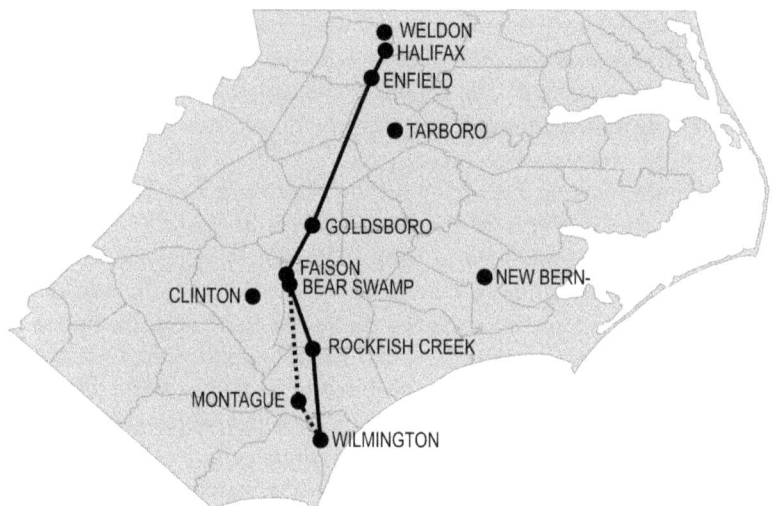

This map of modern eastern North Carolina illustrates Walter Gwynn's Western Route of the Wilmington & Raleigh Rail Road. The names of the places given are current and some are for reference purposes. The solid line represents the accepted variant of the Western Route. The distance is 161½ miles. Walter Gwynn gives this distance in his survey. The railroad crosses Rockfish Creek and continues to Bear Swamp. The dotted line indicates the alternate route from Wilmington to Bear Swamp. The abandoned track of the 1890s Cape Fear & Yadkin Valley Railroad avoids the swamps of the Cape Fear lowlands by passing on the high ground between Moore's Creek and Long Creek as Gwynn described in his 1836 survey. The Cape Fear & Yadkin Valley Railroad turned northwest at Montague. This location is the first point offering the opportunity for a direct route to Bear Swamp over moderate ground. *See* "Extracts from the Report of Walter Gwynn, Esq., Engineer, to the President and Directors of the Wilmington and Raleigh Rail Road Company," *Farmers' Register* (October 1836), 348–351.

Cape Fear River, and proceeded across the "dividing ground" (Eagle Island) at the confluence of the northeast and northwest tributaries of the Cape Fear. It continued between Long Creek and Moore's Creek, and Rockfish Creek, to the head of Bear Swamp. This route would follow the course of the old 1890s route of the Cape Fear & Yadkin Railroad from Wilmington that parallels present-day US 421 to Montague, then followed a direct course to Bowdens.

The Eastern Route differs significantly in that it crossed the Neuse River at Rockford Bridge (N 35.23348; W 77.82112) east of Goldsboro, then crossed Contentnea Creek at Edwards Bridge (N 35.41320; W 77.49667) at present-day Schuffleton on the Green/Pitt county line. It would then continue to Tarboro, and pass through the divide between Deep Creek and Conoconnara Creek, and turn west to enter Halifax below

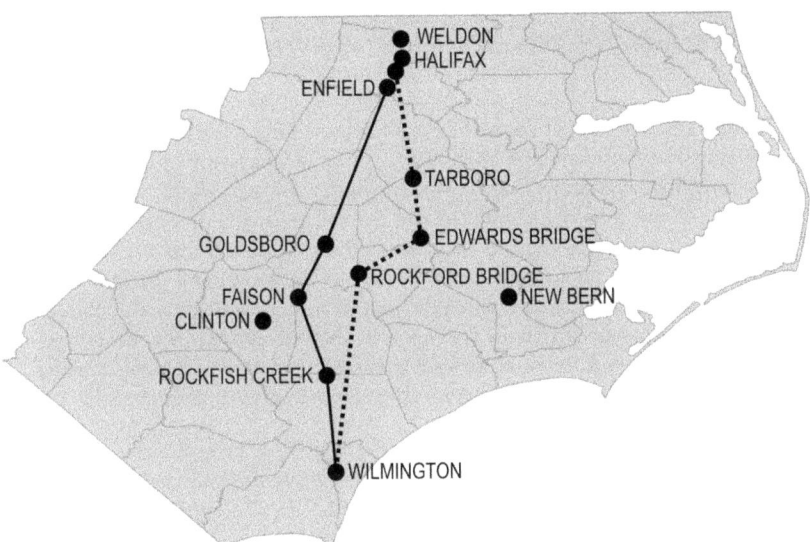

This map of modern eastern North Carolina illustrates Walter Gwynn's Eastern Route of the Wilmington & Raleigh Rail Road. The names of the places given are current and some are for reference purposes. The solid line illustrates the accepted route of the railroad. The broken line represents the Eastern Route. The total distance is 162½ miles from Wilmington to Weldon. This distance matches Gwynn's calculations, and the map given here includes those places mentioned in the report. *See* "Extracts from the Report of Walter Gwynn, Esq., Engineer, to the President and Directors of the Wilmington and Raleigh Rail Road Company," *Farmers' Register* (October 1836), 348–351.

Quankey Creek.⁶ The section of the later Seaboard Coastline Railroad between Scotland Neck to Halifax followed the general path suggested by Gwynn for the northern end of his eastern route. An abandoned section of railroad leading from Scotland Neck to Tarboro via the town of Speed appears to be a favorable continuation of the route south. However, Gwynn's estimate of 162 miles and 1,504 feet of rails does not fit into this model. Starting at "Dry Pond" in Wilmington and proceeding in a direct line to Rockford Bridge, then directly to Edwards Bridge, to Tarboro, to Halifax, and then to Weldon, would be a length of more than 162½ miles.

The company selected the Western Route. It began on the north side of Wilmington at the river rather than at "Dry Pond," and it continued to Faison, where it arced towards Goldsboro (Waynesborough), and continued to Rocky Mount, Halifax, and Weldon. The total length of the route was 161½ miles. The selection of this route is confirmed in the "Proceedings of the Second Annual Meeting of the Stockholders of the Wilmington & Raleigh Rail Road Company" after construction was well under way.

> In laying before you an account of their transactions since the last annual meeting, the President and Directors have the satisfaction to state, that after the most thorough examination of this country through which the road is to pass, its location has been decided and fixed — passing ¾ of a mile east of Waynesborough, crossing the Tar River — through Enfield and Halifax to Weldon; making the total distance between Wilmington and Weldon 161 miles. Having carefully examined the several routes surveyed and reported to them, they concur entirely in the opinion, that the above is the most eligible; and their expectation of its speedy completion, at the original estimate, (as will appear by a communication from their Engineer) are now fully confirmed.⁷

Governor Dudley commenced the work on the railroad by turning the first spade of earth on October 25, 1836.⁸ In November, the *Raleigh Register* carried an article concerning the stockholder meeting held November 7 of that year. Work was to begin at the Halifax division.⁹ The plan involved eventually having two crews working at both ends of the road. The Wilmington crew would put down rail to Faison's Depot and turn north to join with the Halifax crew working toward Enfield. This was determined at the meeting of the stockholders on March 14 and 15 of that year. The first mention of the letting of contracts on the road appeared in the *Carolina Observer* (Fayetteville) in late January of 1837. At that time, the eighty-eight miles of the route from Wilmington to Waynesborough (Goldsboro) had been located, and the company had awarded contracts for fifty-two miles of grading. Contractors had cut a large portion of the timber for the superstructure. By February, the officers of the company were happy to report to their stockholders that the stockholders of the Halifax & Weldon Rail Road Company had agreed to merge their stock with the Wilmington & Raleigh Rail Road Company. The contractor responsible for putting down rails began work in April of 1837.[10]

Contractors, with an average force of 900 laborers, were at work grading the road in early 1837. In addition to the extent of work reported in February, contractors were grading the twelve miles from Halifax to Enfield. The company issued contracts for rail and sills to landowners along 100 miles of the route. By November, fifty-three miles of grading were completed, contractors were grading another forty-three miles, they had put down twenty-three and a half miles of rails, and another thirty miles of rails were in progress. Two Stephenson locomotives had arrived and were being used to carry construction materials. Work on the bridge over the Northeast Cape Fear River, ten miles from Wilmington, was under way. The bridge was 360 feet long with three spans resting on two stone abutments and two stone piers. The water at this location was thirty-six feet deep. The shops and fixtures at Wilmington were under construction. The company's stagecoaches took two and half days to travel from Halifax to the company docks in Wilmington.[11]

In November of 1837, the train was in operation between Halifax and Weldon. This was the first regular train running over a significant distance in North Carolina. The locomotive and cars were in use every day except Sunday and Tuesday to convey passengers as far as the track was open in late December from Wilmington. Twenty miles of track were open on the southern division of the road as far as Armstrong's farm two months later. The daily schedule of departure from Wilmington was pushed back from 11:00 A.M. to 9:30 A.M.[12] In April, the *Wilmington Advertiser* reprinted an article from the *Raleigh Register* on the progress of the road:

> We learn that by the first of May, at farthest, this road will be completed in Teachy's, 3 miles above Rockfish, or 42 miles from Wilmington. One month thereafter, 7 miles more; on the first of July, 5 more; and by the middle of August, 5 more. This will make 59 miles, and reaches the cross roads from Duplin Old Courthouse, and thence to Limestone. It is expected that 20 miles, from Weldon to Enfield, will be opened by the first of June.[13]

The *Wilmington Advertiser* reported on May 4, 1838, "A most dreaded part of the road, the Burgaw Swamp, thirty miles from Wilmington is finished, and the cars will traverse it probably tomorrow." In the same article, it is stated, "A good deal of produce has already been brought to this market by way of the railroad, such as Turpentine, Tar, Bacon, Corn &c." The schedule for departure from the Wilmington Depot was pushed back another hour to 8:30 A.M. by mid–May. In October of 1838, the northern end of the line was in operation as far south as Enfield, and the southern end had extended service to Faison. The company's stagecoaches serviced the 90 miles between Faison Depot and Enfield. Twelve miles of track between Faison and Martin's farm (in the neighborhood of the present-day town of Dudley) was completed by mid–December, and the first train was sent over this stretch of track on December 20, 1838.[14] The remaining nine miles of track to Waynesborough lacked only the iron for completion. Shipped from New York and Philadelphia, it arrived in early 1839. On the occasion of Washington's Birthday in Waynesborough on February 22, 1839, the town was witness to the arrival of the first train as well as the first steamboat, the *E. D. McNair,* to navigate the Neuse River to that point. The union of river and rail transport at Waynesborough was significant in that the steamboat provided a connection to New Bern that served until a railroad was built between the towns. The train brought dignitaries from Wilmington, including the Wilmington Volunteers and their band.[15]

At the third annual meeting of the stockholders held at Waynesborough on the sixth and seventh of May of 1839, the company reported that 103 miles of the line were open. The company had ten locomotives in service and four eight-wheeled passenger cars. Each had a capacity of fifty passengers. Two sections of the line totaling about eighteen miles were expected to be open by July. This left fifty-eight miles of track to be completed. Iron for the railroad was being shipped to Wilmington and Portsmouth. By August, twenty-one miles in two sections were completed, thus reducing the distance between the two divisions to thirty-seven miles. The trains traveled ninety-three miles on the southern division, and thirty-one miles on the northern division. At this time, the stagecoaches ran forty-two miles, but this was reduced to thirty miles when twelve miles of track opened in October.[16]

The opening of the line into the interior of the state improved commerce in both directions. By September, *The Wilmington Advertiser* quoted a report in *The Wilmington Chronicle* that twenty-three freight cars of "merchandise of various kinds" had left the port for the rural markets along the line. Similarly, the opening of the last sections of the road brought the first load of bacon ever from Greene County, a product previously shipped to New Bern. At this time, the stage route had been reduced to thirty miles. On October 11, *The Wilmington Advertiser* announced that the ship *Oberlin* had arrived in New York with a shipment of 575 tons of iron from

England for the railroad, and the same issue reported that a Norris locomotive had been purchased and was expected to be in place at the northern end of the road by early November. On November 4, 1839, the Wilmington & Raleigh Rail Road held its Fourth Annual Meeting (though the Third Annual Meeting had been held in May) in Wilmington. A total of 130 miles of the railroad was reported in use at that time.[17]

In early January of 1840, the *Wilmington Advertiser* published an article that provides details of the progress of the railroad. Trains ran daily over 125½ miles of track from Wilmington to the Tar River, and 29½ miles of track from Weldon to Battle's Depot—a total of 155 miles. This left only 6 miles to be completed. In addition, the *Wilmington Advertiser* includes detail on curves and grades:

> Only 21 1–2 miles 650 feet of this road are curved, leaving the unparalleled amount of 139 1–2 miles of straight road, in a total length of 161 miles. One of these straight lines is 47 miles long; others are 3- 4- 6- 7- 8- and 15- miles in length. The shortest radius of curvature used is 5730 feet and most of the radii arc 12 — 20 and 30,000 feet,— the radius of one curve is 68,240 feet in length — which curve is considered equal to a straight line — The steepest grade on the road is 30 feet per mile — these occur only in approaching the few streams that cross the line — the grades generally are level or near approximations to level grades.[18]

The remaining 30 miles would not be completed until March of 1840. Sprunt gives March 7, 1840, as the day on which the last spike was driven. Burton Alva Konkle states in his biography of John Motley Morehead that the exact time the last spike was driven that day was at 12 P.M., and the first train from Wilmington arrived at Weldon at 9 P.M.. A celebration was held at Wilmington Depot on April 15, 1840. The Wilmington Volunteers provided music for the occasion, and food was provided for a crowd of 550. *The Wilmington Weekly Chronicle* gave a detailed account of the festivities.[19] The following map illustrates the timeline of construction. The complexity of the undertaking is reflected in the company's report to the state on expenditures.[20] The cost of the railroad had been $1,638,812.57 and the cost of the four steamboats and their fixtures had been $270,942.97; thus, the total cost amounted to $1,909,755.54.[21]

The Wilmington & Raleigh Rail Road operated its steamship line between Wilmington and Charleston from 1837 until rendered unnecessary by the completion of the Wilmington & Manchester Rail Road in 1854. The docks of the steamboat packet of the Wilmington & Raleigh Rail Road in Charleston were located at the foot of Laurens Street south of the shipyards.[22]

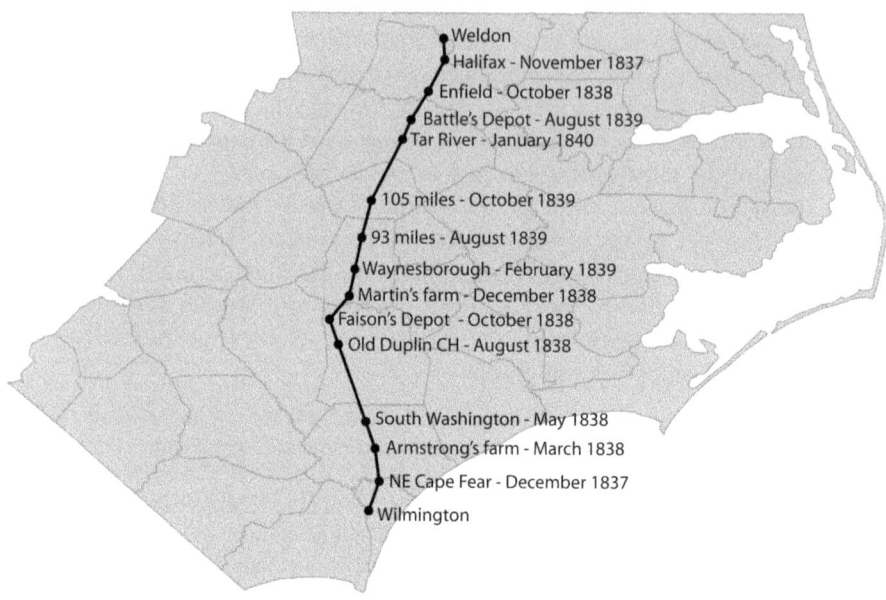

This map illustrates the timeline of construction for the Wilmington & Raleigh Rail Road. Each point represents a section of track that was opened for use based upon available documentation. Construction commenced at both the southern and northern divisions in 1837.

The company owned six ships during this period: the *Boston, North Carolina, Governor Dudley, C. Vanderbilt, Wilmington,* and *Gladiator,* all of which were side-paddle passenger vessels. The steamboat line was, in essence, an extension of the railroad into South Carolina that exploited a pre-established water route, and the railroad was able to provide this service almost immediately. While the steamboat line never carried the volume of the freight of the railroad, it did provide passengers with the most convenient access to the south. At the May 1, 1837, meeting of the stockholders, President James Owen reported that a steamboat had been purchased since their last meeting in February of that year, and it had arrived in advance of the company's stagecoaches.

> Contracts have been entered into for another steamboat, under the supervision of one of the most skilful and scientific builders of our country, and she will be ready in the month of October, at which time we anticipate that 50 miles of the Rail Road will be completed, and furnished with coaches and cars for the transportation of passengers and produce.[23]

The first steamship between Wilmington and Charleston in May was the *Boston*. References to this vessel appear in the annual report submitted by president *pro tem* Alexander Anderson to the Board of Internal Improvement in 1838, along with the financial report prepared by company treasurer James S. Green. The company had paid $58,233.70 for the *Boston*, which was traded to the shipbuilding firm of Watchman & Bratt in partial payment for the new steamship *Wilmington*.[24] During December of 1837, the *North Carolina* was the second steamship to be put into service. This ship had a brief and troublesome beginning with a return to New York for maintenance in 1838[25]; and in May of 1839, she collided with company steamship *C. Vanderbilt* off the South Carolina coast near Georgetown, and both ships were forced to return to Charleston.[26] The captains of both ships were suspended pending an investigation by the company.[27] As a result, Captain Davis of the *North Carolina* was relieved of his command. The *North Carolina* was expected to be ready for service again by the first of June.[28] A year later, on July 25, 1840, the company steamship *Governor Dudley* collided with the *North Carolina* as the two ships were passing. This time, the *North Carolina* was lost. The *Governor Dudley* was the third steamship of the company to be put into service.

In her *Journal*, Frances Anne Kemble included details in her voyage from Wilmington to Charleston on the *Governor Dudley*. Mrs. Kemble and her family set out to the railroad company's docks to board the ship in the afternoon of December 24, 1838. They had only arrived in Wilmington at five o'clock in the morning that same day. Mrs. Kemble, a perennial critic by nature with an almost pathological obsession with neatness, had been subjected to a two-day ordeal on the yet to be completed Wilmington & Raleigh Rail Road. She had been deprived of rest, jostled about on the stagecoach, exposed to the cold wind, and been offered strange, interrupted meals in dirty environments — all in the company of equally miserable strangers. Her experience on the *Governor Dudley* appears to be a relatively pleasant change, though she could not repress the desire to criticize something, the curtains of the sleeping berths.[29]

A more jovial writer, T.A.R., composed a story for the March/April 1843 issue of *Orion, a Monthly Magazine of Literature and Art*, entitled "Locomotion: Or, Lights and Shades of Travel." The tale describes his travel in the company of a friend on the Wilmington & Raleigh Rail Road trains, stagecoaches, and steamboats during 1838. The writer notes that "yellow Jack," meaning Yellow Fever, in the South had caused a "derangement and uncertainty in public conveyances to those latitudes." His observations on the coach ride and the eating arrangement along the route confirm Mrs. Kemble's experiences. T.A.R. notes that it was five in the morning when his company arrived in Wilmington. The steamboat *Governor Dudley* was scheduled to dock at eight, but T.A.R. reported that the steamship had been late for the last three of its tri-weekly trips. After waiting, the writer and his company chartered another steamboat, *Cotton Plant*, to take them as far as Smithville (now Southport), there to meet the *Governor Dudley* with instructions from the "Wilmington agency" to exchange passengers — the *Cotton Plant* returning to Wilmington and the *Governor Dudley* returning to Charleston. The *Cotton Plant* was prepared at one in the afternoon, and was ready to cast off at two. There were at least thirty-four passengers, seven of whom had been waiting for the boat to Charleston for more than a week. The passengers were required to pay for the trip to Smithville, but were reimbursed by the captain of the *Governor Dudley*.[30]

The *C. Vanderbilt* began her service on the railroad's Wilmington to Charleston Packet in December of 1838. Upon adding the *C. Vanderbilt* to their fleet and a contract from the Post Office Department, the company began daily trips to Charleston. In spite of the collision with the *North Carolina*, the ship appears to have required only a new boiler, which was constructed for the ship in the company shops at Wilmington.[31] The editor of the *New Orleans Commercial Bulletin* expressed his satisfaction with the *Vanderbilt* when he opted, in 1849, to proceed north via the steamship line and railroads from Charleston rather than a steamer bound for New York; but also noted that maintaining the steamboat line was a drain on the profits of the Wilmington & Raleigh.[32] The *Wilmington* was built in 1839 in Baltimore and put into service in September of the same year. The builder was Langley B. Cully, and its captain was Charles Ivey. The woodwork was executed by T. Morris & Son, and was perceived to be an example of fine craftsmanship. "We understand that $10,000 or $15,000 more have been expended upon the Baltimore boat than the builders are to receive by the contract."[33] A more detailed account of the vessel's specifications appears in the *Wilmington Advertiser* in late September. The editor derived some of his material from *Lyford's Price Current*, a weekly commercial published in Baltimore.[34] The article includes comments from the captain, Charles Ivey. He stated that the ship's guards were eighteen inches higher above the waterline than other boats. In addition, the wheel buckets were made of iron, and the boiler burnt one cord of wood per hour.[35] The *Gladiator* was the last vessel added to the railroad's steamship line. Built in New York in 1841, it became operational on the Wilmington to Charleston Packet in the same year. Its gross tonnage was 379 tons.[36] The sparse record that has survived appears to indicate that the *Gladiator* performed admirably.

In 1849, the United States Government chartered the steamship to transport troops from Smithville to Palatka, Florida. The officers of the company, under the command of Captain A. Elzey, prepared a card that expressed their gratitude to the captain and crew of the ship.[37]

The steamboats were scheduled to arrive in Charleston at ten o'clock in the morning. It appears from the 1849 annual report that with four vessels operating up to the termination of the packet in February of 1854, the company employed crews for three — three captains, three first mates, three second mates, four first engineers, four second engineers, eight firemen, six wheelmen, nine deckhands, three stewards, three stewardesses, six waiters, three cooks, six knife boys and scullions, and an additional three deckhands that were slaves. The report of James T. Miller, the agent for the company's steamboat line, included in the 1850 annual report of the company a listing of three captains: Smith commanded the *Gladiator;* Bates, the *Governor Dudley;* and Sterrett, the *Wilmington.* The *Governor Dudley,* from the description provided in the report, appears to have encountered hurricane conditions in August of that year, but still performed well. The *C. Vanderbilt* was out of order awaiting the delivery of a new boiler. The following year, at the next annual meeting, the company reported that the *Vanderbilt* has been completely "rebuilt from her keel up," including machinery, to the point of being "a new boat in all but her name." An examination of the earlier 1847 annual report indicates that the *Gladiator* had undergone repairs during the year and was in need of having the copper lining of the hull replaced. The other three ships had been modified to remove a design flaw; the guards were removed to make them more navigable in bad weather.[38]

The end of the Wilmington to Charleston packet came with the competition of the Wilmington & Manchester Rail Road in early 1854.[39] The line had created a prolonged regular commercial intercourse between the ports. It was a *de facto* extension of the Wilmington & Raleigh Rail Road, but it was also a temporary device whose demise was the intended outcome of a planned advancement of rails southward. During the following year, S. L. Fremont, engineer and superintendent of the company, reported at the 1855 annual meeting that "way travel," that is, from one place on the line to another place rather than "through travel," had increased since that steam packet had been discontinued. This was in part due to the reduction of the Wilmington to Weldon ticket from "through" to "way" fare.[40]

The opening of southeastern North Carolina and northeastern South Carolina by the Wilmington & Manchester Rail Road, and the connection between the North Carolina Rail Road and the Wilmington & Weldon

Rail Road at Goldsboro, established a network with a multitude of passenger and freight destinations on the existing line. For example, the long anticipated rail connection between Raleigh and Wilmington was available, and the counties of Brunswick and Columbus to the south of Wilmington acquired access to and from the port by rail. The steamboat packet could fulfill only so much within the limits of time and connections. The accommodations the steamboats offered through passengers stand in stark contrast with the aggravations associated with stagecoach and railroad travel. The intent of the Wilmington to Charleston packet was not recreational, but rather a necessary extension of the Wilmington & Raleigh Rail Road to the ultimate intended length. When the rails were down, the railroad could unburden itself of its steamboats and its obsolete corporate name. In the delivery of the Great Mail, the steamboat connection from Wilmington to Charleston was problematic. It accounted for a significant number of incidents of failure of the mails on the New York to New Orleans Great Mail route, and by 1845 the Wilmington to Charleston steamboat connection was the section of the route responsible for many failures and irregularities of the mails, the major cause being weather related. The Mobile to New Orleans steamboat connection also experienced similar difficulties.[41] In the late 1840s, the Wilmington & Raleigh Rail Road anticipated a rail connection to South Carolina.

> We now confidently look forward to the time, when the Steam Boat line can be dispensed with, as there is every probability that the Wilmington and Manchester Road will be constructed. The completion of this Road would doubtless be of incalculable benefit to our Road, and every Stockholder is therefore deeply interested, in contributing to so desirable a result. The completion of the Wilmington and Manchester Rail Road, coupled with the renewal of our Road with heavy Iron, (while there would be a large diminution of expenses on our line) would secure an increase in speed of 24 hours, between the North and South, a large increase of our business, and safety and certainty, in the transmission of passengers, mail and freight.[42]

The route of the stagecoach line of the Wilmington & Raleigh Rail Road evolved during its brief existence between 1837 and 1840 as the railroad was being constructed. The southern route from Wilmington to Waynesborough followed roads that paralleled the projected railroad. The northern route, however, traversed areas of Edgecombe County (and what would later become Wilson County), and Wayne County that were bypassed by the railroad, particularly, the towns of Tarborough and Stantonsburg. The history of the state route was documented in several period North Carolina newspapers. Frances Anne Kemble's *Journal of a Residence on a Georgian Plantation, 1838–1839* contains an account of travel on the line, and documents from the Post Office Department provide information that is helpful in determining sections of the route.

The acquisition of stagecoaches and horses was mentioned at a meeting of the stockholders of the company held on May 1, 1837, at Wilmington. The following month, an article in the *Wilmington Advertiser* notes that double teams of horses had been stationed along the stagecoach route in advance of the arrival of the coaches. The stagecoach line had proven to be successful after its first month of service. An announcement in the January 3, 1838, issue of the *Raleigh Register* stated that the winter route for the southbound stages of the railroad started at Halifax and included a stopover at South Washington. The May 18, 1838, issue of the *Wilmington Advertiser* and the June 9, 1838, issue of the *Tarboro Press* reported the proceeding of the second annual meeting of the stockholders of the Wilmington & Raleigh Rail Road held earlier that month. The director considered and rejected a plan to change the stagecoach route from "Enfield, by Tarboro, to Stantonsburg, to the route by Rockymount" at this meeting. An article in the October 27, 1838, issue of the *Tarboro Press,* reprinted from the *Wilmington Advertiser,* announced the opening of the section of the railroad from Halifax to Enfield in the north and a section to Faison's Depot in the south. After the last spike of the railroad was driven on March 7, 1840, the stagecoach line was phased out. The stagecoaches were sold to C.W. Hause of Leechville in Beaufort County, North Carolina.[43]

At least three of these pieces of information found in newspaper articles are necessary for this study because they help establish locations along the route that can be associated with the narrative of traveling on the stagecoach line that fill the gaps in Frances Anne Kemble's narrative. A notice from the office of the Petersburg Rail Road Company dated October 27, 1838, announced to planters and farmers sending produce north consigned loads to their agent (Major B.F. Halsey) or the agent for the Wilmington & Raleigh Rail Road Company at Enfield. The *Wilmington Advertiser,* two days before Mrs. Kemble's stagecoach ride, names the southern termination of the stagecoach line in an article. Mrs. Kemble substantiates what the newspaper reports on the southern extent of the railroad. She notes that the stagecoach had traveled about ten miles after a stop in Waynesborough, and that a group of locals had gathered at the place where the stage stops to meet the train from Wilmington to see the locomotive "come up for only the third time into the midst of their savage solitude." An article reporting an example of fish being purchased in Wilmington and arriving in Tarboro the next day by way of the railroad's stagecoaches indicates that the stagecoach line was still servicing Tarboro in late 1838.[44] The two sections of the railroad that were in operation and towns located on the stagecoach route can be mapped out using the information provided in these articles for Mrs. Kemble's trip on December 23, 1838.

Mrs. Kemble, after departing Weldon by train between eight and nine o'clock in the evening, arrives four hours later at the end of the northern section of the railroad.

> Between twelve and one o'clock [in the early morning of Sunday, December 23, 1838], the engine stopped, and it was announced to us that we had traveled as far upon the railroad as it was yet completed, and that we must transfer ourselves to the stagecoaches; so in the dead middle of the night we crept out of the train, and taking our children in our arms, walked a few yards into an open space in the woods, where three four-horse coaches stood waiting to receive us.[45]

Mrs. Kemble's description of a group of men warming themselves by a fire at the end of the railroad most likely was a work crew, and the opening in the woods suggests that railroad construction had advanced a short distance south of Enfield. The log road that her stagecoach traveled that night went through swampland. The stage arrived at Stantonsburg shortly after sunrise. Kemble writes a single paragraph about the night's journey. There had been only a four-hour respite at Weldon from the time she left Portsmouth, Virginia.[46] It is evident from her account that both the Portsmouth & Roanoke Rail Road and the Wilmington & Raleigh Rail Road had subjected their passengers to an unimaginable ordeal to meet the scheduled connections. Mrs. Kemble and her family arrived at Wilmington at 5 A.M. on December 24, 1838, deprived of sleep and adequate nourishment after nearly two days of travel.

The mileage of stagecoach travel appears in the *Wilmington Advertiser* several times between 1838 and 1840. In October of 1838, the stage trip between Faison and Enfield was ninety miles.[47] The modern highway equivalent from Faison to Enfield via Goldsboro, Stantonsburg, and Tarboro (US 117, NC 111, NC 222, NC 33, and NC 44, to SR 1103), is 90.75 miles. However, in August of 1839 the southern division of the railroad had advanced to the ninety-three mile mark (in the neighborhood of Pikeville), and the northern division had advanced to Battle's Depot (Battleboro). The stage route was forty-two miles.[48] The direct distance between these locations is 40.32 miles and the route by modern highways is 42.70 (US 177 and US 301). Stantonsburg and/or Tarborough could not be on the stage route at this point. By October of that year, the southern

III. The Building of a Railroad 75

Map of the progress of construction on the Wilmington and Raleigh Rail Road during 1838, as reported in the area newspapers. The railroad was finished in March 1840. The total length of the railroad from Wilmington to Weldon was 161½ miles. The stagecoach line of the railroad operated during construction. By May 1838, the stage line ran from Halifax to South Washington. A section of rail from Halifax to Enfield was completed in October 1838, and the southern division was completed to Faison's Depot. By the last week of December, the railroad was within nine miles of Waynesborough.

division added twelve miles (near the site of present-day Contentnea Junction), and the train still stopped at Battle's Depot in the north. The stage route was thirty miles.[49] The direct distance between these locations is twenty-nine miles. On modern roads (US 177 and US 301), the distance is 30.43 miles. The obvious empirical conclusion, with some variation, is that the antebellum roads are the foundation of the modern roads; and the route of the stagecoach line of the Wilmington & Raleigh Rail Road closely approximates a set of modern roads. An examination of historic maps can determine whether the road network of the 1830s through 1860s in Edgecombe (Wilson) and Wayne counties contained roads that would allow a route that satisfies the distance conditions.

In 1863, Jeremy Francis Gilmer, a Confederate Army engineer, prepared the *Field Map of Lieut. Koener's Military Survey Between Neuse and Tar Rivers North Carolina*. This map, though drawn more than twenty years later than the completion of the railroad, illustrates the road network and topography of several counties from the Neuse River to the Virginia in fine detail.[50] What is immediately obvious is that many of the roads depicted in this map approximate modern roads in the same counties. These roads are even apparent on the earlier 1833 MacRae-Brazier *A New Map of the State of North Carolina* and the 1865 *U.S. Coast Survey*.[51] Three bridges crossing Fishing Creek are depicted in all the historic maps thus mentioned. The route from Enfield to Tarboro crossing Fishing Creek at the site of Spear's Bridge is 22.49 miles. However, the road from Enfield to Tarboro via Bell's Bridge, and the Tarboro-Stantonsburg Rd. were on post routes: these routes were twenty-four miles from Enfield to Tarboro, and forty-six miles from Tarboro to Waynesboro via Pitts Cross Roads, Oak Grove, and Stantonsburg.[52] That the railroad was able to deliver fish from Wilmington to Tarboro by their stagecoaches in late December of 1838 suggests that a Tarboro stop was on the route. It follows, then, that the best route of the stages would match the post route.

From a casual reading of Mrs. Kemble's *Journal*, it would seem reasonable to assume that the stagecoach traveled south to Rocky Mount, then on to Stantonsburg. However, the section of railroad between Enfield and Rocky Mount traverses the marshland of Swift Creek. This is the type of topography where the early builders of railroad would have driven pilings.[53] These structures would not have been suitable for stagecoaches or any other vehicle other than locomotives and railroad cars. On a modern topographic quadrangle map, US 301 crossing the Swift Creek marshes and all other roads go a considerable distance around it. It would be another eight months before the northern division had carried the railroad over the marshes to Battle's Depot.

For this reason, it is highly unlikely the stagecoach followed the route of the railroad on departing from Enfield. Additionally, one might ask why she did not notice going through Halifax, Enfield, or Tarboro? The railroad was, and still is, located to the west of Halifax. The town of Enfield was not originally oriented on the line of the railroad; rather it was centered along the old road to Halifax that crosses the railroad above the town and continues at an angle to the west. That Mrs. Kemble boarded the stagecoach from here rather than a mile or so further down the track is possible. The likely route would commence at Enfield and Tarboro via Bell's Bridge over the Tar River. Because the rate of travel is ten miles per hour or less, time constraints do not permit a route that crosses the Tar at Teat's Bridge and enters Tarboro. Mrs. Kemble's failure to realize that she traveled through Halifax, Enfield, Tarboro, and Stantonsburg can be attributed to the darkness, her fatigue, and her metropolitan mindset. The stage route from Enfield to Waynesborough was likely the most direct route that falls within the mileage of staging given in available sources. The stage route ended at the time of Mrs. Kemble's journey at a location southeast of the modern town of Dudley in Wayne. It is likely that this site is where present-day Everette Road SE intersects the Mount Olive Road and the railroad. A short distance from this point north on the tracks was the plantation of Colonel Ezekiel Slocomb, a veteran of the American Revolution.[54] This individual is the best match to the unnamed colonel in her text.

The value of knowing the morphology of this rather temporary arrangement and drawing connections to a modern road network is that it provides an identifiable physical context with actual landscapes that aid in the interpretation of archival documents concerning the railroad and narratives, particu-

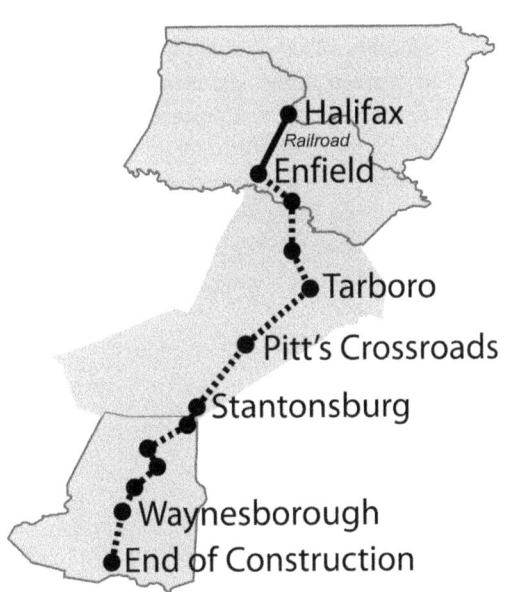

This map illustrates the most probable route of the stagecoach line of the Wilmington & Raleigh Rail Road as of late December of 1838.

larly Mrs. Kemble's often cited *Journal* entries. The use of stagecoaches by the Wilmington & Raleigh allows the railroad to be integrated into the existing railroads and steamboat line to the north and south of North Carolina. While constantly being adjusted as railroad construction advanced, it appears that the stagecoach line was the crucial element that allowed for the most efficient use of the railroad as part of system serving the southern and northern east coast. In the Kemble *Journal* the stages are never late; it is the train. And while the pace of the journey as described by Kemble appears outrageous, it seems possible that the tri-weekly service could not be maintained otherwise. Given that it had taken approximately forty hours from the time she arrived at Weldon until she reached Wilmington, to which can be added a six hour layover at Wilmington and a twelve to sixteen hour steamboat trip to Charleston, it appears that the railroad was running behind on that particular run. It is still faster than the two and a half day stage route from Halifax to Wilmington the railroad operated in late 1837. Insofar as interpreting the impression of North Carolina that Mrs. Kemble records in her *Journal,* knowing the stagecoach route makes the reader aware that most of her travel through North Carolina was through rural Edgecombe and Wayne counties, most of which is still rural today. Because she traveled that section of route at night, she missed Halifax, Enfield, and Tarboro.

The three components of the Wilmington & Raleigh Rail Road during its construction, steamboats, stagecoaches, and railroad, allowed the company to begin service from Weldon to Charleston in 1837. This is about the same time that the Portsmouth & Roanoke was completed. Thus, from the beginning, it was part of an interstate transportation network functioning well even as it was being built.

CHAPTER **IV**

The Technology: Its Origins and History

The proceeding chapter highlights the expertise of Maj. Walter Gwynn and certain of his colleagues. Many of the railroads of North Carolina and Virginia mentioned here were built under the direction of this West Point trained civil engineer. His career in North Carolina and the neighboring states would continue through the antebellum period, and include a number of hydrological projects, bridge designs, and railroad surveys. The American school of civil engineering was still in its formative years when the railroad movement began; the science and craft of this new technology was European, and the emerging tradition of civil engineering in the United States was the agency of its transfer and refinement. The American school possessed both the advantages and defects of the English and French schools of thought that influenced its development.

West Point trained engineers in particular formed the foundation of civil engineering in the United States; and while the states were reluctant to seek government aid in financing public works, they were more than willing to employ army engineers. The passage of the General Survey Act of 1824 and the creation of the Board of Engineers for Internal Improvements provided turnpike, canal, and railroad companies with army engineers. Through projects such as the Baltimore and Ohio Railroad and the Charleston and Hamburg Railroad surveys, engineers such as Maj. William G. McNeill and Lt. George W. Whistler refined the craft of the railroad survey. Throughout the 1830s, Army engineers offered technical support that aided the construction of 1,879 miles of track. The War Department and Congress began the practice of lending Army engineers to these private companies in the mid–1830s. The Topographical Bureau understood that the railroads were of military as well as commercial significance and served the national good. If the army withheld its engineering expertise, these worthy projects would suffer. After the repeal of the General Survey Act in 1838, many of the West Point trained engineers who participated in these surveys would later become presidents, chief engineers, or engineering staff for railroads and canal companies.[1]

The threat of slave insurrections and hostile incursions by Native Americans prompted the War Department to consider the military potential of this new technology; and railroad companies, eager to receive technical aid, were quick to call attention to the logistical value of their particular railroads. The companies gave Army engineers in the service of railroads considerable independence. They located routes to avoid steep grades, "deep cuttings and heavy embankments, and long viaducts." Army engineers, unfortunately, often recommended different track gauges advocated in various textbooks; and acquiesced to advocating the use of less durable wooden rails — at least for initial construction — because wood was cheap and abundant. Walter Gwynn, in his capacity as chief engineer for the Portsmouth & Roanoke Rail Road, advocated wooden rail construction. The government and military did not actively pursue a standard of construction, to avoid the perception of federal interference.[2]

The training of army engineers at West Point followed the French scientific school more than the tradition of British technical artisanship. Col. Claudius Crozet, a graduate of the Ecole Polytechnique and a professor at West Point, emphasized the practical application of mathematics in the curriculum during the early 1800s. The French had made considerable advances in the science of hydraulics. The cadets needed to conceptualize a project in detail and prepare plans before they could build. Crozet introduced Sganzin's *Program d'un Course de Construction,* a textbook on transportation surveying, to his classes in 1816, "the first textbook in America to discuss reservoirs and advocate locks and dams in natural channels." Capt. Dennis Hart Mahan, a West Point graduate and professor of mathematics (1824), continued his study of engineering in France in 1826, and returned to the academy as the best-educated engineer in America. His tenure at West Point continued until his death in 1871. However, the influence of the French school left the U.S. Army Corps of Engineers with a focus on large-scale federally sponsored navigation projects, and out of the political and economical mainstream.[3]

The field of civil engineering attracted some outside the military. Charles S. Storrow, a graduate of Harvard, continued his education in France at the Ecole des Ponts et Chaussees during the early 1830s. During

1831, Storrow visited Britain to examine that country's engineering achievements. There he prepared drawings of the roadbed of the Liverpool and Manchester Railway. These proved their worth shortly after his return to Boston. The Boston and Lowell Railroad hired him as assistant engineer. In 1835, he published his *Treatise* on hydraulic engineering. It was a landmark work in the history of American engineering, and one of the earliest written in English to build on the theoretical advances made in the field by the French. Storrow's work was quickly taken up by Dennis Hart Mahan and became the standard introductory text in hydraulics at West Point, and was cited by Mahan in his own works.[4]

The Ecole Polytechnique graduated engineers that were also concerned with types of engines. Nicholas Leonard Sadi Carnot's *Reflections on the Motive Power of Heat* (1824) was an obscure work cited by the influential French engineer Benoit Pierre Emile Clapeyron, and eventually attracted the attention of William Thomson, Lord Kelvin. Though Carnot did not live to explore thermodynamics beyond the *Reflections*, his later notes suggest a revision of his concepts in a similar direction as those expressed by James Prescott Joule on the conservation of energy.[5] François Marie Guyonneau, le Comte de Pambour, another graduate of the Ecole Polytechnique, published *Traité des Locomotives* (1835) and *Théorie de la Machine à Vapeur* (1844). These works employed a high degree of mathematical facility and remained standard texts for decades.[6] De Pambour's equations are cited extensively in the *Report from The Secretary of War in Compliance with a Resolution of the Senate of 24th January, 1838, with a Report of the Survey of the Charleston and Cincinnati Railroad*.[7]

The transfer of British engineering knowledge to the United States appears to be more direct. Benjamin Henry Latrobe, a British professional engineer, became the engineer for the Philadelphia Waterworks, and he was also the architect of the Capitol. Considered the father of professional architecture and civil engineering in the United States, his American career spanned the years 1796 until his death in 1820.[8] For example, Hamilton Fulton, civil engineer for North Carolina, consulted Latrobe on the possibility of uniting at least two of the great rivers of the state.[9] The British firm of Robert Stephenson and Company at Newcastle-upon-Tyne supplied some of the early locomotives used on the American railroads.[10] The Wilmington & Raleigh owned two Stephenson locomotives.[11] American engineers added some useful modifications to this English equipment, and eventually developed locomotives more appropriate to the topography of the American landscape and the cheap methods of rail construction.[12]

Another example of the application of European technology is that of Horatio Allen, an engineer for the Delaware & Hudson Canal Company, later the chief engineer of the Charleston & Hamburg Rail Road. Allen studied railroad technology first hand while on an iron purchasing mission to England at the behest of the Delaware & Hudson in 1828. Allen was an early advocate of steam power over animal traction. In England, he met George Stephenson, who accompanied him on an examination of the Liverpool & Manchester Railway, and he observed iron rails on wood spaced four feet eight inches apart on the Stockton & Darlington Railway. He placed orders for the Delaware & Hudson Canal Company for three locomotives from Foster, Rastrick & Co. of Stourbridge, and an order for one locomotive from Stephenson. The Foster, Rastrick locomotive, "The Stourbridge Lion," proved to be too heavy for the track of the Delaware & Hudson when it was tested. This was a slight setback. In 1828, Allen accepted the appointment of chief engineer for the Charleston & Hamburg Rail Road. Confident in the future of steam locomotives, he advised the company to build its railroad for steam locomotives from the start. His plan for construction was timber rails topped with iron held in place by spikes. At least eight early English locomotives were used on this railroad.[13]

George Stephenson had used a track gauge of four feet eight inches on the Stockton and Darlington railroad in 1825. The short railroad was adapted as an existing tramway used for carrying coal wagons. Stephenson placed iron on the timbers at the gauge used by the colliery that employed him. He later used the same gauge on the Liverpool and Manchester Railway. He and his son Robert built locomotives for this gauge unless a company ordered otherwise. The British engineer Isambard Kingdom Brunel experimented with the seven foot gauge. He believed the larger gauge would allow the locomotive and car to travel with greater stability and great speeds. The British government commission trials between the different gauges concluded that broad gauge track proved to be superior. However, the officials from the Board of Trade recommended the four feet eight and a half gauge since it was already in wide use.[14] American engineers planning the Baltimore & Ohio visited Stephenson's Liverpool & Manchester Railway in 1829. Stephenson had expanded the gauge by one half inch to allow more room between the rail and the wheel flange. The American engineers came away from the experience with the conviction that the Liverpool & Manchester was the model for their railroad in all aspects, including track gauge. They altered the original plans for using four foot six inch gauge to standard gauge. Other visiting engineers from the United States tended towards round measurements such as four feet nine inches and four feet ten inches. The five foot gauge was widely accepted by American engineers, and its use by the Charleston & Hamburg Rail Road prompted the planners of other southern railroads to adopt the gauge. Other American engineers, impressed by the stability of the ride of the seven foot gauge of the British Great Western Railway, recommended broad gauges to their companies. The six foot gauge was used by the New York and Erie Railroad. Before 1850, the railroads of the United States and Canada would use a large range of different rail gauges.[15]

Methods of rail construction were as varied as the selection of rail gauge. Walter Gwynn, chief engineer for the Portsmouth & Raleigh Rail Road and later, the Wilmington & Raleigh Rail Road, recommended strap-iron wooden rail construction. This consisted of iron bar, two inches wide by one-half inch thick, spiked to heart pine rails resting on oak sills. The sills were notched to receive the rails, and oak wedges held the rails in place.[16]

The Charleston & Hamburg Rail Road used four different methods of construction: two types of sleeper construction, pile construction, and truss construction. The first sleeper construction was the least expensive and suitable for solid ground. Six by ten inch wooden rails were set in ten by twelve inch sleepers spaced six and a half feet apart. The ground was excavated or filled as needed. With the second sleeper plan, the rails were placed three inches into caps, secured with wedges, held in place with a two-inch spike, and the sill was bedded lengthwise nearly to its depth in the ground. The size of the rail was the same. The sills were nine feet long, and the sills were placed three feet from the center of the road under the rails. The sills were nine by nine inches. The rail was held in place by the cap, and the cap was set in the sill. The third construction method used piles. These piles were logs ten to fifteen inches long driven into the ground by a pile driving machine. The company furnished these machines to the contractors working on the road. They had a special spade attachment, much like a posthole digger, that excavated a hole three and a half feet deep. The piles were placed in the hole, and hammered into the soil with a 600 to 1,000 pound hammer falling along guides. The machine stood fifteen feet high, and was mounted on wooden rollers. The piles were driven depths not less than four feet in the ground. They were driven six feet apart transversely, and six and a half feet apart longitudinally. When in place, they were cut to level, and capped with timbers six by nine inches that were nine feet in length. The truss method was used for very high elevations of the track. A foundation of piles had to be placed first. Then an arrangement of four eight-by-ten inch timbers was built into the form of an inverted "W," and capped with a ten by twelve. The bottom sills were twelve by twelve inches. The cost of this type of construction ranged from $6,000 to $10,000 per mile.[17] Strap-iron wooden rail construction was significantly different from the latter method employed using heavy iron rails.

George W. Whistler, also a West Point trained engineer and pioneer in railroad surveying and construction in the United States, was employed by the czar of Russia as a consultant on the St. Petersburg and Moscow Railroad in the early 1840s. In a letter to Count Kleinmichel in September of 1842, Whistler summed up the arguments for and against the use of wide gauges. The advantages included greater stability, a reduction of friction, and the potential for greater speeds. The disadvantages included the increased length of axles, their consequent weight, and the cost of material on the road associated with the greater width. Significantly, he recommended the use of heavy iron rails of sixty pounds per yard supported every three feet. The *chair,* a cast iron fitting between the base of the rail and supporting wood or stone, was commonly used at each bearing point on European railroads of the day, but only on the ends where rails join on American railroads. Whistler recommended, based on his own experiences, that the use of H-rail provided greater stability and economy than the more common T-rail.[18]

The differing selection of gauge, construction methods, and equipment used by the early American railroads is attributable to the diffusion of British technology through the agency of West Point–trained civil engineers. The passage of the General Survey Act of 1824 filled the need for professional engineers for canal and railroad projects by lending Army engineers. The American school of civil engineering was influenced by the scientific French school; however its emphasis on hydrologic problems rather than the new railroad technology led many to seek their knowledge through the few treatises on the subject or through visits to England. The American railroad evolved with built-in disadvantages, particularly different rail gauges and perishable wooden construction, that inhibited the formation of networks.

The techniques of track and roadbed construction recommended by United States Topographical Bureau engineers reflect the evolution of railroad technology. The locomotives of the day, primitive and light weight, were compatible with a number of experimental track construction methods. The most abundant construction material in the eastern United States was timber, and its availability on site along projected routes compensated for the scarcity of domestic iron. In addition, the absence of a suitable network of roads imposed the necessity of commencing construction at a port or river landing. This provided the only effective means of transporting the imported iron, and allowed the railroad to become useful early during construction. The disadvantages of wooden rails include their susceptibility to rot and to insect damage. Drying, cracking, shrinkage, swelling, and warping are universal problems associated with all exterior wooden construction. However, the fact that a thin ridged bar of iron was spiked to the top of the rails created conditions for differential expansion. Regularly subjected to the stress of passing loads, the spikes loosened and the iron detached from the rail, a particularly dangerous situation that came to be known as a "snakehead." In the early years of railroading, civil engineers sought to provide drainage for the railbed through ditching and embankment to preserve the rails as long as possible from the adverse effects of water. The superstructure of the rails was often placed on highly permeable materials such sand or gravel, and occasionally the wood rested on stone. This period of railroad construction also often included a horse path, an idea borrowed from mining and canals that would have practical application with urban omnibuses running on tracks in the nineteenth century. However, it was quickly abandoned by railroads, along with other experimental novelties such as cars equipped with sails to catch the wind.

United States Civil Engineer DeWitt Clinton conducted a survey for a railroad from the Portage Summit of the Ohio Canal to the Hudson River in the early 1830s. He submitted his report to Lt. Col. John J. Abert of the Topographical Bureau on January 26, 1832, and the report was transmitted to Congress on February 29, 1832. His recommendations address some of the problems of early construction techniques.

> I should, however, propose that it should be double track, and that locomotive engines should be used entirely on it, to supercede [supersede] the necessity of the horse path. The rails should also be elevated on suitable blocks, some inches above the ground, to admit of their being freed, in the easiest manner, from the snow and sleets which would lodge on them during winter. The great error of the roads in operation, or building, in this county, is, having the rails nearly on the level of the horse path. I would also propose, in deep cuts, that the roads should have an [a] uniform declivity, to admit of the water which may collect to be drained in the easiest manner; and, on heavy embankments, that the road should be constructed of wood, and that suitable turn outs should be made from one track to the other.[19]

The horse path, however, appears in Walter Gwynn's survey for the Portsmouth & Roanoke Rail Road of 1833. The centers of the sills (crossties) were to be cut for the construction of the path. Though it was a single-track railroad, the drainage ditches were positioned with the idea of allowing space for double-track. When the section of that railroad had been completed between Portsmouth and Suffolk, a large drainage ditch was dug through the Dismal Swamp alongside the path of the track and the excavated material was used to build up the track bed. It was topped with a layer of approximately a foot of sand. Seventeen miles of track were completed by the time Gwynn made his report. He makes mention of Claudius Crozet's estimate of $90,563 for this section of the line, but it had been completed for $75,000.[20] The method Gwynn describes for the section of track between Portsmouth and Suffolk involved placing the sills at least half-way into the ground to accommodate the horse path. This would allow the bottom of the rail to touch the ground, the method that Clinton advised against. The sills on the Wilmington & Raleigh Rail Road originally were buried one-quarter of their height in dirt, under which method the company reported in 1850 that they lasted five to six years. Sills later completely covered with dirt lasted only three years.[21] The method described — excavation and embankment — still is common practice for railroad construction. The excavations cut into the slope of the land.

> The graduated surface of the road-bed in excavations, will vary from 13 to 16 feet in width, the slopes being 45°. The graded surface on embankments will present a uniform width of 12 feet, with slopes of 33½° or 1½ base to 1 perpendicular.[22]

During the course of locating the route of a railroad, then and now, stakes are placed at intervals along a centerline. The stakes placed at 100 feet, starting from the beginning of the road, are called *full stations*, and all others are *plus stations*. For example, a stake set at 5,280 feet (a mile) is number "52 + 80." A profile of the slope of the land is obtained by level-rod readings at each stake and intervening points where the slope of the land changes. This practice is called *profile leveling*.[23]

In the report of the 1837 survey of the Western & Atlantic Railroad in Georgia, Lt. Col. S. H. Long includes a profile map of the route. The base measurement is the level of the Oostanaula River.[24] The route of the railroad began at the Chattahoochee River south of Marietta, Georgia, crossed the Etowah River, and followed the valley of the Chickamauga River to the Tennessee line. Maj. James D. Graham conducted a survey for a railroad from Pensacola, Florida, to Columbus, Georgia, in 1836 that also followed the river course.

> The profile of the route will present inclinations nowhere greater than ten or fifteen feet rise or fall per mile, except to avoid the circuit of the valley of

the Chattahoochee just before it receives the Oochee. In order to gain the valley of the latter stream by a shorter route, the trace of the road will be rendered more straight, but it may be necessary to admit one or two short inclinations not exceeding thirty feet per mile.[25]

The terrain on the Pensacola to Columbus route follows the alluvial basin of the Escambia River from Pensacola to its confluence with the Conecuh in southeastern Alabama. The route parallels the Conecuh to its head and turns east towards Columbus. The river network is oriented north to south. This 210-mile railroad became another victim of the Panic of 1837. Work on the project ceased. Graham estimated that the railroad would cost about $6,800 per mile. The director of the company recommended strap iron wooden rail construction.[26]

Five miles of the Charleston & Hamburg Rail Road used fill, excavation, and ditching in preparation for the track to be placed directly on the ground.[27] Walter Gwynn's survey for the Portsmouth & Roanoke Rail Road gives estimates for these methods for the separate divisions, and details on bridging. The 10 miles between Main Street in Suffolk and Station 290 on the Portsmouth & Roanoke Rail Road contains six truss bridges totaling $600, and four stone drains totaling $1,000. The distance from station 290 to station 525 on the west bank of the Blackwater River (near the present-day town of Franklin, Virginia) contained 20 truss bridges at $1,500, but the bridge across the river had stone abutments and piers at a total of $9,500. Gwynn included a truss bridge at $120 over Buckhorn Run, a bridge over the Meherrin River at $14,500, and several more truss bridges and stone drains totaling $1,600.[28] The overall cost per mile for embankments and excavations varied for the nine divisions of the railroad between Suffolk and the Roanoke. Excavation costs dropped in the 5.43 miles leading to the Nottoway River and approximately four miles before the Meherrin River. The most costly embankment occurred 5.29 miles after the crossing of the Meherrin, followed by a sharp reduction of costs over the 4.46 miles before the Summit at Station 1,406, 12.35 miles from the Roanoke River. The profile of the route from the Meherrin River at the Virginia–North Carolina line to Station 1,288 (5.29 miles) shows an elevation gain of 84.23 feet; however, the climb distance is 2.63 miles. The track runs along the west bank of Cypress Creek until it crosses it south of Margarettsville, North Carolina. A sharp ascent begins on the south bank of the creek. The greatest cost for embankment apparently was incurred in smoothing this grade.

The survey for the Winchester and Potomac Railroad was conducted in 1832, and presented to the Twenty-fifth U.S. Congress in 1838. It contains maps, tables, and associated technical documents that illustrate the science behind the early surveys. The formulas devised by Lieut. Col. Long and James Adamson provide an empirical foundation for calculating grade relative to motive power for strap-iron wooden rail construction and a horse path with sleepers placed four feet apart and six by six inch rails.[29]

The essence of these calculations becomes clear when contemplated in a form that is more familiar. If the carload is at rest, the force acting against the weight of the car from the rails will cancel the normal component of its weight; it is in a state of equilibrium. The sum of vertical forces equals zero, the sum of the horizontal forces equals zero, and the sum of the moments of those forces at any point on the plane is all derived from Isaac Newton's *Third Law*. However, it is possible for an entire structure to be in motion and still be in a state of equilibrium when the individual parts of the structure do not move with respect to each other. Other forces apply to bodies in motion and figure into the equations for statics where necessary.[30] Friction must be added to the parallel (downward component) of the weight on ascent and subtracted on descent. The power of a locomotive had to be calculated so as to fulfill the tasks it was expected to perform on a particular terrain.

Walter Gwynn recommends the use of a five-ton locomotive on the Portsmouth & Roanoke Rail Road, since the grade along the whole extent of the line would not exceed 20 feet per mile. He notes that the performance of this engine at that grade equals a six-ton engine at 30 feet per mile grade.[31] The 1838 report by engineers William Gibbs McNeill and W. G. Williams on the survey for the Louisville, Cincinnati & Charleston Rail Road is one of the most exhaustive reports of the early railroad era, and contains a wealth of information about grades, locomotives, construction, and topography. Drawing from the research of De Pambour, these engineers explored the cylinder, wheel diameter, length of stroke in connection, pressure per square inch in connection with the type of engines required for steep grades.[32]

Even though these documents provide fascinating insights into the science of early railroad technology, the locomotives described therein — five tons, six tons, 12 tons — were still primitive machines. Grades had to be moderate to accommodate these engines and increase their efficiency, and load capacity. The various construction methods including excavating, embankment, piles, and trestlework, smoothed out ascents and descents. As evidenced by some of the surveys for railroad in mountainous terrain, the need for heavier engines made it necessary to space sills more closely. Also, the engineers located the routes along the courses of rivers. For example,

Walter Gwynn's survey for the Wilmington & Halifax (Wilmington & Raleigh) passes through the alluvial plane of the Cape Fear River basin for much of its extent. The directors of the company selected the "Western Route" that proceeds west of the Northeast Cape as far as Faison. Gwynn noted that, outside of bridging a few minor streams, a few excavations of no more than ten feet, and embankments of two or three feet, the railroad could be built in nearly a straight line over level ground.[33]

An examination of the terrain along the route of the Wilmington & Raleigh Rail Road between Wilmington and Faison in the Coastal Plain of North Carolina verifies Gwynn's observations. In most places the modern rails rest on a modest layer of ballast, and it is likely that the original railroad rests on a layer of sand like its counterpart, the Portsmouth & Roanoke Rail Road. The first great obstacle that the railroad had to cross was the Northeast Cape Fear River. As mentioned earlier, this required a 360-foot lattice truss bridge with stone piers. However, the levels of the banks of this section of the river are not steep. The Northeast Cape Fear makes a bend westward approximately six miles east of this position as it makes its way to the confluence with the Northwest Cape Fear. On its way northward to Faison, the railroad follows the high ground on the west side on the Northeast Cape Fear — to use the analogy "cutting with the grain." Outside of crossing the difficult Burgaw Swamp, Rockfish Creek, Stewart Creek, and other minor streams, the line of the railroad is straight. The site of the most extensive section of trestlework south of Faison was at Bear Swamp. It was mentioned in the 1856 stockholders report as the highest trestlework on the entire line. The longest section of trestlework was through Goshen Swamp.[34] This was later filled, and is now a high embankment. At Faison, the line of the railroad takes an arc into Goshen Swamp. There is still an impressive modern wooden trestle crossing Reedy Branch running through Goshen Swamp. Piles were driven into the soil of the streambed, the outer piles set at an angle, a cap put on the piles, and extensive bracing performed.

The landscape changes as the route of the Wilmington & Raleigh Rail Road continues to the Neuse River. Walter Gwynn notes this fact in the report of his survey.

> Here the first undulation in the plane of the road worthy of notice occurs, a descent and immediately an ascent of 30 feet to the mile is unavoidable, and some comparatively deep cutting, and heavy embankments are encountered. Immediately on ascending the valley Goshen, the route reaches a dry, level, open woods through which it passes over Brooks' Branch.... After making a slight undulation in crossing Brooks' Branch, which is a very inconsiderable

This example of modern trestlework is on the line of the railroad near Goshen Swamp. The method is still practiced in railroad construction, and resembles the description of the high trestles on the Charleston & Hamburg Rail Road in many aspects. *See* "General Description of the Charleston and Hamburg Rail-Road," *Farmers' Register* (October 1833), 261–263.

stream, it arrives at the same level, on which it continues to the head of Yellow Marsh; along the margin of which, it descends to the valley of the Neuse River, encountering in its descent, some heavy cuttings, which consist, however, entirely of sand.[35]

Brooks' Branch (or Brooks Swamp) was discussed in the context of the stagecoach line of the Wilmington & Raleigh Rail Road in the previous chapter. The piles and trestlework at Brooks' Branch are those mentioned in Frances Kemble's *Journal of a Residence on a Georgian Plantation*. During her trip south from Philadelphia, Mrs. Kemble traveled on the yet to be completed Wilmington & Raleigh Rail Road. The ravines in her text are in Brooks' Swamp. Today, the high embankments at Brooks Swamp, traversing a distance of approximately 1.3 miles, can be seen south of Dudley, North Carolina. The head of the Northeast Cape Fear commences on the east side of Mt. Olive, and the Goshen Swamp drains into the river. Therefore, a large part of the route of the Wilmington & Raleigh Rail Road follows the course of the Northeast Cape Fear to its headwaters. Between Dudley and Brogden in Wayne County, North Carolina, the excavation is as extensive as Gwynn's report indicates.

The route of the Wilmington & Raleigh Rail Road from the turn at Faison to Weldon follows a different pattern. It crosses two major rivers, the Neuse and the Tar, and a number of small streams such as Nahunta Swamp, Black Creek, and Contentnea Creek. The route of the railroad runs perpendicular to the prevailing stream flow. A railroad that runs parallel to the prevailing stream utilizes the advantage of the level ground of the river floodplains and basin divides. It does not matter if the river is

At Brooks Swamp, about two miles south of Dudley, North Carolina, the railroad passes over two branches running through Brooks Swamp. At the time the railroad was constructed, trestlework was used to cross the swamp. It is likely that the high trestles crossing two ravines described in Frances Kemble's *Journal* were located at Brooks' Swamp (photograph by Dr. Cyn Johnson).

This photograph shows the Neuse River near Goldsboro. The railroad could not make a crossing of the river closer to Waynesborough. The town was eventually moved to the railroad and was renamed Goldsboro.

flowing north to south or west to east. This is apparent from the survey of the Pensacola to Columbia, the Western and Atlantic route, and the Winchester and Potomac route. The railroad has to cross minor tributaries that drain from hillside hollows or higher planes of the river divide. When a route starts running perpendicular to the prevailing stream flow, it might cross from one river basin to another. The relics of prior stream action, hills and declivities, must be cut and filled to make a smooth grade. In the case of the Wilmington & Raleigh Rail Road, it passed over terrain worked by the ancient wave action — scarps and terraces. It passed through Wilson, Edgecombe, and Halifax counties, and through areas of the Coastal Plain Province that contain Precambrian and Paleozoic granitic rock covered by a thin layer of Coastal Plain sediments.[36]

The route of the Raleigh & Gaston Rail Road, however, built through the Northeast Piedmont, encountered bands of Precambrian and Paleozoic granitic rock, lower Paleozoic slates, flows, and pyroclastics.[37] Charles F.

M. Garnett, chief engineer for the company (also the chief engineer of the Western & Atlantic during the early 1840s), mentioned that the presence of rock along the route caused the price of excavations and embankments to be costly. In addition, the railroad had to construct five bridges, of which the one over the Tar River was the highest. These bridges, totaling 3,240 feet in length, cost the company $155,000.[38]

There are distinct differences between railroad construction on the Coastal Plain and in the Piedmont. The task of bridging rivers and streams varies because the stream cross-section through rock and residual soil is different from sand and alluvial clay.

In evaluating the information about terrain for use in route analysis, there are several factors to consider. The first is the location of the route parallel or perpendicular to the prevailing direction of the drainage network regardless of geological province. Second, the location of route on the Coastal Plain differs from that of the Piedmont and mountain terrain in bridging, trestlework, excavation, and embankment because of stream hydrology and soil. Third, crossing major rivers is costly wherever they are located. Coastal rivers will spread out over a floodplain and tend to be shallow, but a bridge there will have a longer span than one crossing at some point upriver. Piedmont rivers will have higher banks and require tall piers. Finally, by early antebellum standards, the weight of a locomotive and the tonnage it is able to haul is proportional to the steepness of the grades along the line; heavier loads require closer spacing of sills.

Could a railroad be built in the early years that could pass between the Coastal Plain and the Piedmont, or the Piedmont and into the Appalachian Province? Walter Gwynn, serving at the chief engineer of the North Carolina Rail Road in 1851, recommended that the route of the railroad should commence at Waynesborough, then pass four miles north of Smithfield and continue to Raleigh. From there it would continue its arc through the Piedmont to Charlotte.[39] The Waynesborough to Raleigh section of the road fulfilled the intentions of those that first proposed a railroad between Wilmington and Raleigh in 1833. On the *Map of North Carolina* of 1882 prepared by state geologist W. C. Kerr and civil engineer William Cain, the Raleigh & Augusta Air Line Railroad extends from Raleigh to the town of Hamlet in Richmond County, not far from Rockingham and on a line to Cheraw. There, it forms a junction with the Carolina Central Railroad on its westerly route to Charlotte. In many respects, it follows the projected route of the Raleigh & Columbia Rail Road. To the north, the Raleigh & Gaston extends from Gaston to Weldon with the Greensville branch of the Petersburg Rail Road removed. The Cape Fear & Yadkin

Valley Railroad, however, extends from Fayetteville past Greensboro into Stokes County rather than to the Narrows of the Yadkin as originally proposed.[40]

Not only does this prove that many of the early plans were viable when the technology improved and the capital was available, many in fact followed their projected route. The Waynesborough to Raleigh segment of the North Carolina Railroad is particularly significant because Walter Gwynn directed the survey. While it is difficult to prove he would have recommended the exact route to the Wilmington & Raleigh Rail Road had the company built its Raleigh branch line from Waynesborough, it is unlikely his sensibilities would have strayed from finding the most efficient and economical route. The deviation of the Raleigh & Augusta and the Cape Fear & Yadkin Valley routes appears motivated by the development of the Chatham coalfields and the domestic iron production. Both railroads intersected at the town of Sanford. The fact remains that since these railroads existed, they have left an impression on the physical landscape that provides reference for models of the proposed railroads of the 1830s that follow their routes.

With iron rails, closely spaced crossties, and heavy 4-4-0 locomotives, all the routes mentioned were possible in the late antebellum and later. Taking a closer look at these routes and looking for the steep grades, deep excavations, and extensive bridging can contribute to determining the technical demands of these routes if they were built during the 1830s.

The first great railroads in America were built with British iron. No reliable source of domestic railroad iron existed. The United States government offered remission of duties on imported iron to railroad companies to encourage construction. As the original rails started to fail after about ten years of use, the railroads returned to the foreign market for new heavy iron rails rather than buy from domestic manufacturers even though the quality of domestic iron had improved, and it was being produced in quantity. American ironmasters began petitioning Congress for a resumption of duties on imported iron, but the railroads mounted stiff resistance. The integration of the manufacturing organizations and financial institutions of Europe, and particularly those of England, continued to recommend their iron to the American railroads throughout the antebellum period. This is a topic often neglected in texts devoted to early railroad development, albeit a significant factor in determining the nature of initial construction and contributing to the financial burden of when the original rails were replaced.

In May of 1849, Dr. Armand J. DeRosset Jr. left on the steamer *America,* sailing from New York to Liverpool to negotiate the purchase of new iron for the relaying of the Wilmington & Raleigh Rail Road. By the end of July, it appears that he had succeeded. The *Wilmington Journal* announced that he had made a contract for 9,000 tons of heavy T-iron, enough to relay 120 miles of the line. The terms of this contract were not disclosed at the time, but they were considered equitable.

The arrival of the first load of 273 tons of T-iron from Cardiff, Wales, arrived at Wilmington, North Carolina, in October on the brig *Albemarle*.[41] The company desperately needed to replace their deteriorating strap iron wooden rails that had been put down in the late 1830s. Years earlier, the Petersburg Rail Road Company, completed in 1833, had to replace their perishable wooden rails. In May of 1843, the Petersburg Rail Road had completed all but two miles of relaying their road with heavy T-iron, as well as nearly completing their bridge over the Roanoke at Weldon.[42] Three thousand tons of iron had to be put down before a specified date or the company would have to pay $75,000 in duties.[43]

A Bill for the Relief of the Petersburg Railroad Company, presented by the Committee on Finance in the United State Senate on January 17, 1843, required that the company provide proof that they had put down all the iron by December 1, 1844. The bill is a continuation of duty free privileges that were granted August 13, 1842, and expired March 3, 1843. Thus the iron had to arrive before that date.[44] One thousand tons were put down in 1842, and an additional two thousand tons had arrived at City Point in February of 1843, and were sent by wagon to the depot to be sent down the road for installation. This was done without an interruption of service.[45] The particular circumstances of the Wilmington & Raleigh Rail Road and the Petersburg Rail Road represent the general state of early railroads built with strap iron wooden construction.

The United States at the dawn of the railroad era was an agricultural nation that had no means of manufacturing iron in the quantities necessary for building railroads; its engineering tradition was in its infancy, and the lack of regional investment capital inhibited most large scale internal improvement projects.

By contrast, Britain, the preeminent industrial nation-state of the early nineteenth century, had developed mass production techniques for the manufacturing of iron; its engineering tradition had established the first standards for locomotive design and railroad hardware. The banking houses of London dominated international finance, and had a reputation for providing investment capital to foreign ventures, both directly and through intermediaries. The first railroad companies in America had little choice but to purchase their iron and equipment from British manufacturers, and to seek part of the necessary investment capital in European bonds. As early as 1828, the Baltimore and Ohio Rail Road Company had prepared a memorial to Congress for a remission of duties on imported iron; the memorial was referred to the Committee on Finance.[46] The remission of duties on foreign iron for railroads soon became a matter of policy. However, its use on American railroads started to become a contentious issue during the 1840s as the domestic equivalent became more available and of comparable quality. The *Memorial of a Number of Ironmasters at Lexington, Virginia, in Relation to an Increase of Duty of Imported Iron,* March 14, 1842, referred to the Ways and Means Committee of the House of Representatives of the Twenty-seventh Congress, states that the iron interests of Virginia cannot sustain themselves without increased duties on English iron.

> Your petitioners feel assured that Virginia is as well adapted for the successful prosecution of manufactures in general as any State in the Union. Our climate, water power, the inexhaustible stores of fuel furnished by our forests and coal fields, and, we will add, the character of our labor, testify to the truth of the proposition, that nature has pointed it out as fitted to be the chosen seat for the manufacture of iron in all forms.... At the present moment, the existing manufacture of iron, so far from being extended, is in peril of extinction, from the diminished rate of duty. This is an evil with which not Virginia alone, but also the other States engaged in the manufacture of iron, are threatened; and these only, but all the States, in its action of agriculture, arts, and commerce, and the general capacity for defence.[47]

It would seem that the Petersburg Rail Road Company could have saved time and expense had it patronized the burgeoning iron industry in Virginia, but it chose to remain with foreign manufacturers. The Virginia ironmasters failed to persuade Congress to alter policy. Ten years later the Legislature of New Jersey castigated the general government for its failure to enact a national policy to support domestic manufacturing of iron while noting that "the principal governments of Europe lavish the most generous encouragement on the production of the mines and various manufacturers of iron."[48] The "generous encouragement" appears to have been reserved for the railroads.

The *Statement of the Amount of Duties on Railroad Iron Refunded, Annually, from the Year 1831 to 1841* reported by the Treasury Department in 1842 amounted to a total of $4,800,183.84 for the entire period. Beginning with $6,847.90 refunded to the Baltimore and Ohio in 1831, the amount jumped to $336,709.19 in 1832 as seven railroads came under construction. The bonds for duties on imported iron were not canceled until the particular shipment of iron had been laid down. The amount for

1833 had dropped to $202,210.70; however, another railroad (Boston) was added in 1834, and the amount climbed to $421,010.34, and continued to rise in 1835 to $529,529.79. The amount for 1836 was $234,194.74; it was $407,517.05 in 1837; $910,011.66 in 1838; and $672,376.86 in 1839. The Wilmington & Raleigh Rail Road was refunded $38,455.65 during this year. It was the only refund for that railroad listed. The amount for 1840 was $688,510.97, and for part of 1841, the amount was $391,264.64.[49] Tables for iron imported under the tariffs of 1842 and 1846 for years 1843 through 1838, including articles, quantities, values, and duties, can be found in the *Letter from the Secretary of the Treasury* dated January 16, 1849.[50] That there was a pressing need for iron products of all kinds that could not be satisfied by domestic manufacturers is apparent. In fact, the need for imported railroad iron was so pervasive during the early days of railroad construction it is not surprising to find that the citizens of Pennsylvania were petitioning Congress for a reduction in duty on this product in 1835.[51] It would take more than petitions and memorials to make domestic iron competitive: the transportation infrastructure had to exist first.

On July 14, 1832, Congress passed an act to refund duties on railroad iron, providing that that it was installed permanently; however, some clarity was needed on railroad hardware. For example, the Baltimore & Susquehanna Rail Road Company ordered 320,000 iron fastenings for their track known as dog-tooth clamps and was erroneously charged the duty as if it were ordinary hardware. The company petitioned Congress in 1837 for remission of duties on such items.[52] Other situations were more serious, and reflected the general derangement of the American economy during the late 1830s and early 1840s.

The State of Michigan had a different problem with their railroad iron. The last of its imported iron arrived in New York on May 10, 1839, and May 23, 1839, and was intended for immediate use; but that state had negotiated its loans with the United States Bank in Philadelphia and the Morris Canal and Banking Company. These banks failed, and because Michigan no longer had the funds to continue the project, the railroad iron would not be put down until 1842; thus the state missed the deadline for remission of duties on the iron. A suit was brought by the United States against James H. Whitney, bondsman for the State of Michigan, and he was ordered to pay $8,428.19 in damages and $50 for the cost of court. In 1844, the State of Michigan sought relief from this judgment, citing the failure of the banks as the cause of the delay, not the negligence of the state.[53]

The predicament in which the State of Michigan found itself in the late 1830s was not precipitated by an isolated event. The early American railroads relied on bonds rather than stock for raising capital because distant investors favored the secure profits they offered. Some companies went directly to London to obtain sterling bonds, and others utilized the agency of large northern banks. The practice continued through the antebellum period.[54] The Deposit Act of 1836, the product of Jacksonian monetary policy, entailed the shift of specie from the economic center of the nation to state banks in order to accomplish the distribution of the federal surplus. Its dispersal disrupted commercial intercourse, and eroded investor confidence at home and abroad. The Panic of 1837, and the subsequent depression that followed, undermined the stability of the American financial market.[55] As a result, the advance of domestic industry was set back; the railroad companies and their shareholders struggled to maintain solvency; and the primacy of British iron and capital was preserved.

The *Letter and Memorial of Isaac K. Lippincott, On the Manufacture of Iron and the Operation of the Present Tariff Laws* of December 31, 1841, noted that under the existing conditions brought about by the closing of furnaces in New York, New Jersey, Pennsylvania, and in all the seaboard states, reduced duties had brought British iron into direct competition with domestic iron. Lippincott recommended the building of a National Foundry as it had been first presented in a report to the House of Representatives on January 12, 1839, and he was especially supportive of the idea of locating such a facility in Lancaster County, Pennsylvania, where there were 102 iron foundries within fifty miles of the town of Lancaster.[56] In the same year, the citizens of Danville, Pennsylvania, had prepared a memorial advocating their region as the site of the National Foundry based upon their proximity to the necessary materials of iron smelting, transportation connections, and their safe removal from the threat of invasion.[57] A report by William Cost Johnson to the Select Committee on the National Foundry of February 23, 1843, titled *National Foundry* is an extensive and fascinating document on this subject that is worthy of further examination; however, the purpose of the foundry is clearly stated within the opening pages. Not only was there a need for a National Foundry for the production of munitions, but such an institution would also establish national standards for iron manufacturing through scientific study and practical experiment.[58]

The proposed revision of the Tariff of 1846 by the Taylor administration brought forth the all too familiar economic complaints of the era, the propping up of northern industry on the backs of the South and the West. For the State of North Carolina specifically, 260 miles of railroad needed to be relayed or built, and tariff duties would make the task unnecessarily expensive. The *Wilmington Journal* expressed these views a month after Dr. DeRossett departed. The writer was referring to the cost of iron for relaying the Wilmington & Raleigh Rail Road.

> Now, taking 50 tons as an average per mile, (an exceedingly low estimate,) we have 32,500 tons of iron as the total amount necessary. This can be procured, we suppose at $45 per ton, $1,462,500 in all. Under such a tariff as the iron men want, it would cost $60, a total of $1,950,000, or a difference of nearly half a million of dollars, out of which North Carolina would be *protected* for the benefit of Pennsylvania. These calculations are made somewhat hastily and without pretending to accuracy in the details, yet we feel certain that the relative proportion of prices will be found pretty much as we have placed them.[59]

The newspaper reported that a comparison of the English iron with American railroad iron manufactured at Danville, Pennsylvania — both used on the Harrisburg & Lancaster Rail Road — found that the American product was tougher; yet it cost about five dollars a ton more than the Wilmington railroad was paying for their British iron.[60] However, it later cited articles in the *Washington Republic* and *New Haven Register* that were more critical of the cost and strength of American made iron: still, the main complaint was that the American product cost more.[61]

The debate over imported railroad iron would continue into the 1850s. Thomas Clingman of North Carolina, during his career in the House of Representatives, spoke at length on the floor on the subject of duties on imported railroad iron, noting that the railroads of North Carolina were in essence public works in which the farmer asks how much he can afford for such improvements and then he purchases shares. Citing the share value of the Wilmington & Raleigh was seventy cents to the dollar, he does not consider North Carolina railroad stock the type of investment for the capitalist seeking large and immediate returns. The railroads enable the farmer to get his produce to market, and yield their dividends in the form of public good, not profits. To these statements, he elicited the concurrence of his fellow representative from North Carolina, William S. Ashe (later president of the Wilmington & Weldon Railroad).[62]

Among the Resolutions of the North Carolina Legislature presented to the Thirty-second Congress was one calling for the abolition of duties on railroad iron.[63] The following year, a convention was held in Richmond for the purpose of persuading Congress to approve a refund of all the duties collected on imported railroad iron between 1851 and 1854 because the duties had been imposed differently for various railroads depending on the rates in force at the time of construction. The amount of the duties totaled $10,072,977.60 on $33,576,592 worth in iron. The *Memorial* of the convention explains these inequities.

> While some States made their railroads when iron was admitted duty free, or when the price of iron was so low was to compensate, in some measure, for the oppressive duty, other States were so misfortunate as to construct their most important works when the duty, added to the high price of iron, rendered it an intolerable burden. If it be just and equitable to encourage railroads by continuing this exemption from duty for a longer period, it is equally so to refund the duties paid by those companies which have borne the pressure of the high duty and the high price combined.[64]

Part of the success of the British product had been the introduction of the hot-air blast in their iron manufacturing. This process forces a reaction between carbon monoxide and iron ore that yields molten iron and carbon dioxide. Lippincott mentioned this method and another discovery whereby anthracite coal could be used in smelting iron when he referred to cheaply made iron from England, Scotland, and Wales. The British had been in the iron business for a long time, and had perfected production in quantity. They had also pioneered railroad technology, and could produce all the specialized hardware that their clients required. Pennsylvania, Virginia, and North Carolina, all rich in the raw materials for iron making, would need decades of organization before their iron manufactories would be ready to mass produce iron rail.

The British could also offer another service that was not readily available in the United States of the 1840s: credit. Dr. DeRosset had gone to England not only to purchase iron, but he also negotiated a mortgage on the company to pay for the iron. The 1850 stockholders report records that mortgage bonds were payable in London, due in 1869. This amount bearing 6 per cent interest was $355,555.56, and was issued for the purchase of iron. The company still had its debt of $222,666.67 in English bonds due in 1858. In addition, the railroad also had bonds due to the United States for duties on the iron in the amount of $39,424.13 payable in annual installments over the course of four years. The government, in 1850, agreed to deduct the amount annually from the company's Post Office contract.[65] The raising of money to pay freight and duties on iron was a key issue at the 1849 meeting of the stockholders. The *Wilmington Journal* reported the proceedings of this meeting.

> *Resolved,* That the Stockholders of this Company will join in a letter of Attorney to the Treasurer of this Company, authorizing and empowering him to sign their names as sureties to such bonds as may be made by the Company, for the purpose of raising a sufficient sum to pay the freight, for

the use of the Road, the amount for which each Stockholder shall be liable to be set forth in such letter of Attorney.[66]

The company was apparently in such want of cash that it had to appeal to the stockholders to endorse bonds for the transportation of their new iron. The amount of the early debt of the company to the English banks for its initial construction made it likely that they would return to finance its reconstruction; and, likewise, the English financiers would rather lend more for improvements rather than risk their investment.

British iron and European capital would remain an essential element of the American railroad economic culture until the Civil War forced a reorganization of production, labor, transportation, and capital to achieve military objectives. It should be noted that there is a difference between the transfer of technology and the creation of an industry. As a case in point, the market for British locomotives in the United States existed briefly. American craftsmen wasted little time in adapting British locomotive technology to the diverse landscapes of the nation and the special needs of its various companies. Even the Wilmington & Raleigh Rail Road had its own foundry for manufacturing replacement parts, and managed to construct a few of its own locomotives.

By contrast, American iron was manufactured by the same class of craftsmen, working autonomously in close proximity to the raw materials, but often removed from the existing transportation network. While they were able to produce iron of the same quality as their foreign counterparts, they lacked the command of capital to produce it cheaply and in quantity. The British had gained experience in industrial capitalism for more than a century: raw materials, manufacturers, labor, transportation, consumers, investors, financial institutions, insurers, and government worked in concert to supply an international market. Only during the post-war period, when the demand for railroad iron would become overwhelming, would the same elements unify to give form to the emerging American steel industry.

The 14 locomotives that ran the line in 1840 were the best of English and American technology at the time. The first two engines, built by the English Stephenson firm, arrived in late 1837. Illustrations accompanying the Wilmington & Raleigh Rail Road's advertisements in the Wilmington newspaper and the impression of the company seal on early documents in the North Carolina State Archives suggest the Stephenson "Planet" class locomotive.[67] The Smithsonian Institution's preserved Stephenson locomotive, the *John Bull,* used on the Baltimore & Ohio Rail Road, is a modified "Planet" class locomotive, as is the reproduction of the Raleigh & Gaston's locomotive *Raleigh* housed at the North Carolina Transportation Museum in Spencer.

Three Norris engines and one Baldwin engine, both made in Philadelphia, are mentioned in the *Wilmington Advertiser,* along with three passenger cars and four baggage cars built by the firm of Betts, Pusey & Harlan, whose shops were located in Wilmington, Delaware. Eight wheels supported these passenger cars, and the engine tenders for passenger trains were also fitted with eight wheels. This arrangement was adopted for reasons of safety, and to reduce the need for frequent stoppages for water and fuel.[68] Another Norris engine was ordered for the northern end of the line. The company also owned locomotives built by D. J. Burr and Company. The 1838 report given by Alexander Anderson, President pro tem of the Wilmington & Raleigh Rail Road, before the North Carolina Legislature's Board of Internal Improvements, provides a detailed account of the company's resources, equipment, and the cost of purchase. Included in the report are the following items: 12 locomotives with tenders, $90,000; 8 coaches capable of carrying 56 passengers each ($2,250 each), $18,000; and 80 burthen cars ($300 each), $24,000.[69]

The paint scheme for the locomotives and cars is a matter of speculation. However, the paint shop inventory of the company included in the annual stockholders reports detailed large quantities of the Brandon paint, also called *ochre,* a clay base containing iron used in preparing paint, including Venetian red, vermillion, chrome green and chrome yellow. Other pigments include India red, vermillion red, chrome green, chrome yellow, and black, suggesting a similar selection of colors to that of the *Raleigh,* but perhaps used in a different way.[70] Assuming the paint scheme was selected early in the history of the company, the locomotive and cars were likely decorated with some arrangement of these cheerful colors.

James Sprunt, in *Chronicles of the Cape Fear River,* provides more details about these first locomotives.

> Twelve locomotives, which were named, *Nash, Wayne* (built by R. Stephenson & Co., Newcastle-on-Tyne, England), *New Hanover, Edgecombe, Brunswick,* and *Bladen* (built by William Norris, Philadelphia, Pa.), *Greene, Halifax,* and *Sampson* (built by Burr & Sampson, Richmond, Va.), etc.[71]

The *Brunswick* was the first engine to run over the entire railroad when it was completed from Wilmington to Weldon, and it was still in service as a supply train in 1858.[72] Another engine that survived into the 1850s was the *Edgecombe.* After 1840, other locomotives were added periodically over the decade. During the Great Fire of 1843, five of the locomotives were damaged.

IV. The Technology

All the Rail Road Depot, buildings, of every description, including five Locomotives, some cars, the bridge over the ravine, and two or three yards of the road where there were several tracks.[73]

Shortly thereafter, the *Wilmington Chronicle* reports that some of the locomotives could possibly be repaired. At the annual meeting of the stockholders held on November 9, 1843, $8,000 was determined to be the cost of replacing provisions, fixtures, etc. due to the fire. This amount seems small compared to the original cost of the $90,000 it took to purchase the original 12 locomotives. However, by that December a powerful new engine was added to the road, and another like it had been ordered, to compensate for the loss of locomotives due to the fire.[74]

> In consequence of the loss of several locomotives by the fire last spring, there has since been a lack of motive power on the Wilmington Rail Road, especially felt in the heavy freight transportation. The deficiency is now however partly supplied, and will be entirely very soon. An engine capable of hauling a train of 6 or 700 bbls. Turpentine, weighing alone 100 to 120 tons, has just been put upon the Road, and another which it is supposed will be able to take along a train of a thousand bbls., or about 170 tons, is expected shortly.[75]

The available surviving record does not provide enough information to determine what happened to all the damaged engines. It might be safe to speculate that they were eventually restored or their salvageable components could have been used in engines made in the company shops.

Mention of four new locomotives, two new coaches, and a large number of "trucks" having been purchased appears in a report of the annual meeting of the stockholders of 1846.[76] During the 1840s, the company acquired a number of new locomotives. The *J. C. Calhoun*, an M. W. Baldwin locomotive, was put into service in 1841. The *James K. Polk*, also by M. W. Baldwin, followed in 1842. The *William A. Graham*, by M. W. Baldwin, and two Burr, Pea & Sampson locomotives, *E. B. Dudley* and *Wm. H. Haywood*, were purchased in 1846; followed in 1847 by the *Perseverance*, by M. W. Baldwin locomotive. During 1850, the company shops built the *J. M. Morehead* and the *Saxapahaw. Mechanic*, a Norris Brothers locomotive, was also added in 1850. This first generation of passenger locomotives was lightweight and managed an average speed of 22 miles per hour.[77] In 1891, Albert Johnson, an engineer whose career had started with the Richmond and Fredericksburg Railroad in the 1830s, gives a description of the early locomotives on the Wilmington & Raleigh Rail Road.

> They had no pilot, no headlight and no cab. English fashion, the driver or engineer stood out in the weather. The first engines on the Wilmington and

Weldon railway weighed ten tons each. They were the Dudley, the Haywood, the Green and the Sampson.[78]

These early locomotives, as with all locomotives built prior to the Elijah McCoy's invention of the "Lubricator Cup" in the late 19th century, had to be oiled frequently during their run. The average oil consumption for these early locomotives was one pint every 10 miles. Other organic lubrications available at time included animal fats that were used as grease, and organic oils. That the railroad became a heavy consumer of tallow and cotton waste is not surprising.

Some of these first generation engines were rebuilt and used for varying tasks until the 1860s. The *Brunswick, Edgecombe, E. B. Dudley, W. A. Graham, J. C. Calhoun,* and *W. H. Haywood*— all put into service between 1838 and 1846 — were rebuilt during the 1850s. Even when they were worn out, the company shops were able to rebuild them. The *Edgecombe,* along with the *Cumberland* and *J. C. Calhoun,* are listed as worn out and irreparable in the 1856 "Consolidated Report of Locomotives." Other older engines listed in this report are the *W. A. Graham,* valued at $1,000 and considered not worth rebuilding. The *Saxapahaw* (a shifting engine built by the company shops in 1850) was valued at $500 and considered worn out; the *W. H. Haywood,* at $3,000 and the *E. B. Dudley* at $800 were considered worth rebuilding. Surprisingly, by 1860, the *J. C. Calhoun* was being repaired and the *E. B. Dudley* had been rebuilt.[79] Between 1851 and 1855, eleven new locomotives were in use. These new locomotives, the second

TABLE 1. LOCOMOTIVES OF THE
WILMINGTON & RALEIGH RAIL ROAD, 1850–55

Name of Locomotive	Builder	Put into service	Usage
J. M. Morehead	Company Shops	1850	Timber
Saxapahaw	Company Shops	1850	Dirt
Mechanic	Norris Brothers Co.	October, 1850	Passenger
Farmer	Norris Brothers Co.	May, 1851	Passenger
Merchant	M. W. Baldwin	June, 1851	Freight
Industry	M. W. Baldwin	February, 1852	Freight
Director	Norris Brothers	February, 1852	Passenger
Quickstep	Norris Brothers	March, 1852	Passenger
Engineer	Norris Brother	April, 1852	Passenger
President	R. Norris & Son	February, 1853	Passenger
Express	R. Norris & Son	March, 1854	Passenger
Treasurer	M. W. Baldwin	May, 1855	Passenger
Guilford	M. W. Baldwin	August, 1855	Freight
Orange	Manchester Locomotive Works	September, 1855	Passenger

Locomotives put into service on the Wilmington & Raleigh Rail Road between 1850 and 1855 (from the 1855 Report to the Stockholders).

generation to be put into service on the Wilmington & Raleigh Rail Road, were truly American machines. They were almost evenly divided between the M. W. Baldwin and Norris Brothers. Norris and Baldwin had developed locomotives that were dependable, durable, and could perform well on less than perfect rail arrangements. American railroads at that time had been built in a quick economic fashion, and many railroads during the 1850s, particularly in the South, were still using strap iron on wooden rail. Others were using an assortment of different iron rail sizes and designs. Even when the "T" rail became the standard, it was manufactured in many weights and sizes. The American railroads were longer than most of their European counterparts and covered diverse terrain. The design had to be such that a railroad could repair a locomotive in its shops.

The American locomotive of the 1850s was twice the weight of its predecessors, weighing 20 to 25 tons, and that weight was distributed over a greater area. The 4-4-0 configuration with its four large driver wheels was the standard American locomotive of the 19th century, and many builders used this design well into the early 20th century. It is worth noting that the durability of Norris locomotives was such that the Seaboard Air Line was using one for instructing engineers in the late nineteenth century, though the company made its last locomotive in 1867.[80] The Baldwin locomotives were equally durable. Following the Civil War, the *Goldsboro* and *Industry* were rebuilt, and another engine, the *Guilford,* had been recovered from the Roanoke River and was being repaired. M. W. Baldwin built all three locomotives. The *Orange,* built by Manchester Locomotive Works in New Hampshire and put into service in 1855, was still in service after the war.[81] The arrival of one of the Norris engines in 1851 is mentioned in *The Wilmington Herald.*

> We take the liberty in connection with this subject of stating that A New Locomotive, from the manufactory of Norris & Bros., has been received by the Company. It is called "The Farmer," a good name, and it looks like a splendid engine.[82]

Angus Sinclair provides a description of several Norris locomotives, quoted from an 1853 article in the *American Railway Journal,* in his book *Development of the Locomotive Engine.* Several Norris locomotives are listed in this article. It is probable that the reporter for *The Herald* saw a locomotive with similar features.

> No 10, by Norris, outside cylinders 12 3/8 inch by 26 inch; 4 drivers 5 feet diameter on truck; heating surface, 708 square feet in tubes, 54 in firebox, and 10 square feet grate area; weight 43,920, of which 26,880 are on drivers.[83]

While the available documentation does not reveal the actual specifications of the *Farmer,* the 1856 report to the stockholders indicates that for the year ending on September 30 the engine ran 11,853 miles, hauled 341 cars, consumed 201 cords of wood, and was in service 79 days. It appears the *Farmer* averaged 59 miles to the cord of wood while hauling 4.3 cars.[84]

By 1856, the Wilmington & Weldon (changed from the Wilmington & Raleigh) Rail Road had ten passenger locomotives, seven of which were built by Norris. The names of these locomotives were *Mechanic, Director, President, Engineer, Express, Farmer,* and *Quickstep.* Manchester Locomotive Works had built the *Orange,* and M. W. Baldwin had built the *Treasurer.* One new passenger locomotive, the *Alexander McRae,* had been built in the company shops. M. W. Baldwin built all seven of the regular freight locomotives. The names of these locomotives were *Guilford, North Carolina, Merchant, Industry, Perseverance, James K. Polk,* and *J. M. Morehead.* The inventory of locomotives given in the annual report to the stockholders in 1860 indicates a total of 26.

TABLE 2. THE INVENTORY OF LOCOMOTIVES FROM THE 1860 W. & W.R.R. ANNUAL REPORT

Number	Name of Locomotive	Names of Builder	Condition	Usage
22	Orange	Manchester Locomotive Works	Running	Passenger
23	Wilmington	Manchester Locomotive Works	Running	Passenger
24	Gov. Bragg	Manchester Locomotive Works	Running	Passenger
17	President	R. Norris & Son	Running	Passenger
18	Express	R. Norris & Son	Running	Passenger
21	Alex. McRae	Company's Shops	Running	Passenger
9	Weldon	Norris Brothers	Running	Passenger
25	P. K. Dickinson	M. W. Baldwin & Company	Running	Passenger
26	Gov. Ellis	M. W. Baldwin & Company	Running	Passenger
19	Goldsboro	M. W. Baldwin	Running	Passenger
14	Director	Norris Brothers	Running	Freight
15	Quickstep	Norris Brothers	Running	Freight
20	Guilford	M. W. Baldwin	Running	Freight
12	Merchant	M. W. Baldwin	Running	Freight
13	Industry	M. W. Baldwin	Running	Freight
4	W. H. Haywood	Burr, Pea & Sampson	Running	Freight
27	Gilbert Potter	M. W. Baldwin & Company	Running	Freight
28	E. P. Hall	Rogers	Running	Freight
6	J. K. Polk	M. W. Baldwin	Running	—
7	Perseverance	M. W. Baldwin	Running	—
10	North Carolina	M. W. Baldwin	Running	—
1	Brunswick	William Norris	Running	—
8	J. M. Morehead	Company's Shops	Running	—
11	Farmer	Norris & Brothers	Laid up	—
3	J. C. Calhoun	M. W. Baldwin	Laid up	—
5	E. B. Dudley	Burr, Pea & Sampson	Rebuilding	—

IV. The Technology 107

This photograph shows the locomotive *S.D. Wallace* (named for the president of the Wilmington & Weldon Rail Road during the Civil War era). The locomotive, manufactured by Rogers, was typical of the 4-4-0 wood burners that were used on American railroads from the late antebellum period to the introduction of heavy steel rails. Unlike British railroad that were built with the idea of creating a "permanent way" during construction, American railroads tended to built to be put to operation quickly. The 4-4-0 locomotive was capable of negotiating the roughness of these railroads well (courtesy New Hanover Public Library, Robert M. Fales Collection).

On the eve of the Civil War, the Wilmington & Weldon Rail Road was outfitted with an exceptional number of first-rate locomotives, and had managed to keep some of the older locomotives in service for maintaining the line. Paul T. Warner's *Motive Power Development on the Pennsylvania Railroad System, 1831–1924,* published in 1924 by Baldwin Locomotives, contains a number of illustrations of locomotives of the antebellum period along with their specifications.[85] In general, the American railroad tended towards purchasing locomotives with the classic 4-4-0 configuration since the four-wheeled leading truck proved its usefulness in negotiating the grades, curves, and other defects in the rails. The pace of construction for American railroads was primary, and the quality of the road was secondary to placing it in operation expediently. By contrast, the English placed an emphasis on extensive excavations, embankments, and quality construction of the rail superstructure to produce the well engineered road, or as they termed it the *permanent way*.

The history of the Wilmington & Raleigh Rail Road parallels the early railroad development in the United States, as a synthesis of European traditions of civil engineering, the transfer of early British railroad technology, and a few West Point trained engineers such as Walter Gwynn established the foundation for railroad construction in the United States. Drawing upon the available scientific research of the day, these engineers were able to ascertain the appropriate use of materials and motive power for a particular terrain. The shape of the evolving network of railroads was anchored to eastern ports and navigable rivers due to a dependence on imported railroad iron. The locomotives, the first of which were imported from the British manufacturers that pioneered the technology, quickly took on a distinctive American character as domestic firms went into production. Originally lightweight and lacking the power to overcome steep inclines, later models were developed to operate on the diverse landscape of America rather than follow the British approach of creating a more uniform railway. The shops of the Wilmington & Raleigh Rail Road repaired their own locomotives and rolling stock, made castings, built a few locomotives, and functioned as a self-contained industrial plant servicing the railroad and the steamboat line. The locomotives, with their colorful names, represent a cross-section of American builders, each chosen for a particular task.

The Wilmington & Raleigh Rail Road was an industrial operation of unprecedented scope in the history of North Carolina well into the 1850s. When completed in 1840, it tested the limit of what could be achieved with primitive railroad construction techniques and low horsepower locomotives. The surviving stockholders reports and other period documents record discrete details on how this system worked, the nature of its deterioration, and how it was improved. Design errors were exposed after years of usage, and the company adopted corrective measures as it rebuilt the road. For these reasons, the history of the Wilmington & Raleigh Rail Road provides an important record of applied railroad technology from a very early perspective. To a great degree, the early technology was also the source of many of the problems the company experienced during the decade following its completion.

CHAPTER V

Conflict and Crisis

Governor Edward Bishop Dudley died on October 30, 1855, in his sixty-sixth year. When the stockholders of the Wilmington & Raleigh Rail Road met on November 8 for their annual meeting — the first under the new corporate name, the Wilmington & Weldon Rail Road Company — Robert H. Cowan delivered a lengthy tribute to Dudley, the company's first president. For Mr. Cowan, recognizing that there were those in the assembly that had lived through days when it appeared their railroad was on the brink of ruin, he felt it would have been more appropriate had one of their number been selected to perform this service. However, the moment did not lend itself to a testimonial, but instead an impressive summation of a lifelong mission of public service that drew its impetus from personal conviction and innate optimism.[1] Dudley was a founding commissioner of the railroad in 1833, and had served its president of the railroad in 1836–1837 and 1841–1847.

By 1855, the Wilmington & Raleigh Rail Road existed as a monument to Dudley's tenacious belief that this great work was both possible and necessary. His commitment to this undertaking as idea and substance was absolute. This fact was demonstrated through acts of intervention in times that would test the fortitude of any leader. Quick to lend his support to the railroad when it was merely an idea, Dudley was a leading investor in the company from the moment the books were first opened in the summer of 1833. James Sprunt would later write that he often neglected his own personal business to attend to the management of the railroad. In 1843, when railroad facilities at Wilmington were destroyed by fire and even local merchants refused to extend credit to the company, Dudley placed his entire private estate as security to engender confidence in the company's solvency.[2] These actions appear consistent with his lifelong commitment to public service from early adulthood.

As governor, Edward B. Dudley was a harmonizing force in North Carolina politics. He focused on practical issues rather than partisan concerns, and entertained a liberal viewpoint. After serving in Congress from 1829 to 1831, he refused to run for another term. In 1830, he had published a circular that opposed the Cherokee removal that irritated some in the western most section of the state. However, when he ran for governor during 1836, his platform was unambiguous. His views on internal improvements made him an attractive candidate in the western counties in spite of being an easterner. He possessed a congenial personality, great wealth, and a tendency to follow his principles doggedly.[3] Gov. Dudley, with the aid of his colleague William Graham, labored to reorganize the finances of the state during the 1836–1837 session of the General Assembly. The central achievement of this session was the two-fifths investment on the part of the state for several railroad projects, including the Cape Fear & Western Rail Road from Fayetteville to the Yadkin River, the Wilmington & Raleigh Rail Road, and the North Carolina Central Rail Road from Beaufort to Fayetteville.[4] This new statute channeled the distribution of the federal surplus into the stock of the railroad companies and the resulting dividends from stocks were to be applied to the fund for public education called the Literary Fund.[5]

Governor Edward Bishop Dudley was the first president of the Wilmington & Raleigh Rail Road and also the first popularly elected governor of North Carolina. He was an early supporter of the concept of a railroad Raleigh between Wilmington and Raleigh; was an unshakeable champion of internal improvements during his governorship; placed his complete fortune behind the Wilmington & Raleigh Rail Road after the disastrous "Great Fire of 1843"; and rendered service to the company till his death in 1855. He, along with John Motley Morehead, William Alexander Graham, and Charles Manly, constitute a block of Whig governors committed to advancing internal improvements in North Carolina lasting from 1837 through 1850 (photograph courtesy of the New Hanover Public Library, Robert M. Fales Collection).

Hitherto, this work has been concerned with the financial, technological, and logistical aspects associated with the Wilmington & Raleigh Rail Road. The one essential element remaining that explains its existence is leadership. History places leaders within the context of events, and affords them considerable credit for the consequences of their actions. Only recently, with the growth of business schools in universities, have the qualities of leadership been subjected to scientific inquiry. The nature of leadership exhibited by Edward B. Dudley in the planning and operation of the railroad should be examined more critically because there existed from the beginning a host of individuals in Raleigh, Petersburg, and places less concerned — all leaders and authorities in their own right — that expected the Wilmington & Raleigh to fail. There were also highly educated men such as Archibald Murphey, Joseph Caldwell, and David Swain that conceived visionary plans for a state system of internal improvements, but failed in their efforts to secure sufficient support to carry their ideas into reality.

The most established of the leadership theories is the *Fiedler Contingency Model* that focuses on leadership styles rather than vague and sometimes contradictory positions built upon the interpretation of personal traits. Beginning in the late 1960s, Fred Fiedler, a psychologist at the University of Washington, asserted the position that leaders with diverse orientations trending either toward task-oriented or relationship-oriented strengths could be effective if the situation was appropriate to their strengths.[6] It is obvious from the oration that Mr. Cowan delivered on the life of Gov. Dudley that *leader-member relations*— respect and confidence the company had in its president — and the *leader position power*— or the power of the position of the presidency of the railroad — both presented a favorable situation for success. According to Fiedler, the third element necessary to determine *situational favorableness* is a well defined *task structure*. To understand the *task structure* of the Wilmington & Raleigh during the tenure of Edward Dudley, one must review the evolution of the organization with the context of the tasks.

The pivotal moment in the organization of the Wilmington & Raleigh Rail Road occurred in the fall of 1835 in the south wing at the residence of Edward Dudley in Wilmington. James Sprunt describes this event as a meeting to secure subscriptions to the stock of the railroad.[7] Its occurrence so close to the meeting of the General Assembly was more than a symbolic gesture of solidarity of the commercial interests of Wilmington in support of the railroad as the bill to amend its charter was taken up once more; it was the projection of the new incarnation of the Wilmington & Raleigh.

The need to obtain the amendments in 1835 was critical. The charter of 1833 required building the railroad to commence three years after ratification of the act to incorporate the company.[8] If the bill did not pass in 1835, some part of the railroad would still have to built by the next session of the General Assembly. Under the original charter, a meeting of the stockholders could not be called until at least twenty days after $300,000 in subscriptions to the stock had been secured.[9] Regardless of what would become of the bill, the commissioners at Wilmington had to act, or the company would be stillborn.

The motivation that initiated the formation of the organizational structure in late 1835 was crisis — the impending session of the General Assembly — and Edward B. Dudley, a politician with experience in the General Assembly and Congress, who possessed the charisma to marshal all the supporters of the project into a working corporation within a few months. That he was also able to garner sufficient popular support to attain the governorship in 1836 is remarkable. That a regional leader can transfer his or her charisma to a higher level of authority in this way is rare.[10] The common need throughout the state, however, was the same as any regional need: economic development would not occur anywhere without improved transportation and a system of public education. In his inauguration address, Gov. Dudley outlined his program explicitly; and his colleague William Graham called for the use of public funds to achieve such improvements.[11] The goals of the Wilmington & Raleigh Rail Road were compatible with the general program of internal improvements, or rather subsumed under it; there was not a conflict of interests.

The unfolding of events following the ratification of the act to amend the charter actually occurred rather quickly, considering its scope. By March 4, 1836, the *Wilmington Advertiser* announced that the company had secured $400,000 in subscription.[12] The first meeting of the stockholders was held on March 14, 1836, a board of directors was elected, and the stockholders selected Edward B. Dudley president. The directors included Andrew Joyner representing interests in Halifax County; James S. Battle, representing interests in Edgecombe County; William D. Mosley, representing interests in Lenoir County; and remaining directors were prominent men from New Hanover County. General Alexander McRae, a civil engineer, was appointed superintendent of the railroad.[13]

The books were opened to receive subscriptions for 2,000 shares of stock with representatives at Wilmington, Norfolk, Portsmouth, Halifax (Halifax County), Nashville (Nash County), Tarboro (Edgecombe), Pitts Crossroads (Edgecombe), Waynesborough (Wayne County), Lenoir County, and Kenansville (Duplin) on March 25, 1836. James Holliday, one of the commissioners at Halifax, was also associated with the Halifax & Weldon Rail Road.[14] A special meeting of the stockholders was called on February 27, 1837, to secure enough capital to qualify for the two-fifths subscription by the state.[15] The first goal of the corporation was to acquire capital; the second was to commence construction as soon as possible.

Walter Gwynn was in the field conducting his survey in April, had completed a large section of it by July, and presented his report to the company on August 15, 1836. Upon his election to the office of governor, Edward Dudley resigned his position as president of the Wilmington & Raleigh Rail Road, and James Owen, also a former Congressman, was elected to take his place. Arrangements had been made with banks by February 1837 to extend credit to individual stockholders on their scheduled installments on their shares.[16] Work commenced on the railroad slowly in October of 1836, but was underway with vigor in January, 1837. The *Boston* was ordered in February of 1837, and arrived in May; and within a month, the stages were put into service.

The characteristics of the leadership style of Edward B. Dudley included highly developed human relation skills, the ability to delegate responsibility effectively, and the vision to perceive the goal within the context of a greater good. Current literature on leadership defines the synthesis of such qualities as *spaciousness* of the leadership mind.

> The leadership mind is spacious, comfortably embracing paradoxes and contradictions, polarities and ambiguities, conflicts and incompatibilities. The leadership mind holds thoughts and attitudes at once. Specifically, the leadership mind is not troubled by contradictory ideas.[17]

The paradoxes were obvious: the railroad would connect with Petersburg and Norfolk, crossing most of the major rivers in the state, contrary to what the committee from New Hanover argued in their response to Gavin Hogg in 1834. The commissioners in Wilmington had to seek support in Edgecombe County, an area noted for its stubborn opposition to internal improvements, in order to break free of their connection to Raleigh interests and fashion a diverse tapestry of alliances within and outside the state.

Brown, Sprunt, and other historians tend to view the period between the incorporation of the Wilmington & Raleigh Rail Road in 1833 and the amendment of its charter in 1835 as a period of inactivity simply because of a dearth of archival documents. To realize the work of leadership that was sustained prior to the fall of 1835, one has only to contemplate how quickly interests in the northeastern counties committed to the project: Walter Gwynn began surveying the route in 1836, and the Halifax & Weldon merged into the Wilmington & Raleigh in 1837. However, the chief problem that the president and directors of the company created for its shareholders, the state included, during its period of constructing the railroad was long-term debt.

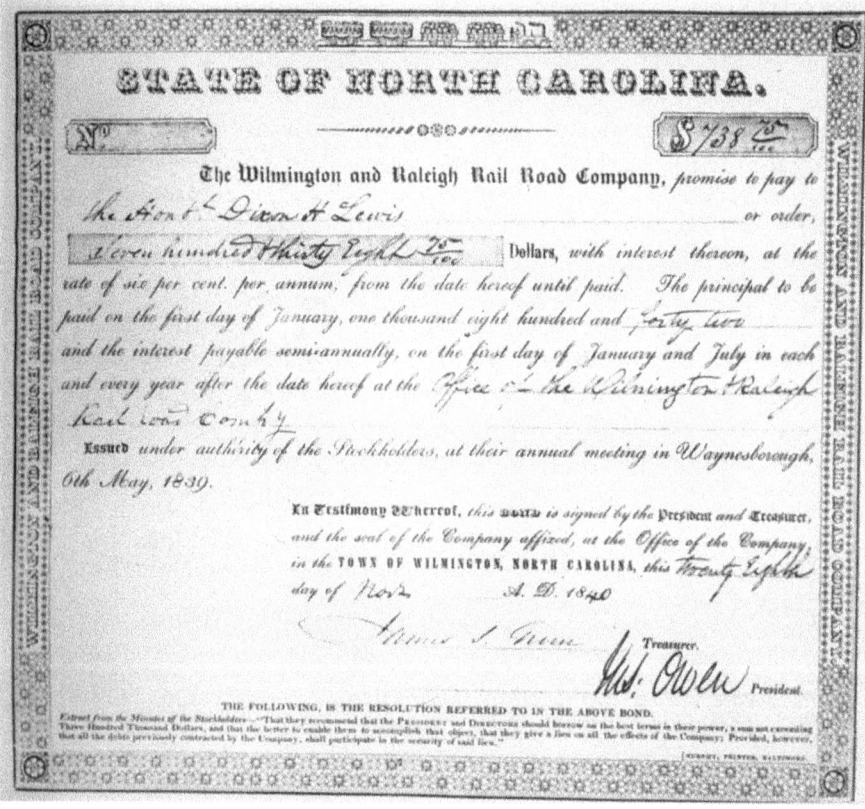

At the annual meeting of the stockholders of the Wilmington & Raleigh Rail Road, held at Waynesborough on May 6, 1839, the stockholders authorized the company to borrow $300,000 to complete the railroad. This bond, backed by the State of North Carolina, accrued 6 per cent semiannually of the principal, which principal was to be paid back January 1, 1842. The Raleigh & Gaston Rail Road also issued bonds endorsed by the state, but defaulted, with the company thereby becoming in essence a state owned railroad until it was reorganized in 1850 (courtesy New Hanover Public Library, Robert M. Fales Collection).

V. Conflict and Crisis

James Owen, the second president of the company, stated in the 1840 annual report that the profits of the company would be used to service debt.

> If we might apprehend disappointment, in our reasonable hope succor from the Legislature, what will be the condition of the company? With a capital of $1,350,000 actually paid in and secured, and property worth over two millions of dollars, the nett revenue, instead of being divided among the stockholders, must be kept back and appropriated to the discharge of the debt; which, being accomplished, will raise the par value of the stock to $150, or 50 per cent. above its original price. To the stockjobber it will afford a rich harvest; but it will prove a cruel blight to the original subscriber who, having contributed his money and his credit, at the most critical juncture of the enterprise, must now, with the prospect of a fair remuneration opening before him, incur disappointment and heavy loss, by the necessity which compels him to a premature sale of his stock.[18]

The company would not be able to declare a dividend for more than a decade. Recalling the observation of Thomas Clingman in 1852 that the shares of the Wilmington & Raleigh were trading at seventy cents on the dollar, it is clear that the value of the railroad was not in its shares but rather in enhancement of commerce. The railroad imposed a single overriding imperative: it had to continue to fulfill its scheduled runs regardless of its performance as an investment. This transformed the task structure of leadership to adapt to new conditions. The goal was no longer the high-energy campaign to build; rather, it became the relentless demands of maintaining an industrial process.

The prevailing economic environment in the nation was discouraging in the early 1840s, and the destruction of the railroad facilities in Wilmington by fire in 1843 eroded confidence in the viability of the company. While the cost of replacing these fixtures and provisions only amounted to $8,000 in a year when the company had reduced expenditures by approximately $49,000, the early estimates for fire loss for Wilmington amounted to approximately $300,000.[19] The commercial and cultural foundation of the town had been shaken by the catastrophe, and ruins at the railroad depot must have projected an impression of defeat that was primarily psychological — a symbol of civic anxiety — and was disproportional to the actual loss. When Gov. Dudley offered his whole estate as collateral to back the credit of the company, the gesture had a salutary effect on both the community and the shareholders beyond providing security to restore confidence in the solvency of the company. Recounted in the oration of Mr. Cowan, it remained a significant event in the corporate history more than a decade later, magnified by the success of the company at the time.

The federal surplus provided the state with the capital to reinforce its policy of investing in two-fifths of the stock of several companies engaged in internal improvements projects. However, the combined effect of this and other economic policies of the Jackson administration created a banking crisis of unprecedented magnitude. Foreign investment evaporated, domestic credit tightened, and the national economy contracted. The subsequent depression lasted well into the 1840s. At the time these events began to unfold, the Wilmington & Raleigh and the Raleigh & Gaston were still under construction. The shareholders who had subscribed in more optimistic times were struggling to make their scheduled installments, and the leadership of the companies implored the General Assembly for relief. To understand the long-term crisis that the early railroads of North Carolina experienced during this time, one should begin by reviewing the origin and nature of the national economic crisis.

The General Assembly enacted *An Act to Aid the Internal Improvements of the State* that directed the surplus revenue towards the purchase of stock in the Wilmington & Raleigh Rail Road and several other projects.[20] North Carolina was slow to obtain a Jacksonian "pet bank" after the distributions of federal deposits from the Bank of the United States in 1833. In 1835, Romulus M. Saunders, a Democrat, successfully persuaded the administration to direct deposits to the Bank of North Carolina.[21]

The individual shareholders of the companies — mostly merchants and planters — experienced the resulting deleterious effects of the Panic of 1837 and the depression that followed. As noted above, James Owen, the second president of the Wilmington & Raleigh Rail Road, described the burden of shareholders in his 1840 report to North Carolina Board of Internal Improvements a few months after the railroad was completed. In the years before the crisis, many of the shareholders had subscribed liberally to the stock of the company. During the downturn, the directors of the company chose to exercise forbearance with the distressed shareholders that were unable to pay scheduled installments on the shares rather than press for payment.[22]

On a larger scale, the economic downturn of the late 1830s influenced the developments of North Carolina's antebellum rail network. Advocates of internal improvements had devised a state plan for a network consisting of intersecting north-to-south and east-to-west corridors in 1833. When the North Carolina General Assembly met in their 1848–1849 session, the state did not actually have a rail network, merely two fragments of a state system of internal improvements that evolved contrary to earlier plans. At this point, both railroads were on the verge of becoming inoperable. The tracks of the Raleigh & Gaston Rail Road and the Wilmington & Raleigh Rail Road, originally constructed with perishable strap-iron wooden rails, needed reconstruction with durable heavy iron.[23] The Raleigh & Gaston was then, for all practical purposes, a state-owned railroad. After the company defaulted on interest payments for state endorsed bonds, North Carolina instituted foreclosure proceedings against it in 1845, and took possession the following year. The state of North Carolina had also endorsed the bonds of the Wilmington & Raleigh Rail Road, and it was the railroad's largest shareholder. The company, though deeply in debt, was profitable and its future prospects appeared encouraging; but the company had yet to declare dividends.

The general economic conditions of the late 1830s through the early 1840s were not the only disruptive force threatening the stability of the Wilmington & Raleigh Rail Road Company. The commercial competition between the Petersburg Rail Road and the Portsmouth & Roanoke Rail Road had escalated into a trade war. The Weldon Toll Bridge was the epicenter of the conflict, and at its conclusion, the entire section of the Portsmouth & Roanoke Rail Road in North Carolina from Margarettsville to the Roanoke River was shut down. Regional ambitions had compromised the integrity of the evolving network of railroads and steamboat lines in the northeast by severing their link to the southern network. All southbound traffic had to pass through Petersburg.

Closer to home, the Great Fire of 1843 that devastated whole blocks of residences and businesses in Wilmington had also destroyed the shops and warehouses of the Wilmington & Raleigh Rail Road. The locomotives and rolling stock at the station were damaged, and sections of the track destroyed. As the periodic bond payments came due for the initial construction of the road, so too did its obligations to the contractors that supplied the labor. The cost of maintaining the steamboat line had increased over the years, the railroad was deteriorating, and whatever increase in revenue the company gained with one was offset by expenditures for the other.

However, railroad development in North Carolina was revived in 1849 when the General Assembly passed legislation for construction of the North Carolina Railroad and for providing aid for the Raleigh & Gaston and the Wilmington & Raleigh to rebuild these railroads with heavy iron rails. Regardless of the productivity of these investments, the state was obliged for the sake of the public good to facilitate the rebuilding of these railroads and lend its support to the long awaited east-to-west trunk line that would bring the existing railroads into a state network.[24] By the mid-1850s, the future of the Wilmington & Raleigh appeared promising.

Many historians have advanced the conclusion that the southern railroads failed to evolve into a coherent network because of undercapitalization, poor planning, nonstandard construction techniques and gauges, and the lack of rail connections between cities and the rest of the country. James A. Ward, author of *Railroads and the Character of America, 1820–1887,* found that many of these assumptions about the inferiority of southern railroads emanate from a narrow scope of research, much of it concerning the network's wartime inadequacies.

Using Albert Fishlow's regional-capital-investment series for railroads and Henry V. Poor's compilation of yearly railway mileage, Ward found that southern railroads met or exceeded the national average capitalization per mile between 1837 and 1842. The lack of standardization of gauge was a problem throughout the Union, not limited to the southern railroads. In addition, he noted the primary function of these railroads was to provide transportation to the nearest market, not to supply the needs of bordering states. He attributed the decline in the gross capitalization per mile in the South after 1842, thus the rate of railroad development, to the region's slow recovery from the nationwide depression that followed the Panic of 1837. The scarcity of technical expertise brought about by service of West Point–trained civil engineers in the Mexican War in the 1840s and construction of the foreign money markets following the outbreak of the Crimean War in the 1850s prevented many southern railroads from upgrading the 1830s technology of their initial construction.[25]

The Panic of 1837 and the Panic of 1857 are the two financial disruptions during the antebellum period that are inexorably entwined with early railroad development in the United States. The first, as noted earlier in this work, delayed the construction of some railroads and prevented many projected railroads from ever going forward. In North Carolina, early plans to build the Fayetteville & Western Rail Road, the North Carolina Central Rail Road, and the Raleigh & Columbia Rail Road evaporated. The Wilmington & Raleigh and the Raleigh & Gaston, both projects that were underway, were the remaining fragments of what could be called the state system of internal improvements. The Panic of 1857, by contrast, had its origins in land speculation brought about as railroads penetrated westward; its impact on the economic condition of the railroads of North Carolina was not pronounced or enduring. The most significant strides in railroad development in antebellum North Carolina had gone forward before the event occurred. In general, the South recovered rather quickly from this national financial downturn.

Andrew Jackson's opposition to the re-chartering of Second Bank of the United States[26] was a key element in the origin of the financial crisis. The Bank of the United States functioned differently from the Federal Reserve Banks that exist today. The private banks were indebted to this central bank rather than acting as its creditors. The Bank of the United States exercised its control of banks by restricting the capital available for lending so that their notes would not depreciate. It was unpopular with state and private banks because it restricted their lending power.[27]

Jackson, in his state of the union message to Congress in 1829, began his attack on the second Bank of the United States after becoming aware of an effort by the bank's supporters to have its charter renewed in advance of its expiration in 1836. He did not want the government to be a stockholder in the bank, yet he wanted the President of the United States to appoint directors to serve on the board of the bank in Philadelphia and its branches. He also believed the bank was engaging in real estate speculation, so he wanted limits set on the amount of time the bank could hold the property it had obtained through defaulted loans; and also wanted the bank to pay state taxes on its branch properties at the same rate used for taxing similar property owned by state banks. Nicolas Biddle, the bank's president, sought Jackson's support for the re-charter bill as Congress considered it in 1832, and agreed to the proposed amendments to the charter.[28] On July 10, 1832, the president returned it to Congress with his veto message.

The Deposit Act of 1836 dispersed all but five million dollars of the federal surplus held in the Second Bank of the United States to the state banks.[29] The timeline of events leading up to the Panic of 1837 began with the ratification of the Deposit Act on June 23, 1836. Supplemental Transfers, meaning interbank transfer of hard currency, commenced on August 1, 1836. The Specie Circular, requiring payment for land held by the government to be in hard currency or backed by it, went into effect on August 15, 1836, and the first and second distributions of the federal surplus occurred on January 1, 1837, and April 1, 1837. New York banks suspended specie payment on May 10, 1837. Shortly thereafter, the Bank of England rejected commercial bills of discount from Anglo-American mercantile houses.[30] The British had invested heavily in the United States during the 1830s. A number of external events in Europe, such as crop failure in England in 1838 and a decline in the demand for British textiles, placed strains on the Bank of England, prompting the bank to borrow gold from France. The liberality of the London money market was constrained.³¹ Railroads and other internal improvement projects, dependent upon the availability of foreign investment capital, failed, were postponed, or were abandoned.

Richard H. Timberlake would address the question of the central bank in the early 1960s after the publication of Bray Hammond's critical work *Banks and Politics in America*. He presented a thesis quite different from Hammond on the demise of early central banking. This is, central banking policy was incompatible with the specie standard. Society resented a central bank in the United States. The development of banks chartered by Congress occurred for fiscal purposes, and "the central banking idea developed residually as an 'external economy' to the public character of these institutions." There was not a safe ground for these institutions to exist. The Treasury was the appropriate repository of public funds, and the authority over currency. The commercial banking activities of a central bank appeared to tend towards a monopoly.³²

Jacksonian monetary policy intersects the history of the Wilmington & Raleigh Rail Road at two critical points in its development. The distribution of the federal surplus brought about through the Deposit Act of 1836 allowed the state of North Carolina to invest in two-fifths of the company stock. However, the depression that followed the Panic of 1837 that was a consequence of the same policy also placed stress upon the shareholders as scheduled installments on their shares came due. Decreased commerce nationwide had an impact on the annual earnings of the railroad.

Railroad development in North Carolina came to a stop, and the two railroads completed in 1840 were far from being a state system that would be accessible to all. Dividends from railroad stock were supposed to help fund public education in North Carolina; instead the railroads became a liability for the state. For example, from 1843 to 1854, the Raleigh & Gaston cost the state $821,856.58 in principal and interest for the bonds it had endorsed.³³ The company was finally reorganized under *An Act to incorporate the Raleigh & Gaston Rail Road Company* during the 1850–1851 session of the General Assembly.³⁴ The Raleigh & Gaston, as noted earlier, became a state-owned railroad after it had defaulted on its bond payments in the early 1840s.

To assume that the Wilmington & Raleigh Rail Road could have fared better if left to its own devices during the 1840s would be naïve. The General Assembly of 1848–49 delivered the salvation of the company on January 27, 1849, in the form of a new issue of bonds endorsed by the state.³⁵

V. Conflict and Crisis

An act concerning the Wilmington and Raleigh Rail Road Company. Provides that the Company be authorized to mortgage the Road for the sum of $620,000 to raise money to repair the same; and gives a priority to this mortgage over the State's holding as former mortgage. Also, extends the credit on the bond of the Company for ten years.[36]

The fragile and perishable wooden rails of the original construction were a liability that limited the earning potential of both railroads; and the state of North Carolina, faced with the potential loss of a valuable transportation resource, had little recourse but to continue its financial involvement.

A reminder of the company's financial situation is quite revealing. The receipts for the railroad of the Wilmington & Raleigh Rail Road Company for 1844 were $158,705.34, while its expenditures were $131,646.15, leaving a profit of $27,059.19; the receipts of its steamboat line were $130,828.41, with expenditures of $71,987.69, leaving a profit of $58,841.32. The total profit of the railroad and steamboats was $85,900.51.[37] The table of receipts and expenditures below is derived from statistics presented at the ninth annual meeting of the stockholders held November 14, 1844, at Wilmington. The average monthly expenditures for the steamboats declined over the four-year period, whereas the expenditures for the railroad had risen from $5,848.01 in 1843 to $10,970.51. The years 1842 and 1843 reflect a decline in receipts. An examination of the proceedings of the annual stockholders meeting held on November 9, 1842, cites several reasons that can be associated with the decline in receipts.

A meeting was held in Washington, D.C., earlier that year between the several companies that served the Atlantic states to establish more uniform rates: a ticket from Baltimore to Charleston was agreed to cost twenty-two dollars.

A cheap, competing route south from New York to New Orleans via Philadelphia, Baltimore, Wheeling, the Ohio River and the Mississippi

TABLE 3. TABLE OF MONTHLY RECEIPTS
AND EXPENDITURES, 1841–44

Year	Railroad Receipts	Steamboat Receipts	Railroad Expenditures	Steamboat Expenditures
1841	$13,552.34	$11,216.69	$10,948.76	$9,213.85
1842	10,736.60	8,496.71	8,818.85	7,825.93
1843	10,175.73	8,672.02	5,848.01	6,499.17
1844	13,225.45	10,902.37	10,970.51	5,998.92

This table shows the average monthly receipts and expenditures for the railroad and steamboats of the Wilmington & Raleigh Rail Road Company for years 1841 through 1844.
Source: *Wilmington Chronicle*, November 20, 1844.

River had been established. A ticket from Philadelphia to New Orleans would cost between thirty-three and thirty-five dollars, and the value of money had appreciated with the improving financial state of the nation. However, the liabilities of the company were problematic.

> It will be seen by the report of your committee that the liabilities of the Company, vary but little from the last year. That about one hundred thousand dollars are required of the old debts to which the creditors are justly entitled, and from their representations stand greatly in need. Many of them have been generously forbearing, but others have indulged in vexatious suits and levied executions on the hire of the negroes employed on repairs, whose attention is daily required to watch over the Road and keep it safe for the passage of the Trains. They were seized and taken away regardless of consequences, in the hope of coercing payment, when the Company had it not. Without provision is made for these debts these scenes will probably be acted over again. The Directors can suggest no other way but an appeal to the Legislature, for the postponement of the payment of the Bond due next January, and the endorsement of fifty thousand more to pay these debts. Having already paid fifty thousand dollars on which the State was security, the further assistance would only place her liabilities at the same amount first granted. Such a measure or some other equally efficient is required in justice to the creditors and for the protection of the credit of the Company.[38]

The liabilities of the company as of October 1, 1845, amounted to $668,817.52. This included $222,666.67 in bonds sold in England; $85,000 owed to the Literary Board with six percent interest; and $250,000 in bonds endorsed by the state bearing seven percent. Also included were $15,000 in bills payable at six percent; $42,272.86 in bills payable at six percent; $12,793 in script bonds to due to contractors; and $3,939.48 on bonds for the hire of slave laborers (the Negro Bonds) due on January 1, 1846. The amount of $18,270 in bonds for slave hire was due on January 1, 1847, and $30,875.08 in payments due for materials and labor to various individuals. In the midst of this complex debt structure, the company sought to have the state relinquish the mortgage it held on the railroad's boats and wharf so that it could borrow more money to extend their rails to South Carolina. In addition, the company wanted to establish a sinking fund — an account dedicated for the purpose of accumulating the funds to pay off a debt — to service their existing debt through a five dollar per share payment from the stockholder beginning in 1847, and lasting for five years. The profits from the company, after paying expenses and the interest on the debt, were to be applied to the sinking fund. The shareholders were to have their contributions to the sinking fund returned with interest after the debt was extinguished.[39]

The year ending September 30, 1847, reflected $331,480.20 in receipts, and $259,912.60 in expenses; the remainder was $71,567.60. Repairs to the road had cost the company $82,479.03, whereas $42,093.11 was spent on repairing the boats. The *President's Report* from the 1847 annual meeting notes that the cost for repairing the boats was very large compared to previous years, and the road repairs would increase because the rails needed to be replaced.

During the summer of that year, a committee from the company traveled north to submit statistics (collected on the counties through which the proposed Wilmington & Manchester Rail Road would pass) to experts who would determine the accuracy of the company's prediction on the profits of its sister road. The experts tended to think the profits would be greater than the company predicted and that the stock of that company would be taken up quickly. The company had in fact pledged to take $100,000 of stock in the Wilmington & Manchester, payable from the sale of its steamboats and other property, when the railroad was completed. The report continues a projection of profit for the new railroad based on the business of the existing railroad for the population of the counties. The population of the counties through which the Wilmington & Raleigh Rail Road passed was 76,850, and the business for the previous year had been $102,243.14. The population along the route of the Wilmington & Manchester was 130,967. Based on the assumption that revenue is proportional to population, the predicted annual income of the new railroad would have been $174,241.73. Some $70,479.62 could be added to this amount for the transport of the mails.[40]

The legislature, however, did not act upon the company's resolution regarding the sinking fund and the need to replace the rails of the Wilmington & Raleigh. By this time, strap-iron wooden rail construction was widely recognized as a built-in flaw that plagued many of the other railroads of the South.

> In the original outlay for construction, the limited means of the Company, no doubt, influenced the Engineer to recommend, and the Board to adopt, the flat Rail. This has been the unfortunate mistake in the construction of many of our Southern Roads, and is the chief cause why they have been unprofitable to Stockholders, while in almost every instance in our county where the Iron Rail has been used, the Roads have proven profitable to the Stockholders. When we look at the business done on our Road, and the great annual increase in freight and local travel, we cannot doubt that if we could command the means to renew the Whole Road with Iron Rail, that the local business alone would support it, independent of the transportation of the Mail and the long or through travel.[41]

The receipts for the railroad and steamboats ending October 1, 1847 were $331,480.20, and expenditures were $259,942.60. The net profits were $71,537.60. The cash on hand left from 1846 was $3,358.56, and the amount in the hands of agents was $7,704.09. This added up to a profit of $82,630.25. However, $27,791.52 had been applied to the reduction of the debt, $37,121.82 was used toward the payment of interest, and $909.42 had been submitted to the Treasurer of State of North Carolina for payment of interest. This, with several lesser expenses, left $8,547.18 in the hands of the treasury of the company. During the period from 1841 to 1847, the number of way passengers — passenger travel between stations on the line — increased from 5,498 to 25,396: the number of through passengers — passengers traveling the entire line through the state — peaked at 14,018 in 1845.

In 1844, the company showed its highest profits at $85,900.51; but in 1846, profits dropped to their lowest level at $28,140.04. During this year, the receipts were $317,822.49, the highest amount to date, and the

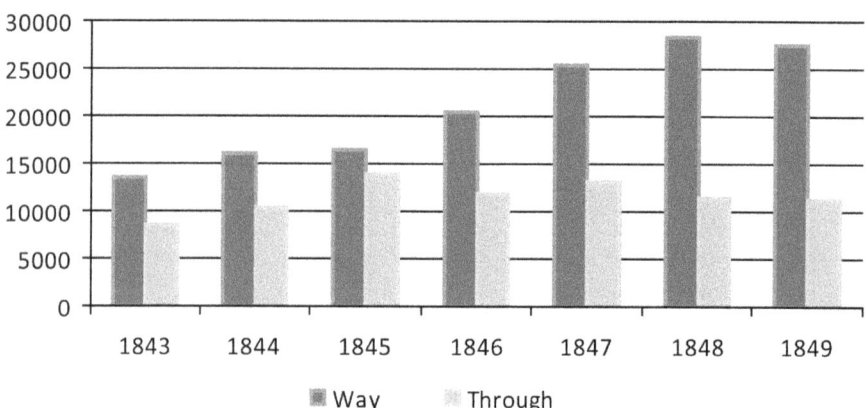

Wilmington & Raleigh Rail Road Passengers, 1843–1849

Throughout the 1840s, the volume of "way" passengers traveling between stations of the Wilmington & Raleigh Rail Road increased dramatically. Data sources: North Carolina, *Report of the Internal Improvement Board to the Legislature of North Carolina* (Raleigh: Seaton Gales, Printer for the State, 1848), 18; Wilmington & Weldon Rail Road Company, *Proceedings of the Stockholders of the Wilmington & Weldon Rail Road Co. at their Twentieth Annual Meeting, held at Wilmington, North Carolina, November 9, 1855* (Wilmington: Thomas Loring, 1855), 26.

number of passengers, 11,885 through passengers and 20,498 way passengers, was high; however, the expenses for their year were $289,682.45. There were 458 people employed by the company during 1847; 203 were slaves on road repairs.[42]

The receipts for the year ending September 30, 1848 included $113,078.22 from through passenger fares, $53,092.04 from way passengers, $12,466.63 for steamboat freight, $51,534.51 for railroad freight, and $77,344.79 for the transport of the mails and rents. The company had been selling its worn out iron rails and copper from its boats, and for this year they received $9,943.31. Their total annual receipts for 1848 were $317,459.50; however, the expenses of the year were $238,133.79. These expenses are broken down into the major categories of transportation, steamboats, and road repairs. The transportation expenses totaled $75,872.13: $13,580.57 for repairing locomotives; $12,754.39 for rolling stock; $43,337.17 for payroll and expenses of this department; and three new passengers cars were added to the rolling stock at a cost of $6,200.00. The steamboat department reported only $8,413.41 in repairs, but the subsistence and pay for officers and crew amounted to $60,012.39. Added to $29,648.14 for fuel, the steamboat department accounted for expenses totaling $98,073.94.

The road repair department reported costs amounting to $63,977.04. Of this amount, $30,146.92 was spent on materials, $25,800.52 on labor, and $8,029.60 for subsistence and clothing for the labor force. Office expenses amounted to $210.68 during that year. Of the remaining receipts of $79,325.71, $35,909.68 was applied to interest on the debt, and $37,195.07 went to the purchase of new iron. This left $6,219.96 in the company treasury.[43]

> It will be seen by a reference to the foregoing statement of the accounts, that a large sum has been expended for New Iron. This was found to be absolutely necessary, to maintain the road in safe running order, for without this outlay, the operation of the Company must have necessarily been greatly embarrassed; as we could not have continued to run our trains over it with regularity or even with safety.— Being satisfied that it was indispensably necessary to the operations of the Company, if not to its very existence, that the Road should be preserved in good condition, your Board has applied to the purchase of New Iron all the means at their disposal, not required for the necessary current expenses of the Company; and being further satisfied that it was false economy to continue the use of the light bar, first laid on our Road, and that permanence and stability could only be hoped for, by adopting a heavy rail in its stead, they have not hesitated to substitute the one for the other.[44]

The Wilmington & Raleigh Rail Road as it existed in 1848 was in a precarious position: the company was carrying $651,783.16 in debt as of October 1, 1848, and paying on the interest; the flat iron, wooden rail system that it had originally adopted was consuming a large portion of the company's receipts in repairs.[45] The company was in need of a further extension of credit to replace the entire 161 miles of the line with heavy iron. The company was at least solvent, and the railroad had experienced a steady increasing of business since its completion.

The failure of the Raleigh & Gaston had taken place because the company did not generate the net profits to maintain the road and make the interest payment on the state endorsed bonds. The company defaulted on its interest payments that came due on January 1, 1843. However, the net profits of the company had been $31,340.15 for 1841 $27,867.07 for 1842; and $23,250.95 in 1843. It was in 1844, when the receipts had fallen to $53,460.77 and the expenditures had risen to $49,470.67, that the net profits of the Raleigh & Gaston had fallen by nearly $20,000.[46] The Wilmington & Raleigh Rail Road had been making its interest payments, but net profits after this adjustment were meager. From the perspective of the investor, the stock of the company was truly "of undetermined value." If the flat iron wooden rails were to continue to be used, the cost of repairs would overtake the profits and the state of North Carolina would find itself running two railroads, paying off the bonds on both, and paying the cost of renewing the rails from the public funds. The latter would have cost the state another half million dollars.

> The cost of relaying our Road (162 miles) with an Iron Rail of 52 lbs. to the yard, at the present price of Iron, from which deduct the value of the old Iron about $84,000, and we have the sum of $516,000. The interest on this sum at 6 per cent, per annum, would be $30,960, which being deducted from 86,252.11—the difference in the expense of the two kinds of rail as before ascertained, and we should make a saving annually of $55,252.11—a sum nearly double the interest of the cost of the heavy Iron. To this add the great additional facilities which such a Road would give to the Company in their transportation, and it must be manifest to any one who examines the subject, that the true economy of the Company would be to substitute the heavy rail.[47]

As stated earlier, the total cost to the state on the accounts of the Raleigh & Gaston Rail Road between 1843 and 1854 had been $821,856.58.[48] The state's role as the largest shareholder in the Wilmington & Raleigh made it a hostage to its own creation, for in this position it was responsible for the health of the railroad just as were the private investors.

It is doubtful that the merchants and planters of the east would have been able to build the railroad to its extraordinary length without the investment on the part of the state. Under these conditions, they were legally bound and socially obligated to promote the success of the railroad.

A Bill Concerning the Wilmington and Raleigh Rail Road Company (North Carolina Senate Document No. 9) provides for the mortgaging of the entire property of the railroad, except its steamboats and the wharf in Charleston, for the relaying of the road in heavy iron.

> *Whereas,* The said Wilmington and Raleigh Rail Road Company is desirous of improving the said Road by relaying it with new and heavy iron, which will greatly enhance the value of the stock held by the State, as well as the individual stockholders, and, *whereas,* to effect that object, it may be necessary for said Company to contract a loan. *Be it therefore enacted by the General Assembly of the State of North Carolina, and it is hereby enacted by the authority of the same,* That the said Wilmington and Raleigh R. R. Company shall be, and are hereby authorized to borrow a sum not exceeding $520,000, for the purposes mentioned, and shall be authorized, if found necessary, to mortgage the Road, and all the property and effects belong to the said Company, for the security of said loan; which mortgage, it is hereby declared and enacted, shall be preferred to the mortgage, and pledge to be executed under the previous provisions of this Act, and all such other mortgages and pledges as may have been heretofore executed by said Company, to secure the State against its loss by reason of her endorsement for said Company, and in case of default by said Company, the said mortgage so to be executed shall be first satisfied.[49]

The same bill gave the state the power to seize the profits of the company if the interest on the bonds were not paid in a timely fashion. Also included was the power to foreclose on the mortgage and sell the road for payment of the bonds, and the transfer of half of the state's stock in the Wilmington & Raleigh Rail Road back to the company for investment in the Wilmington & Manchester Rail Road. The latter provision was dependent on the Wilmington & Manchester first securing $400,000 in subscriptions from other sources. On January 28, 1851, the state exchanged 2,000 shares of Wilmington & Raleigh Rail Road, with a par value of $60 per share, for a like number of shares in the Wilmington & Manchester Rail Road, thus allowing the state to take one of its four directors from Wilmington & Raleigh and place a single director in the Wilmington & Manchester. The state's investment in Wilmington & Manchester was valued at $203,000—more than the State of South Carolina and the Town of Wilmington, but less than the total shares of private investors.[50] Cecil K. Brown had overlooked the significance of the exchange of stock; such an arrangement gave the state leverage in both companies. The report of the Wilmington & Raleigh Rail Road from 1841 to 1849 was printed in the *Wilmington Journal* in November of 1849. The total liabilities of the company as of October 1, 1849, amounted to $637,294.55, including $222,666.67 in English bonds, $250,000.00 in bonds endorsed by the State of North Carolina, $85,000.00 in bonds due the Literary Fund of North Carolina, $16,300.00 due bills payable to banks, and $31,100.30 due to contractors. Negro Bonds for the years 1843 and 1845–1850 amounted to $22,928.99; and the amount due on payrolls was $8,505.16. There remained $793.43 due to contractors on scrip bonds.[51]

The payroll of the company included the following: 471 people worked for the Wilmington & Raleigh Rail Road Company in 1849, of which 235 were slaves included in the Negro Bonds 222 slaves were engaged in repairs to the railroad. By 1860, the company had acquired twelve slaves at a cost of $13,750, but the Negro Bonds due from 1844 through 1860 amounted to $34,806.48. Eleven of the slaves were listed as mechanics and laborers in the shops, or working the depots, and were valued at $13,500 — the report does not explain the twelfth slave. The superintendent's report recommends the purchase of an additional twenty slaves to work the trains and warehouse, noting that the cost of slave hire had risen about fifteen dollar per annum to $210 per slave. That year, the company paid $11,955.30 in subsistence, clothing, and medical care as part of its general expenses. The report expressed discouragement in the white laborers hired due to the difficulty in finding slaves and free blacks. The white laborers tended to quit after they had made enough money to satisfy their most pressing needs.[52]

TABLE 4. STATISTICS FOR YEARS 1841–49

Years.	Receipts	Expenditures	Profits	No. of Passengers Through	Way
1841	$297,228.39	$241,945.34	$55,283.05	9,742	5,498
1842	211,977.48	180,892.65	31,084.83	*	*
1843	257,257.82	179,251.00	78,206.82	8,450	13,574
1844	289,533.75	203,633.24	85,900.51	10,358	16,041
1845	288,493.45	212,091.20	76,402.25	14,018	16,393
1846	317,822.49	289,681.45	28,140.04	11,885	20,498
1847	331,480.20	259,912.60	71,567.60	13,073	25,396
1848	317,459.50	275,228.86	42,130.64	11,456	28,327
1849	310,397.00	245,998.58	64,698.42	11,207	27,575

This table was reproduced from the November 19, 1849, issue of the *Wilmington Journal*. It summarizes the business of the Wilmington & Raleigh Rail Road over nine years. The missing passenger statistics for 1842 are the result of the loss of documents to fire (North Carolina [1848], 18).

The statistics from the 1848 and 1849 annual reports provide enough data to approximate the cost per slave "hire" in payment of the bond, subsistence, clothing, and other needs at $120 per annum. The annual report from 1858 provides a sum of $190 per slave including hire, subsistence, clothing, and medical care per annum.[53]

The recovery of the company from the Great Fire of 1843 appears to have been aided by the intervention of Edward B. Dudley, former governor and then president of the Wilmington & Raleigh Rail Road.[54] The company had spent $8,000 in 1843 to replace "provisions, fixtures &c." destroyed by the fire; and it was reported that the "Machine shop, Warehouse, Offices, &c., are nearly rebuilt" by the end of the summer. The cost of building the shop, warehouse, wharf, and associated buildings at Wilmington had been $56,691.51. The company had fourteen locomotives in 1840, and the total value of locomotives and rolling stock was $170,815.21. The average cost of the locomotives in 1838 had been $7,500 apiece, passenger cars had cost $2,250 apiece, and freight cars cost $300. "Five locomotives and some cars" were damaged in the fire, though it was believed that some could have been repaired. It appears that several engines were not operational, or had been lost, but the addition of a new freight locomotive was supposed to make up for the deficiency in motive power completely. It appears the railroad quickly recovered from this setback.[55] The net profits of the company by year's end were $78,206.82; it was an increase of more than double the previous year's profits of $31,084.83.

Regardless of whatever differences might have existed among the estimated losses, actual losses, and the ultimate expenditures associated with the fire, the loss of the company facilities at Wilmington apparently damaged confidence in the company. The more serious problem had existed before the fire. On January 17, 1843, the Literary Board was authorized to buy up $50,000 worth of the company's bonds that had fallen due on the first day of the year to prevent the company from defaulting. After the fire, the Treasurer of the State of North Carolina had to buy up the issue of bonds due on 1 January 1844.[56] Cowan's statements, in essence, indicated that the company had exceeded its credit limit — so to speak. When Dudley offered his personal estate as collateral for the company after the fire, it was a sure measure of the desperate financial condition of the company.

In an 1843 article entitled "Railroads of Virginia and North Carolina" that appears in the *Farmers' Register,* a writer identified only as a stockholder cites several reasons why the railroads in these states had not be able to declare dividends. In Virginia, the competition between the Petersburg

Table 5. Personnel and Salary Statistics, 1849

Personnel	Salary	Personnel	Salary	Personnel	Salary
President	$2,000 / year	1 Apprentice	$12.50 / month	2 Train hands	$10.00 / month
Secretary and Treasurer	1,500 / year	2 Helpers	18.00 / month	2 Yard hands	8.34 / month
Clerk to the Treasurer	600 / year	1 Helper	12.50 / month	Agents at Depots and water stations, aggregate	2,666 / year
Superintendent of Road Repairs	850 / year	1 Helper	7.00 / month	14 Spike Drivers	182 / year
Assistant for Superintendent	150 / year	1 Boiler Maker	2.25 / day	12 Laborers on Road Repairs	1,524 / year
Steamboat Agent at Wilmington	800 / year	1 Boiler Maker	1.75 / day	4 Black carpenters on Road Repairs	756 / year
Clerk for Steamboat Agent	200 / year	1 Boiler Maker	1.50 / day	6 Hands on Sunday at water stations	78 / year
Steamboat Agent at Charleston, and mail carrier, including wharf hands	1,400 / year	2 Engineers	65.00 / month	8 Hands on Timber Trains	864 / year
		7 Engineers	60.00 / month	222 Negroes on Road Repairs, &c., including those on boats and wharf	18,593 / year
Transportation Agent at Wilmington	800 / year	1 Engineer	25.00 / month		
Agent at Weldon	800 / year	1 Engineer	20.00 / month	3 Captains	1,000 / year
Superintendent of Shops and Machinery	1,000 / year	9 Firemen	20.00 / month	3 First Mates	420 / year
Finishers	2.00 / day	1 Coach repairer in shop	1.00 / day	3 Second Mates	240 / year
Finishers	1.75 / day	1 Coach repairer in shop	.87½ / day	4 First Engineers	720 / year
Finishers	1.50 / day	1 Carpenter on coaches and cars	2.25 / day	4 Second Engineers	480 / year
Blacksmith	2.25 / day	6 Carpenter on coaches and cars	1.50 / day	8 Firemen	192 / year
Blacksmith	2.00 / day	4 Carpenters on coaches and cars	1.25 / day	6 Wheelsmen	192 / year
Blacksmith	1.87½ / day	5 Carpenters on coaches and cars	1.00 / day	9 Deck hands	120 / year
Blacksmith	1.50 / day	2 Carpenters on coaches and cars	.62½ / day	3 Stewards	240 / year
Pattern Maker	2.00 / day	1 Overseer on road repairs	40.00 / month	3 Stewardesses	96 / year
2 Moulders	2.00 / day	1 Overseer on road repairs	35.00 / month	6 Waiters	120 / year
1 Brass Moulder	1.37½ / day	12 Overseers on road repairs	30.00 / month	3 Cooks	180 / year
1 Moulder	20.00 / month	3 Carpenters	35.00 / month	6 Knife boys and scullions	72 / year
1 Apprentice	20.00 / month	1 Painter	10.00 / month	3 Deck hands included in Negro bonds	
2 Apprentices	25.00 / month	5 Conductors on Trains	42.00 / month	10 Wharf hands included in Negro bonds	
1 Apprentice	18.00 / month	3 Train hands	18.00 / month		
1 Apprentice	15.00 / month				

The personnel of the Wilmington & Raleigh Rail Road printed in *Wilmington Journal*, November 19, 1849.

Rail Road and the Portsmouth & Roanoke Rail Road diminished the profits of the Petersburg road while incurring loss to the Portsmouth & Roanoke. The change of route of the Wilmington & Raleigh Rail Road to Weldon to connect with the Portsmouth road deprived the port of access to the more fertile regions of the state west of Raleigh. The Petersburg Rail Road, already ten years old, had to replace its rail with heavy iron, and this would have to be done to all the railroads using strap iron rail construction.[57] It is certain that the strap iron rail construction was a major factor in the companies' financial difficulties, but the assumption that building the Wilmington & Raleigh Rail Road to Raleigh would have opened the port to the produce of the west was mere speculation. The Raleigh & Gaston with "their friends in Petersburg and Richmond" did not see these great profits coming from the west of Raleigh.

The great benefit of both railroads was not seen by the shareholders, but by the citizens of the state. This became unmistakably clear when the particulars were stated by Gov. William Alexander Graham in his 1848 *Message to the Senate of North Carolina.*

> These works, though profitless as stock, have yet given advantages to the inhabitants of the sections which they traverse, of which they would not willingly be deprived ... we must bear in mind, that if these Rail Roads shall cease to operate, and the people in their neighborhood shall be driven back to the old modes of conveyance, that the change will be equal to the imposition upon them, of a tax of certainly Eighty, and perhaps not less than One Hundred Thousand Dollars, per year.[58]

The financial woes of these companies can be reduced to a single problem that was known to all after the failure of the Cape Fear & Yadkin Valley effort: the building of extensive railroads was beyond the means of private capital. That some capitalists, such as the directors of both railroads, could acquire the means by mortgaging their company property did not carry with it the certainty that the profits of the company would be able to service the loans. The State of North Carolina, however, understood that these railroads were actually *public* works in function and could easily become public works in fact.

Something quite different had occurred in Virginia. Regional ambitions had led to the loss of an important rail link that fed into the Wilmington & Raleigh. The trade war between Petersburg and Norfolk was the offshoot of several internal improvement projects. Peter C. Stewart traced the origins of the economic competition to the opening of the Dismal Swamp Canal in his article "Railroads and Urban Rivalries in Antebellum Eastern Virginia." The climax of the struggle came when Petersburg gained control over a portion of the Portsmouth & Roanoke Rail Road's track in North Carolina, and shut the railroad down.

> Towards the end of the War of 1812 Norfolk merchants and North Carolina farmers happily witnessed the completion of the Dismal Swamp Canal, which permitted lighters and other small craft to bring the Old North State's lumber and agricultural products to the Elizabeth River. Narrow and shallow, the canal posed no threat to Petersburg, recently rebuilt after a disastrous fire and entering an era of significant growth as a textile and tobacco-processing center. Unfortunately for the relations between the two towns, the businessmen of Norfolk, noting that they controlled only a small fraction of the total commerce of their own state, tried to secure the tobacco and grain produced in considerable volume in the Roanoke Valley.[59]

Norfolk was able to exercise its early ambitions through investment in the Roanoke Navigation Company and continued support for increasing the depth and width of the Dismal Swamp Canal. The Roanoke Navigation Company, chartered in 1807 for keeping the Roanoke River clear of obstructions, did not commence a comprehensive program of improvements until North Carolina and Virginia re-organized the company under the aegis of both states in 1815. The Dismal Swamp Canal Company, incorporated in both North Carolina and Virginia in 1790, began work on the canal in 1793 and completed it in 1814. The canal improvements were completed in 1828. During the years 1828 and 1829, the improvements to the Dismal Swamp Canal, coupled with the completion of the locks of the Roanoke Canal, allowed produce from the upper Roanoke Valley to bypass the Great Falls and continue to the Dismal Swamp Canal by way of Albemarle Sound. Prior to these improvements, boats would unload produce at the Great Falls, where it would be transported to Petersburg by wagon. Petersburg responded to the redirection of its share of incoming produce to the Norfolk markets by incorporating the Petersburg Rail Road in 1830. The purpose of this railroad was to intercept the produce passing through the Roanoke Canal near its outlet at Blakeley, North Carolina. Since the railroad was partly built in North Carolina, the company had to be incorporated in both states.[60] The railroad was completed in 1833.

Stewart's article provides an account of the Portsmouth & Roanoke Rail Road's control over the bridge spanning the Roanoke River, and the attempt by the Petersburg Rail Road to drive the Portsmouth & Roanoke Rail Road Company out of business with reduced fares. Also, he discussed the advantages of the through ticket from Baltimore via the Baltimore and Norfolk Steam Packet Company. However, the clandestine acquisition of the debt of the North Carolina section of the Portsmouth & Roanoke Rail

Road's track by a Petersburg politician named Francis Rives in 1843 is of particular interest because it illustrates the ultimate outcome of decades of a regional commercial conflict — one that also plagued railroad development in North Carolina. Rives attempted to take up the track, but was thwarted by Walter Gwynn and the Sheriff of Northampton County. Rives was brought to trial in North Carolina, but could not be convicted. The Supreme Court of North Carolina determined that Rives had the right to control the section of track he had acquired. Rives shut down the track (the Petersburg Rail Road was paying him $2,500 quarterly to keep the line closed), and caused the railroad to fail. However, North Carolina would not grant Rives a charter to the track he controlled. Eventually, a new company was formed in Norfolk called the Seaboard & Roanoke Rail Road. The railroad was rebuilt, and service to the Roanoke resumed.[61]

There are several important aspects of the narrative that are missing in Stewart's article. For instance, the closing of Roanoke Inlet in the late 1700s left the Albemarle region of North Carolina without an outlet to the ocean, thus enhancing the success of the Dismal Swamp Canal. Also, the efforts of Petersburg and Norfolk to extend their railroads south of the Roanoke excited sectional rivalries in North Carolina, and upset the state's plans for an east to west railroad; and the State of North Carolina enacted legislation to counter the aggressiveness of the Petersburg interests, and assisted in the restoration of the Norfolk connection.

The maritime commerce of the Albemarle Sound region of North Carolina expanded during the closing decades of the Colonial Era as more land in the vast Roanoke River Basin was put under cultivation. The closing of Roanoke Inlet in the late 1790s curtailed the development of a major port in the state's northeast. Beaufort Harbor and the port of Wilmington were located too far to the south to be beneficial. The Dismal Swamp Canal, completed in 1805 (improved during the 1810s), attracted the produce entering Albemarle to the Norfolk market. As mentioned earlier, the State of North Carolina commissioned plans for reopening Roanoke Inlet, but did not have the resources to undertake such an ambitious project.

The influence of the Petersburg and Norfolk interests on the development of the Raleigh to Gaston route and the Wilmington to Halifax route is apparent in the material already presented; but the details of the outcome of the conflict, with its disruptive effects, require closer examination. By the late 1830s, the Weldon Toll Bridge, with its railroad track, became the focus of the hostilities between the Virginia railroads. This bridge was the only means by which the Virginia railroads could access the Wilmington & Raleigh. The Petersburg Rail Road, upon reaching the

Roanoke River at Blakeley, had hoped to build a bridge there and continue their railroad south. The supporters of the Weldon Toll Bridge Company exercised their influence to prevent the North Carolina Legislature from granting the Petersburg company permission to build their own bridge. The Portsmouth & Roanoke Rail Road purchased the bridge in June of 1838.[62] After acquiring the bridge, the company attempted to establish a joint arrangement for its ownership with the Petersburg Rail Road and the Wilmington & Raleigh Rail Road.

> Through the mediation of a committee from the Board, the Portsmouth Rail Road Company, who had recently become proprietors of the Weldon Toll Bridge, have sold one half of the bridge and rail road from Weldon to Gary's — 4/10 to be paid for by the Petersburg Company, and 1/10 by this company; for which the company's bond is to be given for $10,000, payable three years after the execution of the title deed. A free connection is thereby secured with both the Petersburg and Portsmouth Rail Roads; and the vexatious delays and interruption to which our planters and merchants as well as travelers have been subjected, at the Roanoke will occur no more.[63]

The Petersburg Rail Road backed out of the deal during the ensuing year; and the Wilmington & Raleigh Rail Road Company, disappointed by the prospects of a continuation of the delay in service, contemplated the need for a second bridge near Weldon. The Petersburg Rail Road Company obtained permission to build their bridge, and its construction was under way at the same time the company began the replacement of their rails.[64]

Stewart's article describes how Petersburg politician Francis Rives acquired the debt of the Portsmouth Company on the North Carolina portion of the railroad and then shut it down. The State of North Carolina stopped Rives from destroying the rails, and tried to prevent the loss of an important trade connection. An article in *American Law Magazine,* "Opinion of the Supreme Court of North Carolina in the Case of the State of North Carolina v. Francis E. Rives — December Term, 1844" (July 1845), provides a contemporary view of the controversial legal decisions, and explains the events surrounding the Francis Rives case in more depth than Stewart.

> At the fall term of 1842, of the superior court of Halifax county in North Carolina, Rochelle and Smith recovered a judgment against the Portsmouth and Roanoke Rail Road company for a large debt, to wit: $16,846.80, besides interest and cost. Upon this judgment a writ of *fieri facias* was issued, directing the sheriff of the county of Northampton in that state, against the goods and chattels, lands and tenements of the company. Under this *fi. fa.*

the sheriff went upon the road at Garysburg in Northampton and declared his levy, as follows: "Levied upon the Portsmouth and Roanoke Rail-road, from Roanoke to the depot at Margaretsville and the warehouses at Concord and Margaretsville depots, together with the land on which they are placed." What was so levied on was sold by the sheriff at the road near Garysburg, and Rochelle became the purchaser. When the sale was concluded, the sheriff said to Rochelle the property was his.[65]

Rochelle sold the property to Francis E. Rives, who obtained a deed from the sheriff on December 1, 1843. According to the article, Rives attempted to negotiate a deal with the railroad, but the company and its lawyers did not believe that the sheriff's sale was legitimate. On January 6, 1844, Rives began to dismantle the section of track that he had acquired. In the spring of that year, he was indicted on charges in superior court of Northampton County. The court decision was against Rives based on provisions within the charter of this railroad (and included in the charters of other railroads incorporated in North Carolina) that there was a penalty for injuring the road and the railroad. The privileges granted in the railroad's charter to condemn land and to enter upon adjacent lands for building material implied that the railroad was authorized to act in the public good. The state could not authorize a company to take from private property owners what was rightfully theirs unless it was for the public good. This had been tested in a previous case, *Raleigh & Gaston Rail Road Company vs. Davis*, where the railroad was considered on par with a public road; thus, injuring or obstructing the railroad was akin to doing so to a public road. The court also determined that the company's right to sell the iron and wood of the track ended when it was put down for use; then it became part of the public way and the company would violate its charter if they removed the track for reasons other than its repair or improvement.

The court determined that Rives did not have right to a title, and fined him twenty-five dollars. The court was lenient because Rives acted after consulting a lawyer. In "Opinion of the Supreme Court of North Carolina in the Case of the State of North Carolina v. Francis E. Rives — December Term, 1844," the writer discusses the decision of the Supreme Court of North Carolina that overturned the conviction of the lower court. The higher court determined that Rives had purchased the section of railroad legitimately, and was the rightful owner.[66]

The North Carolina General Assembly of 1844–1845 passed *An Act to provide for the reorganization of the Portsmouth and Roanoke Rail Road Company*.

Whereas the Portsmouth and Roanoke Rail Road Company is laboring under the pressure of heavy embarrassment which greatly injure and impair its public utility, and from which it is represented, that it may be relieved by a new organization, whereby the public interests of the late may be protected and continued, and without injustice to its creditors....[67]

This act allowed the governor of North Carolina — in conjunction with the governor of Virginia — to appoint commissioners to oversee the sale of the railroad, but preserved the rights of those "claiming by purchase any part of the said Rail Road" and the charter of the original corporation and its provisions. The engines and cars had to be sold separately from the road. The purchaser of the bridge and track in North Carolina had to execute a bond with the Literary Fund of North Carolina. The Petersburg Rail Road would have use of the disputed bridge and track to Garysburg on terms set by the governors of Virginia and North Carolina and the commissioners. A majority of the stockholders of the company had to agree to the sale, and the railroad bridge was to be included in the sale to the new company. Further, the act clarified and reinforced penalties for injuring the railroad that were part of the original charter and added "all such acts as are now offences against the State." Another act passed during the 1844–1845 session of the North Carolina General Assembly allowed the Portsmouth and Roanoke Rail Road to turn the railroad bridge into a toll bridge for horse drawn vehicles and pedestrians.[68]

In 1850, the State of North Carolina authorized the Seaboard and Roanoke Railroad Company, the antecessor of the failed Portsmouth & Roanoke Rail Road, to issue bonds, and mortgage the company to John J. Palmer of New York. The mortgage held by the State on the Weldon Toll Bridge would be transferred to the Seaboard & Roanoke Railroad in exchange for bonds on the mortgage. By *An Act Concerning the Seaboard and Roanoke Rail Road* (ratified on January 28, 1851), the Seaboard & Roanoke Railroad was allowed "to change and alter the route of their road from or near Margarettsville" in Northampton County, near the Virginia line, to cross the Roanoke anywhere between Halifax and Weldon. There it would make a connection to the Wilmington & Raleigh Rail Road (the route was not changed), and form a through ticket with other companies. The Seaboard & Roanoke Railroad and Roanoke Railroad (a North Carolina company) was granted the privilege to effect a junction with the Raleigh & Gaston Rail Road. An *Act to Incorporate the Roanoke Valley Railroad Company* is the realization of the proposal contemplated by the citizens of Warren County in April of 1833 — a connection to Weldon. Sections 29 and 30 of this act add a provision for transporting troops in the employment of the State and exempting railroad employees from militia duty.[69] Eventually, all the railroads connected at Weldon.

The idea of the Portsmouth & Roanoke Rail Road was conceived and promoted by Arthur Emerson of Portsmouth as a response to Petersburg's railroad. Petersburg blocked state aid to the railroad in 1833, but failed to repeat their success the following year. However, the choice of inexpensive strap iron wooden rail construction began to fail early. On December 10, 1837, a train derailed because of a loose iron bar and two people were killed in the accident.

When North Carolinian Andrew Joyner became president of the company, he set about making improvements to the railroad and its equipment. The company took on additional debt. The railroad failed to meet the expectations of Norfolk investors at a time when the area's businessmen were experiencing the deleterious effect of Jackson's monetary policy. The fatal debt of the company was to Clements and Rochelle, the builders of the Weldon Toll Bridge. Rives' plot was deliberate and malicious. This is evident by the damage he inflicted on the bridge over Troublefield Creek (N 36.45396, W 77.54260) near Garysburg, and the disposal of iron rails into the same creek. For his efforts, the city of Petersburg would eventually elect Rives as their mayor. Boston investors would acquire what remained of the Portsmouth & Roanoke Rail Road in 1846.[70]

The extension of the Raleigh & Gaston to Weldon was inevitable. The Raleigh interests that aligned with Petersburg made a fatal blunder. Weldon was truly the tollgate to North Carolina. This was made manifest by the construction of the Wilmington & Raleigh Rail Road with its steamboat line to Charleston. The railroad might have remained solvent had it connected to Weldon, as was the original plan of the Roanoke & Raleigh Rail Road of 1833.

In 1877, Walter McKenzie Clark published *History of the Raleigh & Gaston Rail Road Company Including All the Acts of the General Assembly of North Carolina Relating Thereto.*

> The Company was originally chartered in 1835, to run from Gaston to Raleigh. Work commenced soon thereafter. The road was completed through to Raleigh in 1843. It existed under great difficulties until it was finally sold under a foreclosure directed by act of the General Assembly ratified 6th January, 1845. At the sale in pursuance thereof the State of North Carolina, through its then Governor, Hon. William A. Graham, bought the entire property and franchises. It was then run entirely as a State institution until its reorganization under the acts of the General Assembly, ratified January 29th, 1851, and 25th December, 1852 ... The first meeting of stockholders to

organize under the new charter was held at Warrenton, N.C., 11th and 12th September, 1851, when George W. Mordecai was elected President and W. W. Vass, Secretary and Treasurer. The first stockholders' meeting held thereafter met at Henderson 14th and 15th January, 1852, when resolutions were introduced and adopted looking to a connection with the Seaboard Railroad at Weldon. The President also recommended an actual connection at Raleigh with the North Carolina Railroad. The road from Gaston to Weldon and the entire reconstruction of the whole line was completed in 1853. The new bridge at Gaston was completed in 1858. It was burnt down on their retreat by the Confederate forces in 1865, and has not been rebuilt.[71]

During the fall of 1838, the Raleigh & Gaston Rail Road agreed to mortgage "the whole property" of the company to the Literary Fund of North Carolina for the sum of fifty thousand dollars. The Board took $50,000 of the bonds in March of 1839. On June 3, 1839, the Literary Board agreed that the balance of the surplus that belonged to the Board should be used for purchasing the bonds of the Raleigh & Gaston Rail Road, secured by the bonds of the Wilmington & Raleigh Rail Road so as to make the company responsible. The Board purchased $17,000 of Wilmington & Raleigh bonds in August. James Owen, the president of the company, noted in a letter to Gov. Dudley that contractors placed demands on the company at the end of each month, and the stockholders were short on funds because they had not brought in their crops yet; and the company had to pay forty thousand dollars on a shipment of iron. The board purchased more bonds from both railroads that year.[72]

In 1842, the Literary Board purchased bonds for the Raleigh & Gaston amounting to $140,000 as of January 1, 1841, and had increased the amount to $165,300 by December 1, 1842. For the same period, the bonds of the Wilmington and Raleigh increased from $85,000 to $87,000.[73] The Treasurer of North Carolina reported on December 17, 1844, that the state had received $1,433,757.39 of the federal surplus which was dispensed as follows: dispersed for redemption of state stock in the Bank of Cape Fear, $300,000; the Literary Fund, $200,000; Internal Improvement Fund, $533,757.39; and Public Fund, $100,000.[74] *An Act to Authorize the Foreclosure of the Mortgage of the Raleigh and Gaston Rail Road* was ratified on January 6, 1845. The state treasurer was appointed commissioner by the court to sell the railroad. The governor was "authorized and directed to bid" on the railroad for the state.

> That should the Governor of the State, under the preceding section, become the purchaser, for the State, of the road and other property, it shall be the duty of the board of commissioners hereinafter named to appoint a President

and other officers necessary to manage and conduct the same on behalf of the State, until such time as the State can make some other disposition of the same.[75]

The state paid $286,500 in principal and $472,913.10 in interest between 1843 and 1854 on the debt of the Raleigh & Gaston, and $62,443.48 in associated expenses.[76] The Francis Rives affair represented the degree to which the public good could be compromised by unconstrained capitalism.

The victims of the trade war, the Portsmouth & Roanoke and the Raleigh & Gaston, succumbed to the influence of external forces. These included the financial downturn following the Panic of 1837, and the strategic maneuvers of their rivals. However, geographic factors also contributed to their disadvantages. Portsmouth and Norfolk fit the model of what James E. Vance Jr. called "misplaced cities." That is, in colonial times they were well situated to serve the existing settlement patterns and to engage in economic intercourse with Britain. After the Revolution, the former fifteen colonial ports competed for metropolitan status. Each sought to attract the business from the newly settled interior away from mercantile rivals. For some commercial centers, such as those of the southern tidewater of Virginia, inland navigation was suitable during the early years of the nineteenth century. Railroads in the United States were from the beginning designed to enhance the economy and status of the original commercial centers. This model differed from the European one of railroad construction in that the United States railroads exploited the advantages of the existing settlement pattern.[77]

Petersburg was an interior commercial center with access to the Appomattox and James rivers as well as interior land routes. Norfolk had the Chesapeake Bay to the north, and the Dismal Swamp to the south. Its access to interior commerce before the Portsmouth & Roanoke Rail Road was by way of the Dismal Swamp Canal and the James River. Its connection to Baltimore and points north was by way of steamboat. The railroad put it on a competitive plane with Petersburg, and losing it degraded its ability to compete, even as Petersburg strengthened its position by forming a connection to Richmond.

The geographic disadvantages of the Raleigh & Gaston Rail Road are more complex. Raleigh came into existence for political rather than commercial reasons. It was not suitably located for inland navigation. Without an interior railroad connection running south, a through passage to places south was impractical. It was for all intents and purposes an incomplete railroad. The railroad was merely an extension of the Petersburg market into the middle Piedmont of North Carolina. The Raleigh & Gaston did not share the fate of the Portsmouth & Roanoke. While most of the original investors in the railroad were ruined, the railroad itself continued to operate under the management of the state, and that it did not fall into the hands of outside investors is significant. The Wilmington & Raleigh Rail Road, with its steamboat line, was the only continuous route extending south from the Roanoke River: the plan to change its route and merge with the Halifax & Weldon to form 161½ miles of railroad to Wilmington was its strength. Over resistance from Petersburg interests and their friends in Raleigh, these early planning decisions placed the Wilmington & Raleigh in a position to avoid entanglement in the Virginia rival railroads' battle for control of the Weldon Toll Bridge.

The leadership, exemplified by the actions of its president, Edward B. Dudley, during the formative years of the company, was able to negotiate an array of formidable obstacles. These include lobbying efforts by Petersburg, Virginia, in Raleigh to obstruct the change of route, the obstinate commitment on the part of authorities inside and outside the state that promoted grand, but impractical, railroad schemes; the financial crisis that followed the Panic of 1837; the trade conflict between Petersburg and Norfolk, problems associated with the initial construction of the railroad, and events that occurred by accident. Confidence in the viability of the company endured because those in a position of leadership were able to allay the anxiety of the shareholders by offering quickly and effectively remedies to developing problems. The shareholders, including the State of North Carolina, in turn afforded the company patience and forbearance.

CHAPTER VI

Rail Transportation and Economic Growth

During the 1850s, the Wilmington & Raleigh Rail Road became integrated into a network that included two long anticipated connections, the Wilmington & Manchester Railroad and the North Carolina Railroad. This was not the only improvement to the network: work on rebuilding the Wilmington & Raleigh and the Raleigh & Gaston in heavy iron rails was completed early in the decade. As a result, freight and passenger traffic increased as new regions became accessible through the network. Economic development followed on the heels of railroad development as land values increased in the rail corridors, agriculture was transformed, and towns sprang up around the stations.

The evolving patterns of transportation and the characteristics of economic development are the last topic to be addressed in this work. While most of the improvements and network connections were accomplished prior the mid–1850s, their impact was realized on the eve of the Civil War. This chapter will examine and compare data derived from annual reports of the Wilmington & Raleigh Rail Road, along with other sources, to determine the nature of traffic on the railroad before and after connecting lines were built.

Planning for the replacement of the steamboat line to Charleston with the Wilmington & Manchester Rail Road was the last significant event marking the tenure of Edward B. Dudley as president of the Wilmington & Raleigh Rail Road. The Wilmington & Manchester Rail Road Company was incorporated during the 1846–1847 session of the North Carolina General Assembly.[1] Some citizens of Charleston, as expressed in the *Charleston Mercury,* were immediately alarmed that the railroad might take an interior route in the neighborhood of Darlington, Camden, and Sumter; they were also concerned that the Wilmington & Manchester would be built to fifty-six inch gauge rather than the five foot gauge of the South Carolina railroad and that traffic from the North would be diverted west from Charleston.[2] More than a year earlier, at the 1846 annual meeting of the stockholder, Governor Dudley, then president of the Wilmington & Raleigh, had offered a resolution that the company apply to the Legislature to have their charter amended so that they could extend the railroad to Fair Bluff, North Carolina, or to the South Carolina line.[3] This suggests an early inclination to follow an interior route; for Fair Bluff, located southwest of Wilmington and an actual station on the Wilmington & Manchester, was well situated for the continuance of an interior route. There had been early attempts in South Carolina to form rail connections from Charleston to Georgetown and other coastal locations that would have proven more favorable to a continuation of the Wilmington road on a more easterly route.[4] However, by the mid–1840s the interior route offered more connections.

The gauge of the Wilmington & Manchester Rail Road was not as critical an issue as those in Charleston might have thought. The Wilmington terminus of the Wilmington & Manchester was to be located on the west bank of the Cape Fear River opposite Wilmington; bridging the Cape Fear was the real problem. When a Bollman Truss railroad bridge was constructed over the Cape Fear in 1868–69, it accommodated standard and five-foot gauge easily; however, the engineering difficulties encountered with putting down caissons were considerable.[5]

> The Railway Bridge Company are still actively engaged in prosecuting their operations towards the building of the structure over the North West branch of the Cape Fear. The large cylinder, 14 feet in diameter, which gave them so much trouble, was safely sunk into position some weeks ago and now rests upon a firm foundation of rock 37 feet below the bed of the river, and 63 feet below the surface of the water. This Herculean task being accomplished all energies are now directed towards the sinking of the first of the two smaller cylinders, 8 feet in diameter. One section has already been lowered into the water, and ere long we trust this may also rest upon a secure foundation.[6]

The building of such a bridge, as the citation indicates, is quite different from those constructed at Weldon and Gaston. Whereas the underlying rock of the Roanoke River at Weldon is visible above the surface of the water, the foundation of the bridge over the Cape Fear was set in thirty-seven feet of alluvium. In length of span and depth of foundation, a bridging of the Cape Fear River at Wilmington in the antebellum period would prove difficult and expensive. However, Walter Gwynn and L.J. Flemming did design a bridge for the Wilmington & Manchester over the Pee Dee that used cylindrical caissons, a method pioneered in England.[7] Thus the successful construction was not an impossible task.

Without a crossing of the Cape Fear at Wilmington, the gauge of the Wilmington & Manchester had more significance for Charleston and the railroads of South Carolina than it did for the Wilmington & Raleigh Rail Road. Likely, the concerns expressed in the *Charleston Mercury* were aimed at fueling interest in Charleston. The choice of gauge, for practical reasons, should not have been anything other than five feet. If the work were to be aided by the citizens of South Carolina, creating an unnecessary delay for the breaking of bulk at Manchester Junction would have discouraged investment; and throwing up obstacles that would have prevented running the rolling stock of the South Carolina railroads on the Wilmington & Manchester would have inhibited intercompany cooperation. Further, the location of the road to the interior was not as important as in previous times.

The Wilmington & Manchester would terminate conveniently at the center of South Carolina rail commerce. The town rivalries and sectional differences of the past, though clearly perpetual, were less a determining factor in the location of railroads as networks evolved. Access to multiple markets was mutually beneficial to all rival markets. For example, the Charleston market might have lost some commerce from the interior of South Carolina to Wilmington, but it would be gained from the previously unavailable markets along the line of the Wilmington & Manchester.

Work on grading the road for the Wilmington & Manchester began under the supervision of contractor Leonard White on a four mile section between Sumterville (Sumter, S.C.) and Lynches Creek on New Years Day of 1849, and work at the Wilmington terminus began on February 22, 1849, on Washington's Birthday.[8] The railroad was completed in early 1854, and supposedly the last steamboat from Charleston arrived around February 3, 1854. However, the steamboat *Gladiator* was pressed back into service briefly after a flood on the Wateree River topped the railroad trestle.[9]

To understand how this improvement changed transportation on the Wilmington & Raleigh Rail Road, one must begin by discerning transportation patterns from the time the railroad was completed in 1840 up until 1860. The "General Return of Receipts and Expenditures of the Wilmington & Raleigh Rail Road Company from first May to first November, 1840" appears in the company's annual report to the Board of Internal Improvements for that year. This sheet of tabulations breaks down the month-to-month activities of the company in the half-year after its completion. Fortunately, it includes freight volumes and a breakdown of passenger traffic on the line.[10] This is the first document that illustrates the pattern of transportation with the railroad function without interruptions due to construction. Passengers and freight could pass freely along its whole extent. The pattern becomes obvious when this data is graphed.

The volume of "way" passengers, those traveling from one station to another on the line, fluctuated by a few hundred during the six-month period. However, the volume of "through" passengers, travelers using the railroad to pass from one end of the line to the other, displays a distinct pattern over the same period. In essence, "through" passengers were using the Wilmington & Raleigh as a conduit to and from the north and south. During the summer months, the volume of traffic trended toward northern destinations. The pattern reversed in the fall. Overall, the number of "through" passengers far exceeded those making trips along the line. The Wilmington & Raleigh functioned as the rail corridor through North Carolina. Its steamship line completed the connection to South Carolina. The receipts from freight remained nearly flat during this period, while the volume of freight fluctuated by approximately 20,000 tons in both positive and negative directions over the period.

Wilmington & Raleigh Rail Road Passengers, 1840

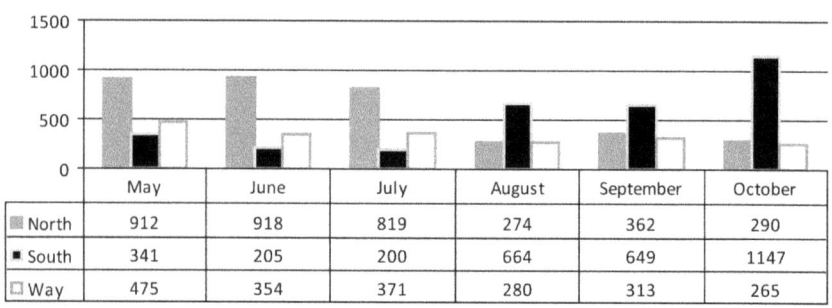

	May	June	July	August	September	October
North	912	918	819	274	362	290
South	341	205	200	664	649	1147
Way	475	354	371	280	313	265

Tabulation of the number of passengers using the Wilmington & Raleigh Rail Road during its first six months of operation after completion displays a pattern of seasonal travel to destinations to the north and south, and a small base of travelers to stations along the line. Data source: North Carolina, "Fifth Annual Report of the President and Directors of the Wilmington & Raleigh Rail Road Company," *Report of the Board of Internal Improvements to the General Assembly,* Document No. 16 (Raleigh: Thomas Loring, 1840), Table B.

W. & R. R. R. Steamboat Line Passengers, 1840

	May	June	July	August	September	October
North	623	526	667.33	558	261.5	237
South	306	322.5	164.25	184	524.33	947
Way	116.5	247	253	215	202.5	130

The number of passengers on the steamboat line of the Wilmington & Raleigh Rail Road for the same period illustrates a similar pattern to the passenger tabulation for the railroad. Way passengers traveled from Wilmington to Charleston (and Smithville). Most were traveling to destinations outside North Carolina. Data Source: North Carolina, "Fifth Annual Report of the President and Directors of the Wilmington & Raleigh Rail Road Company," *Report of the Board of Internal Improvements to the General Assembly,* Document No. 16 (Raleigh: Thomas Loring, 1840), Table B.

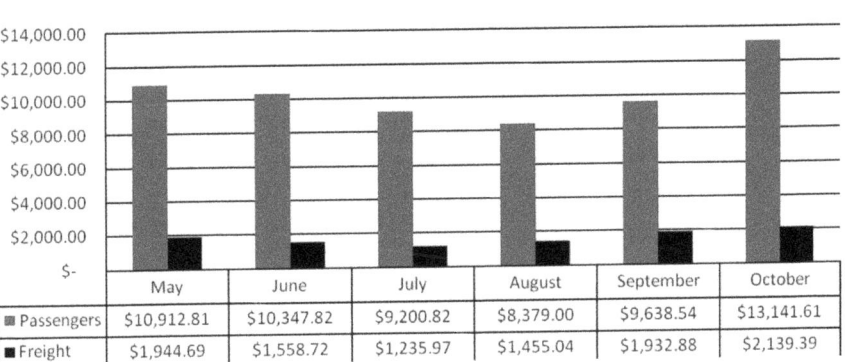

Wilmington & Raleigh Rail Road Receipts, 1840

	May	June	July	August	September	October
Passengers	$10,912.81	$10,347.82	$9,200.82	$8,379.00	$9,638.54	$13,141.61
Freight	$1,944.69	$1,558.72	$1,235.97	$1,455.04	$1,932.88	$2,139.39

Passenger receipts constituted a significant source of revenue for the Wilmington & Raleigh Rail Road during the same six-month period of 1840. Data source: North Carolina, "Fifth Annual Report of the President and Directors of the Wilmington & Raleigh Rail Road Company," *Report of the Board of Internal Improvements to the General Assembly,* Document No. 16 (Raleigh: Thomas Loring, 1840), Table B.

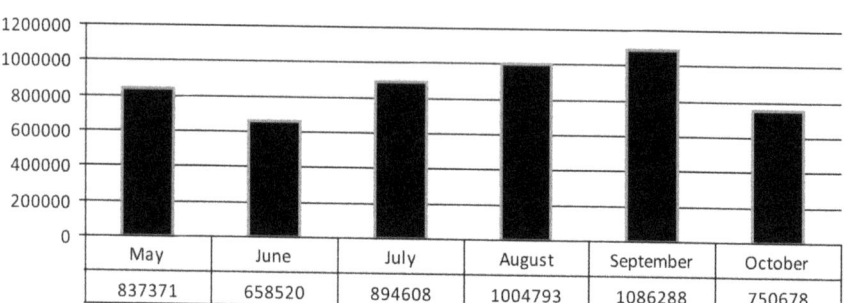

While freight receipts did not vary significantly from month-to-month during the same period, the tonnage of freight increased over the summer. Data source: North Carolina, "Fifth Annual Report of the President and Directors of the Wilmington & Raleigh Rail Road Company," *Report of the Board of Internal Improvements to the General Assembly*, Document No. 16 (Raleigh: Thomas Loring, 1840), Table B.

The gross receipts for the company during the last six months of 1840 had been $152,424.84, but when expenses were deducted, the net revenue amounted to $57,360.61. James Owen, then president of the company, stated that had the net revenue of the half year been divided among the stockholders, the dividend to the state would have amounted to $25,500. But he noted that the total cost of constructing the road had exceeded subscriptions by $684,000. The "available means" of the company included $11,665.57 due from the Post Office Department, $20,738 due from stockholders, $2,963 due from the Petersburg & Portsmouth Rail Road Company and others, $11,922.38 in receivables, and $15,597.33 in the hands of agents. Thus, when these assets are considered, the "pressing demands" on the company are reduced by $62,886.28 to $313,528. Owen recommended that the state guarantee an additional $320,000 in bonds to remedy the company's immediate needs; and pointed out that $1,350,000 in capital had been paid thus far, and that the property of the company was worth $2,000,000. The gross receipts of the company for the six months in 1840 yielded an average monthly income of $25,404 for both the railroad and steamboat line.[11]

Looking forward to the years 1847 through 1860, "way" passengers increased far ahead of "through" passenger travel between 1849 and 1854. By examining the month-to-month passenger volumes for the years 1854–

Wilmington & Raleigh (Weldon) Rail Road Passengers, 1847–1860

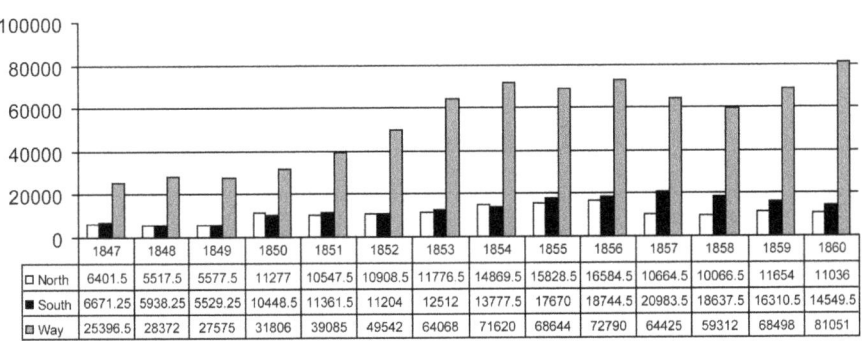

The volume of "way" travel on the Wilmington & Raleigh Rail Road (Wilmington & Weldon) continued to increase through the 1850s. Data source: Wilmington & Weldon Rail Road Company, *Annual Reports of the President and Directors, and the Chief Engineer and Superintendent of the Wilmington & Weldon R. R. Co., with the Proceedings of the General Meeting of Stockholders, November 8, 1860* (Wilmington: Fulton and Price, 1860), 44.

Wilmington & Raleigh (Weldon) Rail Road Passengers, 1854–1855

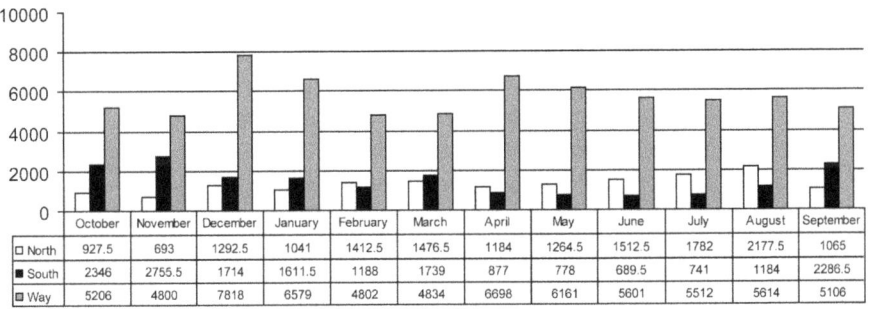

This graph illustrates the passenger statistics on the Wilmington & Weldon Rail Road from October 1854 to September 1855. Data source: Wilmington & Weldon Rail Road Company, *Proceedings of the Stockholders of the Wilmington & Weldon Rail Road Co. at their Twentieth Annual Meeting, held at Wilmington, North Carolina, November 9, 1855* (Wilmington: Thomas Loring, 1855), 20.

Wilmington & Weldon Rail Road Passengers, 1860

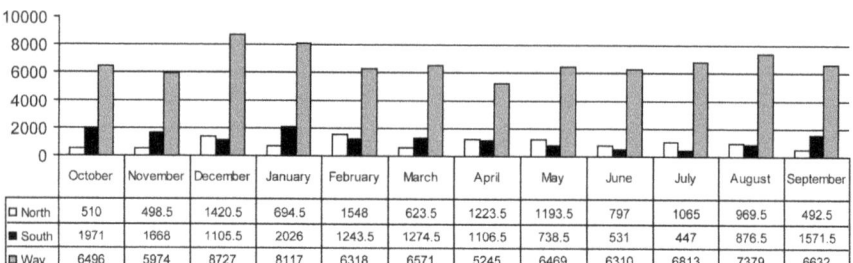

	October	November	December	January	February	March	April	May	June	July	August	September
North	510	498.5	1420.5	694.5	1548	623.5	1223.5	1193.5	797	1065	969.5	492.5
South	1971	1668	1105.5	2026	1243.5	1274.5	1106.5	738.5	531	447	876.5	1571.5
Way	6496	5974	8727	8117	6318	6571	5245	6469	6310	6813	7379	6632

In the last year of the antebellum period, the passenger statistics follow a pattern similar to what had existed five years earlier. "Way" travel, or travel between stations on the line, had increased in the months of February and March. Data source: Wilmington & Weldon Rail Road Company, *Annual Reports of the President and Directors, and the Chief Engineer and Superintendent of the Wilmington & Weldon R. R. Co., with the Proceedings of the General Meeting of Stockholders, November 8, 1860* (Wilmington: Fulton & Price, 1860), 46.

1855 and 1859–1860, it becomes clear that the yearly patterns of both "way" and "through" travel retain seasonal oscillations. Differences between north and south travel through the years were less pronounced by 1860, and the volume of "way" travel had increased.[12] Overall, the growth in "way" travel along the line of the Wilmington & Raleigh (Weldon) Rail Road is indicative of expanding economic development within the counties in the corridor.

The growth of "through" traffic increased between 1854 and 1857. In 1854, the Wilmington & Manchester Railroad replaced the steamboat line of the Wilmington & Raleigh, thus facilitating travel to the South. Still, "through" passenger statistics represent the normal flow of communications between North and South, and the volumes had been constant over the railroad's twenty-year history. The former emphasis placed upon interstate travel in the early plans proved to be less significant when viewing the statistics for later regional travel. While the revenue from "way" travel was less, its volume reflects regional economic growth.

The North Carolina Railroad was completed within ten miles of Raleigh by September 1854, and was expected to be in operation by November.[13] Little mention was made of it in the 1855 annual report of the Wilmington & Weldon; but by the next year, the company witnessed an increase in freight receipts of $42,000 before transportation on the North Carolina Railroad fully organized.

> The North Carolina Rail Road has, as was anticipated by its projectors, been productive of a large increase of business to this Road. The receipts from freight alone from that Road, during the last fiscal year, have been more than $42,000, tho' the business has not yet assumed a form of order and regularity. The citizens of Wilmington foresaw, at an early day, that this great work must be the means of bringing to their town the bulk of the produce of Western North Carolina.—Liberal aid was therefore extended to the work, for which they may now, if they will, reap a plentiful harvest. With 43 miles of Rail Road distance in their favor, it is impossible for any market town beyond the limits of the State to compete with them successfully for this trade. This Road is, however, open to all. *Free trade* is the policy of its messengers. Those who prefer going to Portsmouth or Petersburg can do so by this Road, via Goldsboro' and Weldon, upon the same terms they can come here. That is, the cost for transportation to Weldon is the same as it is to Wilmington. Arrangements were made in May last, with the North Carolina Rail Road Company, to run freight trains through from Charlotte to Wilmington, so that we can now guarantee the most prompt delivery of freight in the West or East. A similar arrangement will soon be perfected with the same Company and the Sea Board and Roanoke Company, by which freight from Portsmouth can reach points West of Raleigh as soon and as cheap as by any other route.[14]

The advantage of the 43 miles, the direct distance between Raleigh and Goldsboro, gave the farmers of the middle Piedmont more market options than sending their produce to Petersburg. This had always been the case on the Wilmington & Raleigh: farmers had the choice of Petersburg, Portsmouth, or Wilmington. Goldsboro, having become a receiving point for cotton, received 6,104 bales in 1860, and all but one bale of that was delivered to Wilmington. The other stations along the line of the Wilmington & Weldon received far less.[15] This fact supports the statement that the connection to the North Carolina Railroad would place Wilmington ahead of the out-of-state competition.

The decline of freight and passenger travel on the Wilmington & Weldon Rail Road in 1858 can be attributed to the Panic of 1857, and the directors acknowledged this in their 1858 report to the stockholders.[16] The national recession that followed the Panic of 1857 lasted from one to one and a half years in most of the eastern commercial centers, and its impact was also felt in rural communities. In the interior, westward expansion was disrupted as railroads failed and their bonds fell in value. The initial cause can be traced to the failure of railroads in the Western lands, mortgage defaults of the same lands that followed a period of land speculation, declining commodity prices, and a lack of liquidity in the Eastern banks, because of the declining value of mortgages and railroad bonds that could be unloaded.[17] The contemporary reader is familiar with this type of financial downturn. It differs from the Panic of 1837 in that it was driven neither by the ideology of decentralization of capital, nor the power struggle between intractable rivals such as Jackson, Biddle, and their supporters. Speculation was the root cause of this economic downturn, and its evolution was propelled by a few notable unforeseen events. However, that merchants, banks, and railroads in the South were more effective in coordinating their response to the recession than other regions is worth noting.[18]

The freight receipts for the Wilmington & Raleigh Rail Road/Wilmington & Weldon Rail Road steadily increased from 1847 to 1860, with plateaus between 1852–1853 and 1857–1858. Between 1854 and 1860, traditional products of the Coastal Plain region, such as naval stores, went into decline as cotton continued its rise. Wheat and flour production spiked during 1857–1858, but declining demand for grain forced down prices at the end of the Crimean War.[19] However, the market for cotton increased. By 1860, the total receipts of the company from all sources were $500,209.56, the greatest amount to date.[20] The relaying of the Wilmington & Raleigh's rails in the early 1850s had contributed to the company's efficiency, but connection with the North Carolina Railroad had also enhanced its service.

Wilmington & Raleigh / Wilmington & Weldon Rail Road Freight Receipts, 1847–1860

Year	Dollars
1847	$48,762
1848	$51,535
1849	$57,015
1850	$71,051
1851	$93,349
1852	$110,194
1853	$112,582
1854	$130,464
1855	$142,349
1856	$154,158
1857	$157,451
1858	$157,832
1859	$161,667
1860	$185,204

The freight receipts of the Wilmington & Raleigh Rail Road (later the Wilmington & Weldon Rail Road). Data source: Wilmington & Weldon Rail Road Company, *Annual Reports of the President and Directors, and the Chief Engineer and Superintendent of the Wilmington & Weldon R. R. Co., with the Proceedings of the General Meeting of Stockholders, November 8, 1860* (Wilmington: Fulton and Price, 1860), 33.

Table 6. Commodities Transported on the Railroad, 1854–60

Year	Cotton (bales)	Flour (barrels)	Turpentine (barrels)	Wheat (bushels)
1854	7088	270	31712	1196
1855	13575	4991	34713	3052
1856	12935	15084	30531	67510
1857	12954	20248	28277	71611
1858	19058	14065	29059	84295
1859	23553	12952	27060	52112
1860	31256	11215	23323	7416

The volumes of the commodities are expressed in different units: bales, bushels, and barrels. The rise in cotton volumes is the most significant trend.
Data source: Wilmington & Weldon Rail Road Company (1860), 39.

Table 7. Land Value for Several North Carolina Counties, 1815 and 1833

County	Land Value in 1815	Land Value in 1833	Amount of Decrease	Percentage Decrease
Beaufort	$810,819	$605,040	$205,779	25%
Bertie	1,350,096	995,809	354,287	26%
Bladen	554,276	435,645	118,631	21%
Brunswick	516,189	289,277	226,912	44%
Camden	412,618	272,539	140,079	34%
Carteret	385,131	276,016	109,115	28%
Chowan	645,360	497,921	147,439	23%
Craven	1,787,931	691,646	1,096,285	61%
Cumberland	1,293,805	942,721	351,084	27%
Currituck	343,473	232,185	111,288	32%
Duplin	729,097	550,812	178,285	24%
Edgecombe	1,926,572	1,524,986	401,586	21%
Franklin	916,713	716,220	200,493	22%
Granville	1,161,446	901,545	259,901	22%
Greene	549,244	382,964	166,280	30%
Halifax	2,061,540	1,569,893	491,647	24%
Hertford	830,081	606,206	223,875	27%
Hyde	813,287	238,615	574,672	71%
Johnston	846,865	632,947	213,918	25%
Jones	711,020	399,702	311,318	44%
Lenoir	724,996	333,491	391,505	54%
Nash	703,034	518,871	184,163	26%
New Hanover	1,293,399	998,902	294,497	23%
Onslow	605,153	416,192	188,961	31%
Perquimans	563,021	445,351	117,670	21%
Pitt	1,399,719	961,499	438,220	31%
Randolph	891,207	712,392	178,815	20%
Rowan	2,176,720	1,389,009	787,711	36%
Sampson	769,301	528,104	241,197	31%
Tyrrell	332,014	247,141	84,873	26%
Washington	437,512	227,072	210,440	48%
Wayne	1,144,620	770,431	374,189	33%

The greatest loss in land values in North Carolina between 1815 and 1833 occurred, with the exception of Randolph and Rowan counties, in the counties east of the fall line.
Data source: Charles L. Coon, *The Beginnings of Public Education in North Carolina* (Raleigh: Edwards and Broughton, 1908), 622–623.

TABLE 8. LAND VALUE FOR SEVERAL NORTH CAROLINA
COUNTIES, 1833 AND 1850

County	Land Value in 1833	Farm Value in 1850	Amount of Increase	Percentage Increase
Beaufort	$605,040	$605,014	-26	0.00%
Bertie	995,809	1,209,847	214,038	21.49%
Bladen	435,645	882,413	446,768	102.55%
Brunswick	289,277	521,059	231,782	80.12%
Camden	272,539	981,280	708,741	260.05%
Carteret	276,016	151,900	-124,116	-44.97%
Chowan	497,921	794,615	296,694	59.59%
Craven	691,646	778,301	86,655	12.53%
Cumberland	942,721	1,295,053	352,332	37.37%
Currituck	232,185	736,357	504,172	217.14%
Duplin	**550,812**	**1,407,443**	**856,631**	**155.52%**
Edgecombe	1,524,986	2,030,223	505,237	33.13%
Franklin	**716,220**	**832,196**	**115,976**	**16.19%**
Granville	**901,545**	**1,406,027**	**504,482**	**55.96%**
Greene	382,964	767,803	384,839	100.49%
Halifax	**1,569,893**	**1,546,642**	**-23,251**	**-1.48%**
Hertford	606,206	616,879	10,673	1.76%
Hyde	238,615	1,141,635	903,020	378.44%
Johnston	632,947	1,025,006	392,059	61.94%
Jones	399,702	467,271	67,569	16.90%
Lenoir	333,491	1,191,461	857,970	257.27%
Nash	**518,871**	**629,556**	**110,685**	**21.33%**
New Hanover	**998,902**	**1,002,957**	**4,055**	**0.41%**
Onslow	416,192	536,676	120,484	28.95%
Perquimans	445,351	1,032,968	587,617	131.94%
Pitt	961,499	1,115,174	153,675	15.98%
Randolph	712,392	1,031,503	319,111	44.79%
Rowan	1,389,009	1,071,546	-317,463	-22.86%
Sampson	528,104	1,804,729	1,276,625	241.74%
Tyrrell	247,141	319,493	72,352	29.28%
Washington	227,072	367,882	140,810	62.01%
Wayne	**770,431**	**1,613,294**	**842,863**	**109.40%**

By 1850, many of the same North Carolina counties that had experienced a decline in land values between 1815 and 1833 showed a higher cash value for farms than previous land values. Of these counties, those through which the early railroads passed, with the exception of New Hanover and Halifax, showed high farm values relative to earlier land values (in bold). Beaufort, Brunswick, Carteret, Craven, Onslow, and New Hanover are coastal counties. Randolph and Rowan are Piedmont counties.

Data sources: Charles L. Coon, *The Beginnings of Public Education in North Carolina* (Raleigh: Edwards and Broughton, 1908), 622–623; United States, *The Seventh Census of the United States: 1850* (Washington, D.C.: Robert Armstrong, 1853), 318–319.

Between 1815 and 1833, land values had declined significantly.[21] The counties that experienced the greatest loss in land values, with the exception of Randolph and Rowan counties, were east of the fall line. An examination of the cash value of farms, from *The Seventh Census of the United States* for the same set of counties shows a substantial increase in the value of agricultural land in 1850 relative to general land values in 1833. The routes of the early railroads passed through several that had shown increases in farm value.[22]

By 1860, the cash value of farms in the 32 counties that had the greatest decrease in land values in 1833 increased from their 1850 cash values.[23] Most increased by double, and some by three times. The median increase across the whole group was 90.87 percent. By this time, several railroads had been built in these counties, or were under construction. These included the North Carolina Railroad that passed through Carteret, Craven, Lenoir, Wayne, and Johnston counties in the east; and in the Piedmont, Rowan County, one of the two counties to the west on the original list. The Wilmington & Manchester Railroad passed through Brunswick County, and the Wilmington, Charlotte, & Rutherford Railroad passed through Bladen County. The Wilmington & Weldon Railroad had built a branch line to Tarboro in Edgecombe County. Now, nearly all these counties were within a reasonable distance of a railroad, or could access one by river. The economic significance of the east to west corridor was fully demonstrated by the increased farm values. That it was the agency of economic development in the Piedmont is well known. However, in the east it brought the Wilmington & Raleigh (Weldon) and the Raleigh & Gaston into a network.

The increased volume of cotton transported on the Wilmington & Raleigh (Weldon) Rail Road during the 1850s was documented in the company's annual reports. Agricultural data from the Census of the United States for 1840, 1850, and 1860 illustrate the changing proportions of cultivation of this crop in the counties on the route of the Raleigh & Gaston, the Wilmington & Raleigh (Weldon), and also in the neighboring county of Wake. The two railroads share Johnston County as a neighbor. Wake, Franklin, Granville, and Warren counties, and the neighboring counties of Chatham and Orange counties, were within the service area of the Raleigh & Gaston Rail Road. New Hanover, Duplin, Edgecombe, Nash, and Halifax counties were on the route of the Wilmington & Raleigh (Weldon) Rail Road.

Cotton is not the type of crop that a farmer would cultivate in great quantities if there were not a specialized market for it. In 1840, Wake County produced 2,391,996 pounds of cotton, 14 percent of the output of the counties having access to railroads for the same crop, whereas the counties along the route of the Raleigh & Gaston and the neighboring counties around Wake County cultivated very little cotton. Petersburg, Virginia, was a center for cotton processing, and the only market within a reasonable distance for this product. Though these figures were recorded

TABLE 9. FARM VALUE FOR SEVERAL NORTH CAROLINA
COUNTIES, 1850 AND 1860

County	Farm Value in 1850	Farm Value in 1860	Amount of Increase	Percentage Increase
Beaufort	$605,014	$1,130,020	$525,006	86.78%
Bertie	1,209,847	2,061,153	851,306	70.36%
Bladen	882,413	2,244,488	1,362,075	154.36%
Brunswick	521,059	755,766	234,707	45.04%
Camden	981,280	1,865,734	884,454	90.13%
Carteret	151,900	411,945	260,045	171.19%
Chowan	794,615	989,606	194,991	24.54%
Craven	778,301	1,376,387	598,086	76.85%
Cumberland	1,295,053	1,536,839	241,786	18.67%
Currituck	736,357	1,175,495	439,138	59.64%
Duplin	1,407,443	3,131,621	1,724,178	122.50%
Edgecombe	2,030,223	4,974,920	2,944,697	145.04%
Franklin	832,196	2,453,250	1,621,054	194.79%
Granville	1,406,027	3,457,365	2,051,338	145.90%
Greene	767,803	1,658,998	891,195	116.07%
Halifax	1,546,642	3,699,426	2,152,784	139.19%
Hertford	616,879	1,321,818	704,939	114.28%
Hyde	1,141,635	1,700,075	558,440	48.92%
Johnston	1,025,006	1,750,771	725,765	70.81%
Jones	467,271	963,266	495,995	106.15%
Lenoir	1,191,461	2,432,030	1,240,569	104.12%
Nash	629,556	1,736,608	1,107,052	175.85%
New Hanover	1,002,957	1,381,687	378,730	37.76%
Onslow	536,676	1,337,923	801,247	149.30%
Perquimans	1,032,968	1,537,770	504,802	48.87%
Pitt	1,115,174	3,052,010	1,936,836	173.68%
Randolph	1,031,503	1,791,483	759,980	73.68%
Rowan	1,071,546	2,924,631	1,853,085	172.94%
Sampson	1,804,729	3,110,749	1,306,020	72.37%
Tyrrell	319,493	455,845	136,352	42.68%
Washington	367,882	704,919	337,037	91.62%
Wayne	1,613,294	3,012,511	1,399,217	86.73%

This table illustrates the increase in the cash value of farms from 1850 to 1860 in the same counties that had the worst decline in land values between 1815 and 1833. All the counties in bold type have railroads running through them, including Randolph and Rowan in the Piedmont.

Data source: United States, *The Seventh Census of the United States: 1850* (Washington, D.C.: Robert Armstrong, 1853), 318–319; United States, *Agriculture of the United States in 1860* (Washington, D.C.: Government Printing Office, 1964), 104, 108.

in the 1840 census after the Raleigh & Gaston was completed, this might explain both the appeal of the Raleigh to Gaston route and the resistance that erupted when the commissioners of the Wilmington & Raleigh sought to change the route. By 1850, almost all of the counties were producing less cotton than they had in 1840. Orange County was the exception, producing 253,437 pounds in 1840, increasing to 922,000 pounds in 1850. Wake County decreased cotton cultivation to 823,600 pounds by 1850.

TABLE 10. COTTON CROPS IN POUNDS IN NORTH CAROLINA
COUNTIES WITH RAILROADS, 1840, 1850, 1860

County	1840	1850	1860
Chatham	399,728	276,000	320,000
Duplin	1,346,229	184,400	468,400
Edgecombe	2,445,000	1,238,800	7,655,200
Franklin	538,320	352,000	1,069,200
Granville	479,499	30,400	51,200
Halifax	2,905,573	696,000	4,172,800
Johnston	401,169	301,200	1,156,800
Nash	5,210,724	138,000	1,102,400
New Hanover	28,566	1,200	52,000
Orange	253,437	922,000	339,200
Wake	2,391,996	823,600	2,444,800
Warren	380,954	66,000	62,800
Wayne	402,175	134,000	1,624,800

This table shows the volume of cotton cultivated, in pounds, from the United States Census for the counties on the Raleigh & Gaston, and the neighboring counties around Wake County; and the counties through which the Wilmington & Raleigh (Weldon) Rail Road are included.
Data sources: United States, *Compendium of the Sixth Census* (Washington, D.C.: Thomas Allen, 1841), 180; United States, *The Seventh Census of the United States: 1850* (Washington: Robert Armstrong, 1853), 321; United States, *Agriculture of the United States in 1860* (Washington, D.C.: Government Printing Office, 1864), 105, 109

However, the volume for Wake increased dramatically by 1860 after the North Carolina Railroad was completed.

The proportions of cultivation within this set of counties show increased percentages for the low volume counties such as Chatham, Franklin, and Johnston; and decreased percentages for the high volume counties such as Edgecombe, Halifax, and Wake. The spatial distribution of this commodity is less concentrated at nodes, and concentrations of volumes are developing on the periphery. Edgecombe, Halifax, and Wake counties emerge as the leaders in cotton cultivation in 1860. However, Wake County had not increased much above the 1840 volume; Halifax County had increased cultivation by over a million pounds, and Edgecombe County was over five million pounds. The percentages show the high proportion of production in Halifax and Edgecombe Counties. Wayne County had more than tripled its volume after 1840, and Johnston County production had doubled. Johnston County decreased volume by approximately 100,000 pounds in 1850, but increased it to 1,156,800 pounds in 1860. As mentioned earlier, Goldsboro had received 6,104 bales, or 2,441,600 pounds, of cotton in 1860. The counterfactual model of an early railroad connecting Waynesborough to Raleigh through Johnston County could have been productive. On the weight of the data presented on just one commodity, cotton, the large volumes cultivated in Johnston and Wake in 1840 could have passed half the distance to Waynesborough. From there, the farmer could direct it to one of three markets, Wilmington, Petersburg, or Norfolk.

In Section 26 of *An Act to Incorporate the Wilmington and Raleigh Rail Road Company,* passed by the North Carolina General Assembly in 1833, the company was permitted to open the tracks to use after each ten miles were completed.[24] This section of the act explains the spacing of most of the depots and water/wood stations along the line: some towns on the line appear between ten and twenty miles apart. The depots in towns that were established before the railroad tended to have the track running on the outskirts of town. Examples include Halifax, Enfield, Waynesborough, and South Washington. Towns that grew up around the depots, such as Mt. Olive, Freemont, and Elm City, have the tracks running through their center streets. The railroad built a warehouse in some locations early, such as at Warsaw (Mooresville Depot) in 1838.[25]

The *MacRae-Brazier Map of 1833* lists only six towns or named locations between Wilmington and Weldon that existed prior to the railroad that would eventually become railroad towns — South Washington, Wrightsville Post Office, Waynesborough, Rocky Mount, Enfield, and Halifax.[26] Not listed on the map, but existing in 1833, was Duplin Cross Roads (later Wallace), the site of a post office. By 1858, stations listed with their agents between Wilmington and Weldon included Marlboro, Leesburg (now Willard), Teachey's (now Teachey), Magnolia (formerly Strickland's Depot), Warsaw, Bowdens, Faison, Mount Olive, Dudley, Everettsville, Goldsboro, Pikeville, Nahunta, Black Creek, Wilson (formerly Toisnot Depot), Joyner's Depot, Rocky Mount, Battleboro, Enfield, and Halifax.[27] Waynesborough was moved about a mile east closer to the railroad and was renamed Goldsboro after Matthew T. Goldsborough, the principal assistant engineer of the southern divisions of the railroad during its construction. Other railroad towns in that year, without station agents, included Northeast, Ashton, Rocky Point, Burgaw (formerly Cypress Grove post office), Duplin Cross Roads (latter Wallace), and Rose Hill.[28] South Washington also moved closer to the railroad, and is now known as Watha.

The railroad development was, above all, one moment in the historical geography of capitalism. The steam locomotive was a technological tool for reorganizing spatial and temporal relationships with the landscape to maximize capital.[29] By the close of 1854, the Wilmington & Raleigh Rail Road transformed the economy of eastern North Carolina into a catchment for exploiting the agricultural and commercial potential for the region. The economic environment of the Wilmington & Weldon Railroad was finally assembled: increased production of traditional crops, the cultivation of new crops, the establishment of new towns, and greater market access.

The Wilmington & Weldon Railroad Company was the new corporate name for the Wilmington & Raleigh Rail Road when the stockholders met in 1855. This was not the result of a purchase, merger, or reorganization into a new corporation. The change of name was merely the expression of a geographic reality: the main line of the railroad terminated at Weldon, and the contemplated branch to Raleigh was no longer necessary since it was included in the North Carolina Railroad. However, the most substantial change marks the end of the history of the Wilmington & Raleigh and the beginning of the Wilmington & Weldon in that the railroad from this point forward would exist within the context of a continuous rail network. Decades after the Civil War, the company discovered documents prepared by Gov. Dudley that outline the policy for an interstate rail network that would finally be realized as the Atlantic Coast Line Railroad.[30]

The antebellum rail network of which the Wilmington & Weldon Railroad was not without flaws, and some of these came about as a result of incidents that marred early railroad development in North Carolina. The trade conflict between the markets centers of Virginia had a disruptive effect on the development of the early railroads in North Carolina. The individual railroads of Virginia interfered in the planning of these railroads, and insinuated themselves into the politics of North Carolina. This was apparent during the discussions concerning the North Carolina Railroad in 1849, and would have dire consequences during the Civil War.

The incorporation of the North Carolina Railroad had overcome significant obstacles — the State of North Carolina had committed to subscribing to two thirds of the three million dollars required to build it. However, the presence of delegates from the Virginia commercial towns at the Internal Improvements Convention at Greensboro — the North Carolina Railroad was the central topic of interest at this convention — was a cause for concern for easterners. An article in the *Wilmington Journal* voices concerns over the Virginia towns gaining more resources from the west and central regions of North Carolina.

> We hope that we will not be assailed with the hackneyed outcry of being illiberal, or "behind the age," when we aver, that had not the North Carolina Railroad project been presented to us as a State work — as eminently North Carolinian in its inception, character and tendencies — we would have opposed it "tooth and toe-nail" from the start — nay more, we feel perfectly

confident, that had it not appealed to the State pride of the Legislature, it would never have become a law. When it was introduced, the *partizans* of the Charlotte and Danville Road, backed by the Virginia interest, were knocking at the door of the Legislature for a charter to connect those two points. It was as a substitute for this project, which would have cut the State in two, and carried all its central and western trade to the Virginia markets, that the Central Railroad bill was passed. Nothing but a desire to build up a market within our own borders — to foster our own trade — to avert the impending ruin of our own public works already constructed, and to prevent the draining of our own resources to swell the commerce and prosperity of our neighbors at the price of our own increased impoverishment, could have overcome the scruples which existed against the State's becoming farther involved in any projects of internal improvement which, as they must in some measure, be confined in their effects to special localities, should, if possible, be constructed by those who expect to be the peculiar recipients of the benefits to be derived from them. Such being the facts of the case, we cannot regard without jealousy and apprehension, the strenuous efforts which are being made in advance to divert the work from the legitimate object, and make it subservient to the interests and wishes of our Virginia rivals. We notice lately the holding of town meetings in Petersburg, upon the subject of appointing delegates to the Greensborough Convention, and we also notice the presence of Ex-Governor MOREHEAD, of this State, who made a long speech on the occasion, setting forth the vast accession of trade which the Central Road would bring to Petersburg. We have noticed the same disposition among many of the leading politicians of the West, with whom the idea seems to be gaining ground that Petersburg or Norfolk is the real point to be reached. The people of the East — the friends of the Wilmington & Raleigh Railroad — those who feel any interest in the property which the State holds in the Road — should look to this matter. If, instead of being a State project, having its outlet within our own borders, it is to be converted into a mere feeder for Virginia markets, we can see no earthly use in the people of the State going into debt to the amount of two millions of dollars to build it; nor in individuals subscribing their money for the benefit of rivals, who will not thank them.[31]

There was also resistance expressed in the east to the recommendations presented by Gov. Graham that the Raleigh & Gaston should be connected to the Danville & Charlotte Rail Road to form a continuous interior corridor south via the Charlotte & Columbia Rail Road.[32] If the railroad maps in *The Railroads of the Confederacy* by Robert C. Black III are examined, at a glace it becomes obvious that a Charlotte to Danville railroad would serve the interests of Richmond and Columbia rather well. Both the Charlotte & South Carolina Railroad and the Richmond & Danville Railroad were built to a five foot gauge. The North Carolina Railroad was built to 4' 8½" gauge, and the connection between Danville and Greensboro was not built until the Civil War was underway. The result of this different track gauge confounded General Beauregard's attempt to move his troops and equipment into North Carolina during February of 1865. The locomotives and cars of the Charlotte & South Carolina would have to be abandoned as he moved northward.[33] By contrast, Walter Gwynn had touted the strategic advantages of the Wilmington & Raleigh Rail Road in the report on his 1836 survey of the route in the event of suppressing an insurrection or defense against a coastal invasion. He was correct in this assessment: the Wilmington & Weldon Railroad would continue to supply the Army of Northern Virginia from the port of Wilmington until the city was abandoned by Confederate forces after the fall of Fort Fisher on January 15, 1865.

The topic of the Civil War fits appropriately in the history of the Wilmington & Weldon Railroad, and could easily constitute a single volume. However, there is one aspect of the history of the Wilmington & Raleigh Rail Road that is particularly pertinent to the study of its later incarnation. The Wilmington & Raleigh was built using slave labor; it used slave labor in its operation and improvements, and provided new opportunities to expand the institution. While this chapter has explored the role of the railroad in expanding the economy of North Carolina, it should also be pointed out that the railroad helped align the interests of the state with neighboring states that were dependent on the slave economy, and those desiring it in the west. This was apparent before railroad development had advanced significantly. An item of interest that was brought up at the *Virginia-State Convention* was the expansion of slavery into the western territory of the state as the pace of internal improvements advanced.

> And again, Sir, the course of industry in the west, does not require slave labor; slaves will be found in the grain-growing and tobacco country alone. This is not now the character of the western country, until a general system of roads and canals, shall facilitate their access to the market.[34]

The speaker, Judge Abel Upshur, earlier noting the eastern slaveholders paid 30 percent of the taxes, continued by stating that their taxes would also pay for roads and canals until the residents of the western regions provided a return on the investment.[35] The investment in the railroads in the South would involve more than the tax dollars of slaveholders; it would prove to be a tangle of foreign and domestic capital that would foster a dependence on the commodities produced through slave labor.

Significance

The significance of the Wilmington & Raleigh Rail Road within the context of American railroad history rests on three aspects of its planning and construction that can be termed "pioneering": it was a well-planned and remarkable accomplishment of civil engineering, testing the limits of what could be done with early railroad technology; the organization and financing of the railroad was structured around an arrangement that would later be termed a "public-private partnership"; and with the use of a company owned steamboat packet making schedule connections between Wilmington and Charleston, and its use of a stagecoach line during construction, the Wilmington & Raleigh Rail Road provides an early success example of multimodal transportation. Its influence upon economic development in eastern North Carolina and the evolution of state transportation policy contribute to the significance of this railroad within the context of the history of North Carolina; and by creating a continuous corridor from the Roanoke to Charleston, it transformed commerce and communication on the Eastern seaboard. There are ample reasons to justify the assertion that its development was a pioneering achievement. Thus, it follows that it should be the object of continued vigorous research both archival and applied.

General Conclusions

State investment in railroad projects was necessary. The amount of private investment capital available was insufficient to support the construction of extensive railroads. In addition, as evidenced by the Panic of 1837 and subsequent depression, an event that significantly hurt both the shareholders of the Raleigh & Gaston and the Wilmington & Raleigh, the role of the State of North Carolina as shareholder and/or owner ensured the survival of the railroad even though private investors were ruined.

The conditions for railroad development in North Carolina during the 1830s, including intrinsic and extrinsic factors, were favorable for building the first railroad from the coast to the interior of the Coastal Plain, and/or north-to-south within the Coastal Plain, preferably connected to a port. Routes through the Piedmont would be difficult, technically and financially; and passing north-to-south from Virginia to South Carolina would involve constructing a greater length of railroad. The "Metropolitan Route," for example, is particularly attractive because it connected all the cities of the Piedmont, and branch lines could be extended from this trunk to the coast. To construct it in the 1830s would necessitate creating several

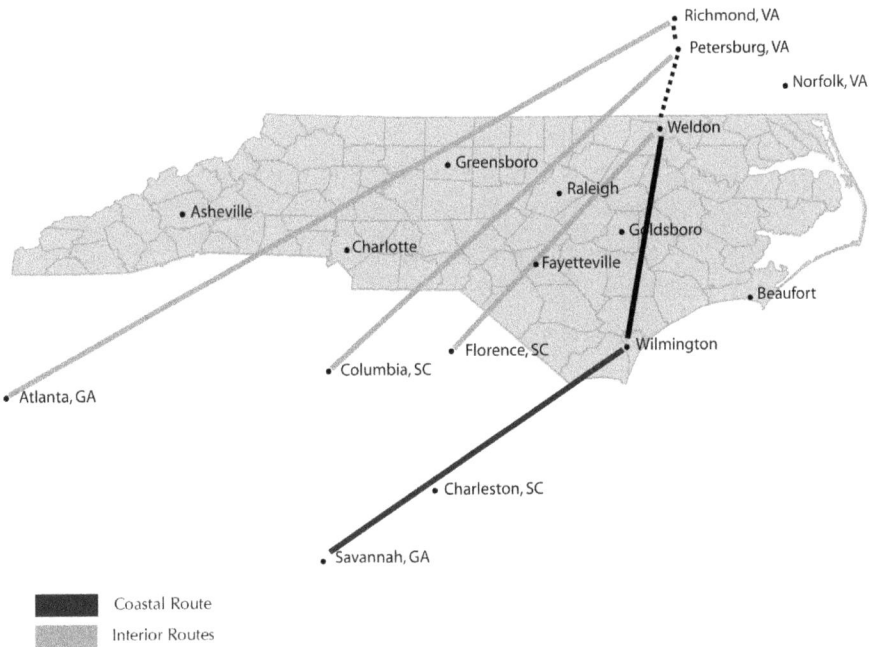

Coastal Route
Interior Routes

This map illustrates the direct distances between the commercial centers in Virginia and the closest commercial locations in South Carolina and Georgia passing through North Carolina. The line to the port of Wilmington is the shortest distance. The length of railroad needed to be built was less if the connection between Wilmington and Charleston was made by steamboat.

companies operating in different states, and an incredible quantity of iron would have to be put down before it would pass through the length of North Carolina. The Wilmington & Raleigh Rail Road, by contrast, could use its steamboats to continue service to South Carolina. It proved to be the logical railroad route to build through North Carolina because it was the best use of the available resources.

The first period of railroad development was influenced by the desire of the Virginia commercial centers of Norfolk and Petersburg to gain control of the agricultural output of the Roanoke River Basin. The completion of the Dismal Swamp Canal, in combination with the earlier closing of Roanoke Inlet, allowed Norfolk to enjoy trade with the lower reaches of the Roanoke Valley through Albemarle Sound. The opening of the Roanoke Canal around the Great Falls of the Roanoke gave Norfolk an advantage over the interior market of Petersburg because the produce from

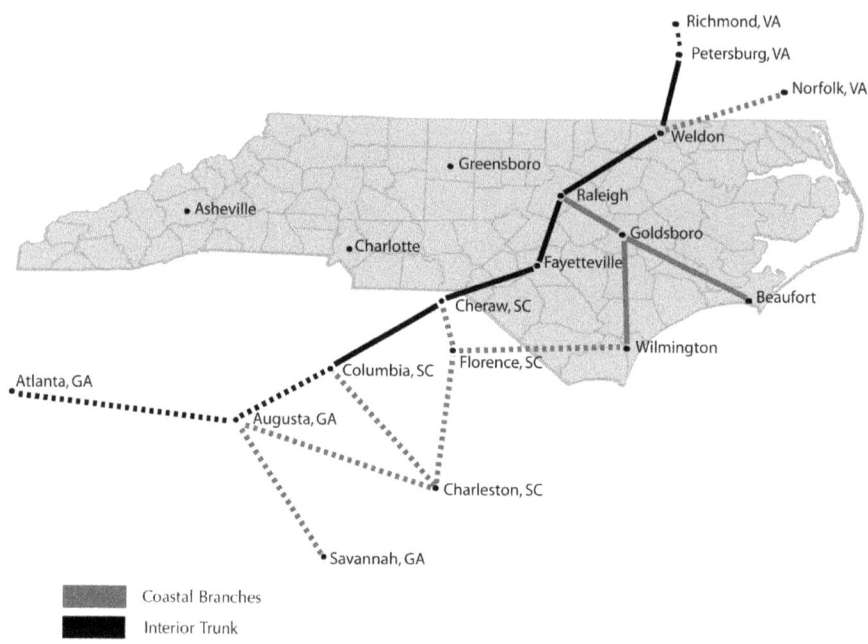

Coastal Branches
Interior Trunk

The ambitious "Metropolitan Route" concept, shown as a dark line, appears to be the most efficient corridor for connecting the major cities of Virginia, North Carolina, South Carolina, and Georgia. In theory, one can see how well the original route of the Wilmington & Raleigh and the proposed route of the Raleigh & Columbia fit within this model. However, constructing such a railroad in the 1830s would have been next to impossible. Aside from the technical complications associated with the railroad construction methods in use at that time and the lack of available investment capital, its greatest weakness was that it could not function as intended if sections of the central track were missing.

the upper reaches of the Roanoke could proceed to Norfolk without breaking bulk at the falls. Formerly, wagons would transport these products to Petersburg. The building of the Petersburg Rail Road to Blakeley, opposite Weldon at the Roanoke Canal, gave Petersburg the advantage in 1833. The construction of the Portsmouth & Roanoke Rail Road, along with its arrangement to use and later purchase the Weldon Toll Bridge, shifted the advantage to Norfolk in 1837. The incorporation of the Halifax & Weldon Rail Road in 1833 threatened to allow the Portsmouth & Roanoke Rail Road to extend farther into North Carolina.

The pivotal event during this period was the blocking of the Petersburg Rail Road's petition to the General Assembly of North Carolina by the friends of the Weldon Toll Bridge Company to build a bridge over the Roanoke near Weldon. From the letters written by Charles F. Osborne, president of the Petersburg Rail Road, to Edward B. Dudley, president of the Wilmington & Raleigh Rail Road, in early 1836, it is apparent that Mr. Osborne had little faith in the bridge building company or its bridge. After completing the railroad to the Roanoke in 1833, the Petersburg Rail Road was left unable to act, waiting for a bridge that would not be completed for years, if at all. The Petersburg Rail Road opted to support the building of the Greensville & Roanoke Rail Road instead. This railroad was a spur of the Petersburg Rail Road to be built to a landing above the Great Falls for the purpose of intercepting produce before it was transported through the Roanoke Canal, and to continue their reach into North Carolina through their affiliate, the Raleigh & Gaston Rail Road. The Portsmouth & Roanoke Rail Road, surveyed in 1833, anticipated the completion of the Weldon Toll Bridge and the railroad to occur at the same time, and the reach of that railroad would continue through the Halifax & Weldon Rail Road. In name, these early Virginia railroads were public works, but in essence they were instruments of trade warfare, *economic stream piracy*.

Letters by writers "Roanoke" and "Petersburg," published in the *Wilmington Chronicle* years after the Wilmington & Raleigh was granted the amendments to its charter, testify to active resistance put forth by interests in Raleigh and Petersburg upon learning that the Wilmington & Raleigh Rail Road would go to Weldon. To understand why investors in the Piedmont would not support the building of a railroad between Wilmington and Raleigh that would enhance their commerce is difficult. Unless they labored under the illusion that investors in the east would undertake the project anyway, or they anticipated greater profits from connections elsewhere, the notion that interests in Raleigh would reject forming a connection to Wilmington without cause seems unlikely.

A scenario that seems more plausible, but difficult to verify, is that the investors at Wilmington and their associates in the eastern counties perceived an obvious opportunity. Their railroad could join with the Halifax & Weldon Rail Road, taking advantage of the existing Weldon Toll Bridge to connect to the Virginia railroads, and use the port of Wilmington to establish immediate connections to the south. While the *Memorial* of the November 1833 convention on internal improvements advocated a monumental plan to expend five million dollars on a state system that would relegate the port of Wilmington to an outpost off the main line, and Gavin Hogg, in his report of the Selection Committee on Internal Improvements, denigrated the commerce of the port, a few advocates in the east took the "go it alone" approach. The books were opened to subscriptions at a meeting at the home of Edward B. Dudley in Wilmington prior to the meeting of the General Assembly in 1835; and with the passage of the amendments to its charter, eastern interests took control of the company. The interests in Raleigh and Petersburg were of course blindsided. A bill to charter the Raleigh & Gaston Rail Road was introduced quite unexpectedly during the 1835–1836 session of the General Assembly.

The years 1834 and 1835 appear to be a critical period in railroad development in North Carolina, but unfortunately the record of the actions of individuals involved is less than transparent. While a more in depth examination of this time was beyond the scope of this study, archival research focused on the private correspondences and other non-public resources might illuminate the missing events that transpired during the planning process.

Regardless of the particulars, the changing of the route of the Wilmington & Raleigh was a sound planning decision because it utilized existing advantages: it could be set in operation early, and it constituted with its steamship line a completed and economical route connecting south. By contrast, the Raleigh & Gaston had immense disadvantages. Some were rooted in the mythology of the so-called "Metropolitan Route" through the interior advocated by Colonel Long and others. The success of the Raleigh & Gaston and the Greensville & Roanoke depended on the construction of the Raleigh & Columbia Rail Road. If there were a first law of planning, it would be *never* to undertake a commercial project that cannot function profitably as a "stand alone" entity in the event that the projected works of others never materialized. The building of the Raleigh & Columbia Rail Road would have involved putting down a greater length of track than the Wilmington & Raleigh, and would have required the transportation of iron from the coast and sources of capital from South Carolina. When the line was completed to the North Carolina state line, a considerable distance to Columbia would remain.

This, however, is not the only flaw of the Raleigh & Gaston. It was incorporated in haste without an appeal for state investment, and it was undercapitalized. The chief logical obstacle of the company was that it had to build its own bridge over the Roanoke River, and receive shipments of iron and equipment via Petersburg. The Wilmington & Raleigh could receive iron and equipment at both ends of construction, Norfolk and

Wilmington. It could also offer a "through ticket" to Charleston while still running stages. For an unbiased position, in spite of the state's extraordinary efforts to preserve the Raleigh & Gaston at that particular time, the railroad was a lost cause from the moment that the Post Office Department awarded the contract for the "Southern Great Mail" to the Wilmington & Raleigh in 1838. Yet, as early as 1835, had the investors in the Raleigh & Gaston put their support behind the established Roanoke & Raleigh Rail Road with a route that would have formed a connection near Weldon and was slated for state investment, the outcome might have been less dire. This was, decades later, a connection that determined the future of the Raleigh & Gaston, and the route has survived to this day. History has consumed the Greensville & Roanoke Rail Road, the old town of Gaston, and the bridge over the Roanoke built by the Raleigh & Gaston Rail Road Company.

When Francis Rives began to dismantle the Portsmouth & Roanoke Rail Road, the State of North Carolina had no recourse but to intervene. While failing to secure a conviction of Rives, the state blocked his petition for a charter, and aided the reorganization of the Portsmouth company. This was the proper action, for Rives and his masters in Petersburg compromised the trust of the State of North Carolina: not only was the taking up of the track of the Portsmouth & Roanoke Rail Road an affront to the people of North Carolina who had become dependent upon it for their convenience and commerce, but it also overlooked that the state had granted the privilege of its existence in the first place. In his message to the Legislature of North Carolina during its 1846–47 session, Governor William Graham explained the problems that the Petersburg Rail Road had created by paying Rives to keep the section of the Portsmouth & Roanoke in North Carolina inactive. At the time, the General Assembly of Virginia had enacted legislation to withdraw the rights granted to the purchasers of the Portsmouth & Roanoke Rail Road if the State of North Carolina revoked any privileges granted to the Petersburg Rail Road by North Carolina in its charter due to its participation in shutting down the Portsmouth & Roanoke.

> In other words, the Petersburg Company, in effect, bought from him the disuse of the Portsmouth Road, and paid him a consideration for withholding from the public the conveniences for which the Legislature had authorized its construction. The right of the individual party to this agreement, thus to dispose of his interest, under decision of the Court, is not denied; and had the other contracting party been a natural person, it would never have been questioned, however great be the inconvenience of the loss of the

Road. But in my view, a corporation, the mere creature of the Law, must look to its charter, for privileges not for restrictions: what is not authorized to it, is denied; and by consequence, the Petersburg Rail Road Company, permitted by its charter only, to construct a Road from that Town to its Southern terminus, and to transport on the same, had no right either to participate in the profits of transportation on the Portsmouth Road, or to suppress transportation thereon. Regarding this contract as designed for the destruction of the Portsmouth Road, to the end that the other might have a monopoly of the business done by both, and as such a public injury and transgression of its own corporate rights by the Petersburg Company, and perceiving that that Company had made no reports to the Legislature of this State, of its operations within our limits, as was expressly required to be periodically done, by the Act of its creation, I directed the Attorney General to file an Information against them in Supreme Court, and required them to show cause why their charter should not be declared forfeited. At the last Term of that Court, judgment was rendered in the case for the defendant. The opinion announcing this decision is accessible to you, and to it, you are referred, to determine whether any new process shall be instituted in the premises, or whether any new Legislation be need, to prevent mischiefs in like cases for the future.[36]

Through this conflict, which has garnered little attention, one can see the evolution of a state policy. The commercial conflict between Norfolk and Petersburg represented an extreme of *laissez faire* capitalism given scope in an underdeveloped nation to the point where regional centers behaved as slightly more constrained versions of Italian city-states presided over by a merchant ruling class. The interstate nature of the Petersburg Rail Road and the Portsmouth & Roanoke Rail Road, and their respective roles in north to south communications and commerce involving the well-being of other railroads and states, would necessitate a diminution of all parochial ambitions.

After surviving the economic downturn of the early 1840s, the Wilmington & Raleigh Rail Road needed to rebuild the entire railroad in heavy iron. The original strap-iron wooden rail construction deteriorated over a period of about ten years, and proved to be a liability for the early railroads. In January of 1849, the North Carolina Legislature approved a mortgage on the company for the purpose of rebuilding the railroad in heavy iron. Also in that year, work commenced on the Wilmington & Manchester Railroad, a connection to the railroads of South Carolina that would replace the less efficient steamboat line of the Wilmington & Raleigh.

With the completion of the Wilmington & Manchester and the connection established to the North Carolina Railroad at Goldsboro, the Wilmington & Raleigh was integrated into a network of railroads that branched into the Piedmont of North Carolina. The railroad attained its mature condition, with accompanying profitability, by the mid–1850s. Measurable economic growth within the rail corridor was the result of improvements to the Wilmington & Raleigh and network development. Growth would continue for the remainder of the decade.

The corporate name of the company was changed to the Wilmington & Weldon Railroad Company in 1855. While the nature of the corporation remained unchanged, North Carolina and the United States in general were changing. The Wilmington & Weldon Railroad Company would play a crucial logical role for the Confederate Army during the Civil War, rebuild its railroad and network connection during Reconstruction, construct new branch lines, and eventually, through mergers and consolidation, would become part of the Atlantic Coast Line Railroad before the end of the century. The era of the Wilmington & Raleigh Rail Road Company, for practical purposes in consideration of extensive railroad development in the late antebellum, extends from 1833 to 1854, and seamlessly joins the era of the Wilmington & Weldon Railroad Company.

The most fascinating of the topics that could be explored concern the transformation of the political and cultural life of antebellum North Carolina that can be directly attributed to the building of the first railroads in the state. Railroads reorganize the function of space into points on a line, and time becomes a measure of distance between points. Railroad development required capital; and when completed, railroads still proved to be voracious consumers of capital and resources in every phase of their operation. They facilitated market expansion and production, but the weight of their debt necessitated that the growth curve be positive. The routines of commerce and culture are forced to synchronize to the unrelenting cycles of the regular runs of the railroad. With the interests of North Carolina vested so deeply in the stock of its railroads and ever expanding program of railroad development on the eve of the Civil War, one must pose the question of how this situation impelled the motives of political objective. This must be addressed in some future study on the history of the Wilmington & Weldon that encompasses the era of the Civil War and Reconstruction.

Appendix A

The Railroad Land in Wilmington

The sites recommended in the 1836 survey suggest locations for the Wilmington Depot and company docks different from the site that was eventually selected. The Western Route of Walter Gwynn's 1835 survey of the Wilmington & Raleigh Rail Road begins in an area of Wilmington known as "Dry Pond."[1] John MacLaurin writing under the *nom de plume* Senex, Jr., described "Dry Pond" as a place "bounteously full of water in the wet season and guiltless of moisture in the dry, that sat placidly on the snow-white sand amid the scrubby oaks and prickly pears and wire grass," located on the southern boundary of Wilmington. The site of John Barnes' farm was located beyond "Dry Pond" at what would become the block bounded by Wooster, Queen, Seventh, and Eighth streets. The east-to-west boundary of Wilmington extended from Fifth Street to the Cape Fear River; and the north-to-south boundary extended from Campbell Street to "Dry Pond." The farm covered approximately five acres and MacLaurin describes it as a "little plot of bald sand-hill land."[2] Gwynn's survey continues by indicating the route continues "due north to the head of market street" and east toward a "Love Grove" where it crosses Smith's Creek.[3] MacLaurin gives the location of the head of Market Street as between Seventh and Eighth streets, and Love Grove Plantation as being on Smith's Creek.[4] The survey continues over level ground to Prince George's Creek, crossing between the Burgwyn dwelling and mill, and continuing to the Northeast Cape Fear River near the site of the old bridge. The Burgwyn plantation was located near Prince George's Creek east of the Castle Haynes estate across the county road.[5] The western route continues from the Northeast Cape Fear for forty-seven miles to the head of Bear Swamp, cross both Rockfish Creek and Stewart Creek; passing west within two and half miles of South Washington and seven miles of Kenansville. With the exception of the section of the route in Wilmington, the track from Smith's Creek to the Northeast Cape Fear River appears to conform to the survey. An alternative to this route provided in the survey begins at the timber pens on the west side of the Cape Fear River at Wilmington, and then extends one mile where it "crosses over and passes along the dividing ground of the Cape Fear and the Northeast Cape Fear to the head of Long Creek. The tracks would follow the divide between Long and Moore's creeks, and between Moore's and Rockfish creeks with crossing of Turkey and Stewart creeks, finally reaching the head of Bear Swamp.[6]

The Deed

The Wilmington & Raleigh Rail Road had acquired a number of parcels in New Hanover County that were consolidated into a single deed in 1840. The parcels in this deed are listed below in chronological order.

I

M. McKay conveyed to the Wilmington & Raleigh Rail Road Company by a deed dated April 19, 1834, the southwest corner parcel of Lot 22 of the Marsden Campbell Plot (drawn up by Alexander MacRae). The parcel measures 165 feet fronted by the northern boundary of town, from the southwest corner of Lot 22 running east to a parcel owned by Pompy Mazell, and 66 feet parallel to Front Street. There was another parcel associated with this deed, also in Lot 22 of the Campbell Plot, that fronted the boundary of town on the south, Front Street on the west, and Second Street on the east, and Lot 23.

II

A parcel containing approximately six acres was conveyed by Robert S. McCombs by a deed dated November 18, 1836, to the Wilmington & Raleigh Rail Road. The lot, located 430 feet from the town line on the south side of Market Street, extended on the north side of Market Street. For the description in the deed, the parcel appears to be two blocks, 20 poles squares (330 feet by 330 feet), with an additional 60 feet, and the northern side of the north parcel is angled at 80 west.

III

P.K. Dickinson conveyed by a deed dated December 1836 the lots 132 through 134 A on the west side of Front Street in the town of Wilmington to the Wilmington & Raleigh Rail Road. The length fronting the street was 198 feet.

IV

A deed dated December 4, 1836, conveyed by A.A. Wanett to the Wilmington & Raleigh Rail Road lots 3, 4, and 5 of the Campbell land at the northwest corner of the northern boundary street, beginning 132 feet from the corner, continuing 198 feet on Front Street, then 135 feet west towards the Cape Fear River.

V

William Calder Frederick and Edwin Kidder conveyed to the Wilmington & Raleigh Rail Road on December 3, 1836, a parcel measuring 66 feet by 135 feet referred to a lot number 2 in the Campbell plot located 66 feet from the northwest corner of the street on the northern boundary of town.

VI

A parcel of 150 acres, less one-fourth acre reserved to John D. Jones for a tomb and house, in Love Grove, was conveyed to the Wilmington & Raleigh Rail Road on February 14, 1837. The beginning of this parcel was at a stake on the bank of Smiths Creek on the old ferry landing a little above or nearly opposite where the causeway leads to the ferry or bridge, then running 3° west a distance of 18 poles (297 feet), then 187 poles (3,085.5 feet) "to a stake at the crossing of the old road," then turning 50° east and proceeding 180 poles (2,970 feet) "to a spruce pine at the corner of Campbell's field," then 46 poles (759 feet) to "a cider on the creek bank growing among some lime stones partly above the ground there down the various courses of the creek to the First Station."

VII

E.E. Piece and William Armstrong conveyed a parcel to the Wilmington & Raleigh Rail Road on November 15, 1837 containing 561.5 acres. It is described as beginning at a pine stump on Smith's Creek then running 80° east a distance of 213 poles (3,514.5 feet), then 10° west 340 poles (5619 feet) to a stump near Hugh Cowan's gate, then west six poles (99 feet) to a swamp stream, then following the western branch of the stream 42 poles

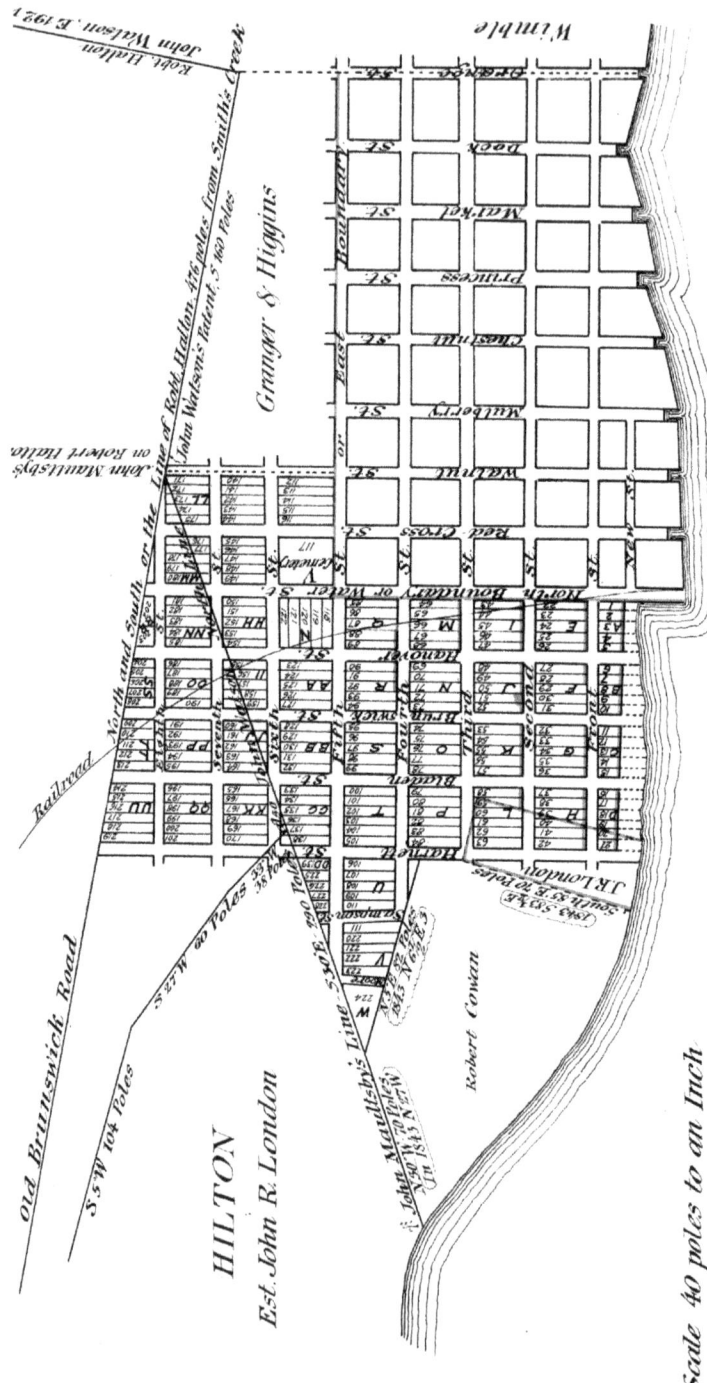

(693 feet), then west 298 poles (4,917 feet) to a stake in a bay, then 206 poles (3,399 feet) east, then, turning 86° a distance of 84 poles (1,419 feet) to a pine on the south side of the branch, then east 150 poles (2,475 feet) to the First Station.

VIII

P.W. Fanning conveyed to the Wilmington & Raleigh Rail Road by a deed dated December 23, 1839, a parcel beginning near the northern boundary of town, 77.5 feet to an alley then eastward running to an alley 130 feet, then 77.5 feet southward parallel to Second Street, then westward 130 feet to the beginning of the tract.

All the parcels are within New Hanover County, and the consolidated deed can be found in the office of the Register of Deeds for New Hanover County.[7] The original plot of the Campbell lands prepared by Alexander MacRae can be found on page 250 in Book BB in the office of the New Hanover County Register of Deeds. In 1915, civil engineer J.L. Becton prepared a new drawing of the survey.[8] This drawing is available in the digital image collection maintained by the New Hanover County Public Library. This is a useful tool for interpreting the deed.

A closer examination of the 1840 deed brings to light several items of interest. The oldest of the deeds incorporated in this deed is the 19 April 1834 McKay parcel. The acquisition of this property predates the company's 1835 charter. The lots of the Marsden Campbell plot comprise the railroad's land on the east bank of the Cape Fear River. Marsden Campbell's plantation was named Clarendon and the division of his land into individual parcels follows a scheme of block of 330 feet square separated by streets of 66 feet in width. Each block is divided into five 66 feet by

Opposite: In 1915, civil engineer J.L. Becton prepared a new drawing of the faded map found on page 250 in Book BB in the office of the New Hanover County Register of Deeds. The original incorporated the survey of the Campbell lands undertaken by Alexander MacRae, and reference to its lot numbers can be found in the consolidated deed of 1840 for the Wilmington & Raleigh Rail Road (New Hanover County Register of Deed, *Book Y*). Also mentioned in the deed are references to the Cowan property, the "old Road" (Old Brunswick Road), and Smiths Creek. Lots 2, 3, 4, and 5 of the Campbell Plot, on Nutt Street between Campbell (north Boundary of Water) and Hanover streets, and Lots 22 and 23 of the Campbell Plot, at the corner of Front and Campbell streets, were sites of the railroad's first facilities (courtesy New Hanover Public Library, Robert M. Fales Collection).

330 feet lots that are in some cases subdivided into lots that are 66 feet by 165 feet.[9] The original scheme of the Campbell Plot is preserved on modern parcel maps because the railroad occupied this land for over a century and none of it was subdivided into smaller parcels. This section of the railroad property bounded by Front Street, Third Street, and Red Cross Street preserves the divisions of the Campbell Plot. These are the 330 feet by 300 feet blocks, the five 66 feet by 330 feet lots, the 66 feet by 165 feet subdivided lots, and the 66 feet wide streets. The "old road" referred to in the deed dated February 14, 1837, appears to be McRae Street. Sprunt places the location of the Cowan plantation "Paradise" on the bluff beyond Harnett Street; and the land below the bluff at Bladen Street was a swamp.[10] The old road presumably led to the causeway and old ferry landing mentioned in the same deed. If so, it appear that this public road was preserved.

The deeds compiled into the consolidated deed, dated September 11, 1840, include parcels on Market Street deeded to the railroad by Robert S. McCombs on November 18, 1836, that have no relationship to any railroad facilities or extent of track in the railroad's history. While the remaining deeds were incorporated in the railroad's property and remained so well into the twentieth century, and they are all located on the northern boundary of town, the Market Street parcels are remotely located, and appear to have been sold off at some point.

The site of the depot and shops was not chosen until early 1837.[11] The company had acquired lots at the river in early December. The lots on Market Street were acquired in November, three months after Walter Gwynn's survey was submitted. Further, it seems unlikely that the railroad, in 1837, could have foreseen the need for acquiring so much land on Smith's Creek for what would become the Upper Yards. Hypothetically, the company may have considered placing their railroad depot at the head of the town's main street, and running track along the eastern boundary of town to the southern boundary. In this instance, the docks at the foot of this boundary could be used for the steamboat line. It would seem probable that the dimensions of the parcel, beginning 430 feet from the eastern boundary at Fifth Street, would form a polygon that abuts a track arrangement of a north-to-south section extending from Market Street to the southern boundary of town; and a section, extending from Market Street to the southern tip of the lands that would become the Upper Yards, which paralleled the angle of the old road.

On a modern street map of the City of Wilmington a line can be drawn from Castle Street (the Dry Pond area) to Market Street along Seventh Street, and another from the corner of Seventh and Market streets, along the line of the old road (McRae Street) to the western edge of the Upper Yards. This seems to be a reasonable interpretation of Walter Gwynn's recommendation of the tracks through Wilmington. The survey of the parcels found in the 1840 deed is a little more difficult to interpret: the deed includes references such as "thence No. 82 East 360 feet" and "then No. 12 west 40 poles." These markers are not helpful. However, the size of the parcel conveyed to the railroad was approximately six acres.[12]

The acquisition of the town lots on Front Street from P.K. Dickinson and the riverside lots outside the northwest boundary of town from A.A. Wanett, William Calder Frederick and Edwin Kidder in December of 1836 indicates that the company intended to locate its docks on the northern boundary of town. These lots are situated around the Front Street Bridge and extend to the Cape Fear River, and are bounded on the south by Red

A small stream has always flowed down from the ridge between Fifth and Sixth streets to the Cape Fear River. After the railroad facilities at Wilmington were abandoned during the 1980s, it returned to the surface when the drainage in the cut of the inclined plane went unmaintained. This photograph, taken in November 2000 near the bridge at Third Street, shows leaves floating on pooling water behind a dam of debris.

Cross Street, the former northwestern boundary of Wilmington. The east bank of the Cape Fear River was much closer to Front Street in the 1830s: according to the Wanett deed, the low water mark was 135 feet from Front Street at this location. The bridge at Front Street crossed a ravine in which a small stream one coursed. The stream extended towards the Upper Yards; and since the tracks at the Wilmington facilities were abandoned in the 1980s, the stream has emerged again since the drainage system at the tracks ceased to be maintained. This stream is also mentioned in the deed dated February 14, 1837, in the consolidated deed of 1840 as a creek with partially exposed deposits of limestone leading down to the First Station. As of early 1837, the railroad had six acres at Market Street, its docks at the Cape Fear outside the northern boundary of Wilmington, a few lots on Front Street, and 150 acres at Love Grove.

The abundance of space in Love Grove would seem a likely place to set up the shops; however, in order that the locomotives and ships could be maintained together, the railroad began building the shops and depot close to the river.[13] The land deeded to the company by Piece and Armstrong in November of 1837 covers 561.5 acres. As stated earlier, four town blocks amounted to ten acres; thus, forty bocks would amount to one hundred acres. The total land conveyed to the company by this deed was equal to 244.6 blocks — nearly equal to fifteen square blocks. While some of this land was necessary for the railroad facilities, the likely use for this land may have been for wood.

The Nicholas Schenk *Diary* notes that the railroad company built a trestle from the bluff to the docks to deliver wood to the steamboats.[14] The company's steamship *Wilmington,* for example, burned a cord of wood an hour.[15] The amount of space the railroad facilities occupied, and the blocks through which its track cut, are a small fraction of the land the company acquired. The stockholders report of 1860 provides a total of 5,596.625 cord used in its "Consolidated Report of the Service of Locomotives" for the year and lists twenty-two stations.[16] The 1855 stockholders report states that six to eight stations were used for taking on wood and water; and the average passenger train used 5,918 cords per year at forty miles per cord, and a freight train would use 2,975 cords per year at 29 miles per cord.[17] Thus, it can be assumed that at least one-tenth of the wood consumed must have been loaded at or near Wilmington before the locomotive had to be refueled. This would mean that between 500 and 600 cords per year had to be cut at Wilmington. Over a period of twenty years of operation, the volume of wood from Wilmington, by these estimates, would have been between 1,280,000 and 1,536,000 cubic feet. The land above Campbell Street, the site of the railroad cut, was woods and swampland, and the land on the eastern boundary was woods.[18] However, situating the docks, warehouse, shops, and depot at the river on the northern boundary of town was advantageous. The distance between the company docks and what would later become the Upper Yards was approximately 2.74 times shorter than the distance by rail and road to the river on the southern boundary. It would also take 1.7 times the length of track; and based upon the cost of Gwynn's survey of the Portsmouth & Roanoke Rail Road, the track across town would have cost the company approximately $6,700 with no particular advantages.[19]

The landholdings of the railroad would prove useful over its history of usage at Wilmington. The first passenger depot would be located on Nutt Street near the company docks. After the Civil War, when the Cape Fear River was spanned by bridge, the Wilmington & Weldon would establish connections with the Wilmington, Columbia, and Augusta Railroad and the Carolina Central Railroad. In the 1870s, the company would add a depot on Eighth Street between Bladen and Brunswick streets. In the 1880s, the depot was located on Front Street between Campbell and Hanover streets. The land at Love Grove would eventually become the vast Upper Yards as the Wilmington & Weldon and its associated railroads were merged into the Atlantic Coast Line Railroad with Wilmington being its headquarters.

APPENDIX B

The Depot Site at Wilmington

Research for this volume began in the autumn of 2000 as an assessment of architectural and archaeological resources at the old Wilmington Depot site for a class assignment while the author was a graduate student at the University of North Carolina at Wilmington. The primary goal was to assemble a history of the railroad from its beginning to the time when Wilmington became the headquarters of the Atlantic Coastline Railroad, and try to place it within the context of American railroad history. Supposedly, with this historic foundation in place, one might be able to connect existing structures to historical documents (such as the stockholders reports) and identify likely sites for archaeological inquiry. After a decade of research, the author has concluded that this approach is inappropriate for this particular site for the following reasons: (1) extensive grading and filling by the railroad at different times radically altered the physical landscape so as to obliterate the architectural and archaeological context of prior periods; (2) archival documents — reports, newspapers, maps, drawings, and photographs — prior to the 1880s rarely provide enough information to construct a complete image of the site at any point prior to the first Sanborn Fire Insurance Map in 1884; (3) the railroad structures were added to, built on top of, or demolished to suit demand with unusual frequency; and (4) the remaining 19th century ruins, mainly retaining walls, can be dated to different periods of construction on the site, but the historic district of Wilmington has many such walls that hold back earth where historic structures still exist. An illustration of the problem can be found through examining the 1860 stockholders report.

The twenty-fifth annual meeting of the stockholders of the Wilmington & Weldon Rail Road Company convened at the court house in Wilmington on Thursday, November 8, 1860. Five years had passed since the company's corporate name had been changed, but in the sense of ownership, it had remained the same railroad. A feature of the annual reports before the Civil War was the list of stockholders on its opening pages. Listed there were a few names from Portsmouth, Norfolk, and Petersburg in Virginia, a few in New York, Florida, South Carolina and Pennsylvania, but most were from North Carolina. Represented in large number were shareholders from Tarboro. The Wilmington & Weldon was on the verge of completing its branch line to that town from Rocky Mount. All that remained was the completion of a bridge over the Tar River. It was to be completed by October 1, but the deadline had been extended for improvements to the bridge. All along the railroad, more trestlework had been replaced with embankments, and drainage of the rail bed had been improved. During the year, American made rails had been used in quantity, old laminated rails were being renewed in the company shops, and 60,000 double-lipped rolled chairs — improved hardware for seating the rails — had been installed, with an order of another 20,000 expected.[1] Other improvements that year included the completion of the bridge at Rockfish Creek and the filling in of the extensive trestlework at Battleboro. Contracts for the installation of brick and iron culverts had also been arranged.[2]

Improvements in the facilities at Wilmington had been ongoing during the 1850s. In 1854, the company completed a carpentry shop at the site measuring 166 feet by 31 feet that contained a stationary engine for driving saws, a planer and a tenoning machine. A stone wall was constructed between the inclined plane leading to the water and the yard above, and foundations had been prepared for a large shed at the company's wharf.[3] During 1855, at Wilmington, the company rebuilt the retaining wall near its warehouse, began filling in the marshes at the Cape Fear River, using 10,000 cubic feet of earth, to create a permanent wharf, and built a company hospital and quarters for slaves near the depot. New passenger depots were built at Wilmington and at Weldon, and the depot at Wilmington added a dining hall. The company invested in half the cost of a steamer, the *W. W. Harllee,* to ferry passengers across the Cape Fear to the Wilmington & Manchester Railroad.[4] A report given in the *Wilmington Journal* describes the new facility in detail. It is quite remarkable, considering the primitive accommodations afforded passengers in the early days of the railroad, to find modern conveniences such as steam heating, hot and cold running water, and gas lighting.

This view of the Wilmington Harbor from Point Peter on the east bank of the Cape Fear River, a detail from a larger drawing in *Gleason's Pictorial Drawing-Room Companion* of 1853, may provide clues to the appearance of the Wilmington depot site prior to the Civil War. If the artist's rendering is accurate, the Neoclassical building at the right (1) was Front Street Methodist Church. Front Street, being higher than Water Street, was supported by a retaining wall (2), above which one can see a horse drawn dray (3) followed by pedestrians approaching the bridge at the intersection with Red Cross Street. The long two-story building at left (4) is in the general area where the steamships of the railroad company docked and is probably the company warehouse. The structure above and behind it (5) on the level of Front Street may have been the company shops. If the drawing is accurate, the depot would have occupied Lots 2 through 5 on the Campbell Plot, or most of Block 245 on the Wilmington town plot. The shops would have been located in Block 246 (courtesy New Hanover Public Library, Robert M. Fales Collection).

The whole affair is some 280 by 80 feet, with abundant space on the South side for the several passenger trains and platforms for the passengers, while the North side is occupied by a neat bar-room, with all the "modern improvements"—a dining saloon 96 by 26 feet, capable of seating 200 persons—the victuals being kept warm by steam, and the dining room, and indeed, the whole establishment, warmed by the same agent. There is a gentleman's sitting-room, 40 × 26; ladies sitting-room, 20 × 26. Between the ladies' and gentlemen's sitting-room is the ticket office and agents room, and next to the ladies' sitting-room is the ladies' dressing-room, and several bath-rooms, with hot and cold water and shower baths. Next, again, we find the baggage room, the barber's shop and gentlemen's wash-room and baths. Of course, there are other indispensable conveniences not requisite to mention, the supply of water throughout is plentiful and of the best quality, with a good head. The whole establishment is lighted by gas. The kitchens are connected with the main building by a passage or corridor. By the improvement of the grade the passengers on landing from the boat go immediately into the cars instead of clambering up the hill as they used formerly to do under all weathers. The whole arrangement is neat, tasteful & convenient and does away with all occasion for clamor on the part of that most clamorous of all classes, the traveling community.[5]

Ascertaining the location and appearance of most of the antebellum structures at the Wilmington depot facility is difficult to do with certainty. There are few drawings and photographs of the depot from the 19th century, and nearly all show parts of the facility as it existed in the post–Civil War period. The line drawing of the Wilmington Harbor from *Gleason's Pictorial Drawing-Room Companion* of 1853, a portion of which appears opposite, shows a view of the town from Point Peter on the east bank of the Cape Fear River. Some structures depicted in this drawing are readily identifiable. One can see the Methodist Church (1) with its classical columns and pediment—without its belfry—located on North Front Street, the closest antebellum landmark to the railroad. Farther north (left) on the level of Front Street is what appears to be a hip-roof building (5) with a lantern (a structure fitted with windows to let in light). This would likely be the company shops. There appear to be at least two other buildings at this level. Below, there is a completely unfamiliar structure (4) at the Nutt Street level, two stories in height with sixteen columns and, from south to north, eleven visible windows on each story, an archway, and a section on the north side without visible windows. If the archway can be interpreted as opening to Hanover Street and the south corner was at the corner of Nutt at the base of the inclined plane, this would suggest that the rear of the building faced Front Street. If the rendering of the artist can be trusted, this building was likely the company warehouse. The warehouse is mentioned several times in Wilmington newspapers before and after the Civil War. In 1843, after the Great Fire, the *Wilmington Chronicle* notes that the company plans to add a second story to the building.[6] In 1868, Captain John F. Devine, the master machinist for the company, prepared plans for converting the old warehouse into offices.[7] S.L. Fremont, engineer and superintendent of the Wilmington & Weldon, presented a petition to the town in 1871 for putting down track along Nutt Street to establish a connection with the Wilmington, Charlotte, and Rutherford Railroad.[8] The old warehouse was torn down in late 1875.[9] After its destruction, new track added for the Wilmington, Columbia & Augusta Railroad cut through its massive foundations.[10] The turntable and the bridge over Fourth Street (Boney Bridge) mentioned in the 1860 stockholders report appears in an article from the *Wilmington Star* in early 1876. The old turntable, located adjacent to the train shed in the yard, was removed during a phase of new construction.[11]

There exists one undated photograph of the old company shop. Mechanics pose in front of a brick structure with at least four visible arched bays with three circular openings above and between each arch. The new shops were constructed in 1883. Another useful photograph was taken of the depot in the mid–1880s. It shows the antebellum stone retaining walls at the inclined plane,[12] the railroad dining hall, the uncovered iron bridge on Front Street, the train shed, and the new shops that were constructed in 1883. In the lower portion of the photograph, one can see a wood burning locomotive pushing a boxcar with the lettering of the Wilmington, Columbia & Augusta Railroad painted on its side. The lower story of the railroad dining hall is unusual with its corner wall extending beyond the surface of the south wall. The doorway on this side is four steps above ground level. The doorway at the top of the stairs on east side appears to be new construction, as does the brick added to the stone wall that serves as the foundation for the kitchen attached to the dining hall. The dining hall, appearing to be built in the Italianate style so popular in Wilmington during the 1850s, appears to be of later construction if the lower stories are the remains of the ancient warehouse. What remains exposed today are the odd masonry of the foundations below the kitchen, and the great retaining wall of the inclined plane. The 1860 stockholders report, however, mentions something completely at variance with the concept of an expansive warehouse facility. Here it is mentioned that the warehouse is too small, should be made of brick, and would be better used as a shed for lime and guano.[13] The map produced by Colonel William J. Twining, chief engineer of the Department of North Carolina following the capture of Wilmington in 1865, presents

This photograph of the mechanics of the shops of the Wilmington & Weldon Rail Road was taken before the new shops were constructed at Wilmington in 1883. The craftsmen of the shops not only repaired locomotives, cars, and rails, they also built several locomotives. The shops had a foundry, a boiler shop, a coppersmith shop, a blacksmith shop, a car shop, a finishing shop, a carpenter shop, and a paint shop in the years before the Civil War. The stockholders report of 1856 list provides a complete inventory of materials and tools for each shop. *See* Wilmington & Weldon Rail Road Company, *Proceedings of the Stockholders of the Wilmington & Weldon R. R. Co., at their Twenty-First Annual Meeting held at Wilmington, North Carolina, November 13, 1856; with the Reports of the President and Directors, and the Engineer and Superintendent* (Wilmington: Thomas Loring, 1856), 17–20 (courtesy New Hanover Public Library, Robert M. Fales Collection).

other problems. A large structure is shown extending from Red Cross Street to the bridge at Front Street, and another structure extends from the other side of the bridge to Hanover Street and then east to the corner of Nutt Street. The entire structure depicted on the map might well be a continuation of the retaining wall.[14]

The changing of the physical landscape from the time the railroad acquired the property continuing on into the present is not the type of landscape archaeologists usually encounter.[15] Normally, one might expect to dig down through the layers of history. At the Wilmington Depot site,

some of the oldest artifacts have been found where the land has been filled. An old link pin coupler was found during construction of the Coastline Convention Center near the 1900 ACL Freight Office. This artifact is now preserved in the Wilmington Railroad Museum. More recently, in 2009, during excavation for a new parking deck for Cape Fear Community College east of the bridge on Front Street — the location of the "unsightly

The Depot Site at Wilmington

The antebellum retaining wall in the inclined plane is the oldest known construction at the Wilmington depot site that can be readily associated with a primary source. This photograph, taken in November 2010, shows sections of concrete culvert that will be used in the latest construction on site. The former inclined plane was trenched to install drainage.

Opposite top: This photograph is the earliest known of the depot at Wilmington. It was taken sometime between 1883, when the new shops that appear here were completed, and 1889, when the iron bridge first appeared in the Sanborn Fire Insurance Maps. The passenger shed in this photograph appears to have been built in 1876, and the iron bridge in 1880. The floor under the railroad dining hall on the left side of the photograph shows evidence of being part of an earlier structure, and the stone retaining walls are mentioned in the 1854 stockholders report. *See The Wilmington Journal,* November 13, 1854 (courtesy New Hanover Public Library, Robert M. Fales Collection).

Opposite bottom: The section of wall once supported part of the railroad dining hall. It appears that brick was added to the stone wall to serve as a foundation for its construction. This photograph was taken in November 2000. The wall can still be seen on the north side of the Cape Fear Community College Nutt Street parking deck.

miasma-breeding marsh"—construction workers unearthed a section of strap-iron still spiked to its wooden rail. It has now been preserved and mounted for display at the museum. This also has been preserved by staff of the Wilmington Railroad Museum, and is now on display.

Today, the site of the railroad facilities at Wilmington has entered a new period of usage as new buildings are constructed for the expanding campus of Cape Fear Community College. Recent excavation has exposed once buried sections of the monumental stone walls that the railroad built near Hanover Street. There is, however, a limit to what can be known from a site with such a history rooted in change. At the beginning of the era of the Wilmington & Raleigh Rail Road, the company acquired agricultural land at the north end of town for its facilities. Originally, they altered only where they built facilities and put down track. A traveler, before the construction of the inclined plane in 1843, descended from the railroad track located on the bluff down a flight of stairs to a boardwalk over the marsh to the steamboats at the company docks. After 1843, the trains came down through the inclined plane to the depot on Nutt Street. The area on the bluff was the location for the shops. By the mid–1850s, the railroad had commenced its first efforts to fill the marshland at Nutt Street, and expand its land fronting the river. Its depot facilities were becoming more modern with gas light, hot and cold running water, and a dining hall for passengers. On the eve of the Civil War, shops and offices, (and perhaps the location of the company hospital and barracks for slaves)

Opposite top: Mark Koenig, executive director of the Wilmington Railroad Museum, is shown with a section of strap-iron rail mounted on a reproduction of a wooden rail. The strap-iron, dating to early history of the Wilmington & Raleigh Rail Road, was recovered during excavation for the Cape Fear Community College Nutt Street parking deck. The iron rail was recovered with its spikes intact. Before the construction commenced on the former depot site, Mr. Koenig and the maintenance department of the college recovered a considerable number of significant artifacts from different periods in the history of the railroad. These are now part of the museum's collection.

Opposite bottom: Construction in November 2010 near the bridge at Third Street in Wilmington exposed the massive stone walls that the railroad constructed on the north side of Block 247 separating its facilities from Hanover Street. The section of the wall closest to Third Street was once topped by another wall of brick with closed-in window openings. Building upon the stone wall which was already there, the Wilmington & Weldon built two workshops for constructing cars during the latter decades of the nineteenth century in this corner of the block.

were likely located on the bluff, yet this can only be inferred by the track layout on historic maps and the physical dimensions given in the stockholder reports. At the end of the era of the Wilmington & Raleigh Rail Road, passengers still had to take the ferry across the river if they wanted to continue south on the Wilmington & Manchester Rail Road.

The transformation of the facilities and the physical landscape assumes a larger scale during the 1870s. The Wilmington & Weldon and the Wilmington, Columbia, and Augusta constructed a new brick Union Station at Eight Street. Doors, windows, wainscoting, and other materials were salvaged from the old Union Depot on Nutt Street of the new facilitiy.[16] In 1876, a new passenger shed was built at Front Street near the railroad office and shops. The grade from the Union Depot to the Cape Fear River was reduced from 106 feet per mile to 52 feet per mile, the old depot on Nutt Street was removed, and waterfront property of the company was extended using the dirt from the grading.[17] By November of 1880, the iron bridge over the ravine on Front Street was completed to connect to the passenger depot on the north side. A new wood working shop was nearing completion, and a roundhouse, built on the former site of the old wood work shop, was expected to be completed by the summer.[18] It follows that near all of the structures depicted in the first photograph of the depot are from the post Civil War period. The only exception might be the buttressed granite retaining wall at the ravine. The only evidence supporting that conclusion is found in the documents that mention a wall being built there during the mid–1850s, and the fact that granite like it was quarried at a site near Elm City on the line of the railroad during the same period. The granite used in these walls is different from the ruin of granite wall remaining at other locations on the site.

The exact appearance of any part of the depot site and facilities of railroad at Wilmington, at any point prior 1880, remains speculative. One is left with the prospect of studying artifacts that appear from time to time, and attempting to associate them with the periods of significance in the history of the railroads of Wilmington.

Chapter Notes

Abbreviations

NCSA The North Carolina State Archives

NHCL The collection housed in the North Carolina Room located in the New Hanover County Library at 201 Chestnut Street, Wilmington, North Carolina 28401

RSUSA *Records of the States of the United States of America: North Carolina [microform]: A Microfilm Compilation Prepared by the Library of Congress in Association with the University of North Carolina ... Under the Direction of William Sumner Jenkins* (Washington, DC: Library of Congress Photoduplication Service, 1949).

SLNC State Library of North Carolina, Government and Heritage Library

UNCCH The North Carolina Collection, housed in Louis Round Wilson Library at the University of North Carolina at Chapel Hill

UNCW Special Collections, housed in William Madison Randall Library at the University of North Carolina at Wilmington

WRMC Wilmington Railroad Museum Collection

Introduction

1. The term "Great Mail" refers to the primary route of mail going in a particular direction. It is analogous to the trunk of a tree with many branches, or a river with many tributaries.

2. The most authoritative work on railroad development in North Carolina is *A State Movement in Railroad Development* by Cecil K. Brown. This work, published in 1928, does not contain enough detail on the origin or early history of the Wilmington & Raleigh Rail Road. *Chronicles of the Cape Fear River, 1660–1916* by James Sprunt, published in 1916, rarely cites sources and contains the recollection of local residents. While his narrative is rich in detail,

the greater context is often obscured by local pride.

3. Wilmington & Weldon Rail Road Company, *Proceedings of the Stockholders of the Wilmington & Weldon Rail Road Co. at their Twentieth Annual Meeting, held at Wilmington, North Carolina, November 9th. 1855* (Wilmington, NC: Thomas Loring, 1855), 51, New Hanover County Library, North Carolina Room (abbreviated hereafter as NHCL), NC 385 W, 1855.

> Article 2 of *An Act Concerning the Wilmington and Raleigh Rail Road Company*, ratified by the North Carolina General Assembly on February 14, 1855, the corporate name of the company to be changed to the Wilmington & Weldon Railroad Company.

4. John Owen, *Message of His Excellency John Owen, to the General Assembly of North Carolina*, (Raleigh: Lawrence & Lemay, 1829), 3–5, in Records of the States of the United States of American: North Carolina [microform]: A Microfilm Compilation Prepared by the Library of Congress in Association with the University of North Carolina ... Under the Direction of William Sumner Jenkins, Washington, DC: Library of Congress Photoduplication Service, 1949 (abbreviated hereafter as RSUSA), N.C. D. 1, Reel 1, Unit 1.

5. North Carolina, *The Revised Statutes of the State of North Carolina passed by the General Assembly at the Session of 1836–37* (Raleigh: Turner and Hughes, 1837), 349–352, NHCL, NC 348.756 N.

Chapter I

1. "On the Schemes for Rail Roads in North Carolina," *Farmers' Register* (April 1836), 766.

2. "Desultory Remarks on Rail Roads, and Other Public Improvements," *Farmers' Register* (March 1836), 684–685.

3. "On the Schemes for Rail Roads in North Carolina," Ibid., 766–767.

4. "Rail Road in North Carolina," *Farmers' Register* (May 1836), 35–38.

5. United States, *Railroads—Atlantic to the Mississippi* (Washington, DC: 23rd Congress, 1835), 51–52.

6. "On the Rail Roads of North Carolina, and the South Generally," *Farmers'* Register (July 1836), 140–141; "On the Rail-Roads of North Carolina, and the South Generally," *Farmers' Register* (October 1836), 342–343.

7. *Raleigh Register*, January 12, 1827, April 10, 1827.

8. Peter C. Stewart, "Railroads and Urban Rivalries in Antebellum Eastern Virginia," *Virginia Magazine of History and Biography* 81 (1973), 3–22.

9. John L. Larson, "'Bind the Republic Together': The National Union and the Struggle for a System of Internal Improvements," *The Journal of American History* 74, No. 2 (September 1987), 363–387. The debates surrounding the Bonus Bill of 1817 records the exhaustive effort on the part of Congressmen John C. Calhoun and Henry Clay to seek the application of federal funds for road and canal improvements. Albert Gallatin had proposed a national system of roads and canals in his *Report of the Secretary of the Treasury on the Subject of Roads and Canals* in 1808. Calhoun and Clay had hoped to see this plan put into action. As the bill made its way through Congress, it was weakened by amendments that compromised its design — shifting control of such projects away from the federal government and distributing funds to the states according to population. President James Madison vetoed the bill. The future of a national system of internal improvements was curtailed, and the responsibility fell upon the states to take up their own programs of public works. The federal government, with the exception of projects on national interest, was relegated to the role of providing technical support.

10. Richard L. Morton, "The Virginia State Debt and Internal Improvements, 1820–38," *The Journal of Political Economy* 25, No. 4 (April 1917), 343, 349, 356–359, 361–362, 366.

11. Robert D.W. Conner, *Antebellum Builders of North Carolina*, (Greensboro, NC: North Carolina College for Women, 1923), 31; North Carolina, *Report of the Committee on Inland Navigation, Submitted to the Legislature of North Carolina, November 30, by Archibald D. Murphey, Their Chairman* (Raleigh: Thomas Henderson, 1815), 7, RSUSA, N.C. D. 25i, Reel 1, Unit 1.; North Carolina, *Mr. Murphey's Report to the Legislature of North-Carolina on Inland Navigation, December 1816* (Raleigh: Thomas Henderson, 1818), 18. RSUSA, N.C. D. 25i, Reel 1, Unit 1.

12. Archibald D. Murphey, *Memoir of the Internal Improvements Contemplated by the Legislature of North Carolina and on the Resources and Finances of the State* (Raleigh: J. Gales, 1819), 17–19, RSUSA, N.C. D. 25i, Reel 1, Unit 1.

13. North Carolina, *Report of Sundry Surveys, Made by Hamilton Fulton Esq. State Engineer, Agreeably to Certain Instructions from Judge Murphey, Chairman &c. and Submitted to the*

General Assembly, at Their Session in 1819, (Raleigh: Thomas Henderson, 1819), 5, 8, 21–32, 42–44, 49, RSUSA, N.C. D. 25i, Reel 1, Unit 1.

14. North Carolina, *Annual Report of the Board of Public Improvements of North-Carolina to the General Assembly, November 27, 1820; together with Mr. Fulton's Reports to the Board, On the Public Works Projected and Carrying on Throughout the State During the Present Year*, (Raleigh: J. Gales, 1820), 1–37, University of North Carolina at Wilmington, William Madison Randall Library, Special Collections (abbreviated hereafter as UNCW), F258.N86, 1820.

15. North Carolina, *Annual Report of the Board of Public Improvements of North-Carolina, to the General Assembly, November 26, 1821; together with Mr. Fulton's Reports to the Board, and Other Papers in Relation to the Improvement of the State* (Raleigh: J. Gales, 1821), xix–xxiii, 13–29, 38–41, 62–67, UNCW, F258.N86, 1821.

16. "Internal Improvements of North Carolina," *North American Review and Miscellaneous Journal*, 1821, 16–37.

17. James C. Burke, "Antebellum Plans for Reopening Roanoke Inlet," *The North Carolina Geographer* 17 (2009–2010), 17–25.

18. Alan D. Watson, *Internal Improvements in Antebellum North Carolina* (Raleigh: Office of Archives and History, North Carolina Department of Cultural Resources, 2002), 81–85.

19. John Owen, *Message of His Excellency John Owen, to the General Assembly of North Carolina* (Raleigh: Lawrence and Lemay, 1829), 4, RSUSA N.C. D.1, Reel 1, Unit 1; Cecil K. Brown, *A State Movement in Railroad Development* (Chapel Hill: University of North Carolina Press, 1928), 12–13.

20. William S. Price, Jr., "Nathaniel Macon, Antifederalist," *North Carolina Historical Review* 81, No. 3 (July 2004), 297, 290–291; William S. Price, Jr., "Nathaniel Macon, Planter," *North Carolina Historical Review* 78, No. 2 (April 2001), 209–210; Thomas E. Jeffery, Jr., "Internal Improvements and Political Parties in Antebellum North Carolina," *North Carolina Historical Review* 55, No. 2 (April 1978), 114; Herbert S. Turner, *The Dreamer, Archibald DeBow Murphey, 1777–1832*, (Verona, VA: McClure, 1971), 69; William E. Dodd, *The Life of Nathaniel Macon* (Raleigh, NC: Edwards and Broughton, 1903), 388–309).

21. Harry R. Merrens, *Colonial North Carolina in the Eighteenth Century: A Study in Historical Geography* (Chapel Hill: University of North Carolina Press, 1964), 19–31.

22. North Carolina (1821), 22–23.
23. North Carolina (1820), 2.
24. North Carolina, *Annual Report of the Board for Int'l Improvements, November 28, 1829* (Raleigh, NC: Lawrence and Lemay, 1829). RSUSA N.C. D.1, Reel 1, Unit 1.

25. Roanoke Navigation Company, "Report on the Progress and Present Condition of the Affairs of the Roanoke Navigation Company," *Annual Report of the Board of Internal Improvement* (Raleigh, NC: Lawrence and Lemay, 1831). RSUSA N.C. D.1, Reel 1, Unit 2.

26. Charles L. Coon, *The Beginnings of Public Education in North Carolina* (Raleigh, N.C.: Edwards and Broughton, 1908), 539.

27. North Carolina, (1821), xx–xxviii.
28. Roanoke Navigation Company (1831), 6.

29. "Progress and Conditions of the Petersburg and Roanoke Rail Road," *Farmers' Register*, May 1834, 758; "To the Stockholder of the Petersburg Rail Road Company," *Farmers' Register*, May 1834, 758–759.

30. "Domestic," *Richmond Enquirer*, September 3, 1833, in *America's Historic Newspapers, 2004*. NewsBank and/or the American Antiquarian Society.

31. *The Newport Mercury*, December 28, 1833, in *America's Historic Newspapers, 2004*. NewsBank and/or the American Antiquarian Society.

32. "Rail Roads in the South," *New-Hampshire Gazette* (Portsmouth), August 20, 1833, in *America's Historic Newspapers, 2004*. NewsBank and/or the American Antiquarian Society.

33. *Letter Book of Governor David L. Swain* (1834), 264–265, North Carolina State Archives, G.L.B. 30.

34. "Virginia Legislature," *Richmond Enquirer*, January 21, 1834.

35: "Virginia Legislature," *Richmond Enquirer*, January 28, 1834.

36. "Rail-Road from Fayetteville and Salisbury, N.C. to Norfolk," *The Richmond Enquirer*, September 1, 1829.

37. James Sprunt, *Tales and Traditions of the Lower Cape Fear, 1661–1896* (Wilmington, NC: LeGwin Brothers, 1896), xlvi–li.

38. William P. Cumming, *North Carolina in Maps* (Raleigh: Division of Archives and History, North Carolina Department of Cultural Resources, 1966), 28–29.

39. Frederick L. Olmsted, *A Journey in the Seaboard Slave States with Remarks on Their Economy* (New York: Mason Brothers, 1861), 322–332, UNCW, F213. O523, 1861; William P. Cumming, Plate X, Plate XIII.

These locations appear on the Mac Rae-Brazier Map of 1833 and the United States Coast Survey Map of North Carolina of 1865 (Cumming, 1955, Plate X; Plate XIII). Banks and Barkclaysville are on the modern North Carolina roads SSR 1006 followed by SSR 1769, together named the "Old State Road." The Old Stage Road begins outside Raleigh on US 401, and continues to Erwin, where it joins SR 217.

40. Frederick L. Olmsted, 308–369. Olmsted describes the transition between the coastal plain soils and the Piedmont soils, and the crops associated with each, between Weldon and (Old) Gaston on the roads following the south bank of the Roanoke. His experience with the poor operation of the stagecoach between Weldon and Gaston, the inadequate upkeep of the roads, and inaccurate scheduling of the train from Raleigh to Gaston belie serious organizational problems between the different railroads providing a "through ticket" south. In addition, Olmsted notes that the Raleigh & Gaston Rail Road had new "U" iron rails, but its cars were "old, dirty, and with dilapidated and moth-eaten furniture"; and the intervening agricultural land between Gaston and Raleigh appear "unproductive." Outside Raleigh, Olmsted examined cornfields and spoke with a farmer who considered twenty-five bushels (per acre) of corn a large crop, but the average crop was about fifteen bushels. The farmer stated that it cost too much to take the corn to market. Olmsted had been on foot ahead of the stage, and had not yet walked ten miles south of Raleigh. His observations on the road from Raleigh to Fayetteville are of particular interest. Olmsted mentions two places along the route that help identify his route, Bank's Plantations and Mrs. Barkley's. At Mrs. Barkley's, he observed turpentine and rosin production. It is likely, owing to fact that the Cape Fear River was about half the distance from the Barkley farm than Raleigh, the output of these works would have eventually found their market at Fayetteville (then downriver to Wilmington), rather than the Petersburg market. The last ten miles of the journey were on a plank road. Olmsted witnessed the arrival of wagons of produce from the western counties during his visit at Fayetteville, and notes that some had come from as far away as the Blue Ridge. These wagons, drawn by as many as six horses, could hold a load of about seventy-five bushels of grain. The wagons also carried cotton. He notes that the plank roads are a significant improvement in safety and efficiency in the transport of produce, and suggests that the region's farmers might prefer this mode to railroads. However, he cites a story he heard from a farmer near Raleigh who sold his grain for a higher price by sending it to Petersburg by train rather than selling it locally; and he mentions both the efforts to build a railroad from Fayetteville to the coal field in Chatham County, and the town's somewhat wasteful investment of $100,000 in 1820 to make the upper Cape Fear fit for navigation. When he departs Fayetteville by steamboat for Wilmington, he observes that the greater portion of the freight that was taken downriver to the port was turpentine.

41. "Railroad from Wilmington to the West," *Wilmington Journal,* June 16, 1854: "We had an opportunity recently of hearing from one of the most liberal and intelligent merchants which that or any other community can boast of, that he favors a rail road from Wilmington to Fayetteville to connect with our Western Road to the Deep River Coal Mines, and thence to the N.C. Road at the Eastern terminus of the Western extension. And we learn that a correspondence has been going on between himself and a gentleman here on the subject. And further, we understand from the paragraph which we quoted in our last from the Wilmington Journal, that some such views were presented to the late meeting in that town to consider of the proposed road to Charlotte. These facts induce us to say a few words, which in their absence we should consider wasted, in support of the connection via Fayetteville. There was a time when we thought the idea of a rail road from Wilmington to Fayetteville was supremely ridiculous. That was when no *successful* rail road existed in the State, and when the experiment of running a rail road on the banks of a navigable stream had not even been made, much less shown to be eminently successful; and when our means could be better employed than opening a channel where Nature had already placed one which answered the purpose tolerable well, to say the least. But that time is past."

42. "For the Journal," *Wilmington Journal,* July 3, 1854: "It seems to me that there are two important sections of North Carolina to be *tapped* by local Roads, in the first instance; but one of these local Roads will become a great line from East to West. That is, the region of the country from Fayetteville, West, through the coal and iron counties of Moore and Chatham, to Salisbury, requires at this moment a local Road to Wilmington, through Fayetteville."

43. North Carolina, *The Report of the Committee on Int. Improvements on the Cape Fear and*

Deep River Navigation Company (Raleigh, NC: W.W. Holden, Printer to the State, 1855), 7, NHCL. "We cannot omit to mention, that from testimony before us, that a fatal blow will be given to these vast resources, should the Bill now before us, or some other suitable measure of relief, be rejected by the present General Assembly, for we are assured by Mr. McLane, that he is under express orders from his employers, to remove the force and machinery of every kind, under his charge, now on Deep River, and to abandon the coal field, if the Legislature refuse to grant the necessary relief, inasmuch as water transportation is so much cheaper and more desirable for coal than Railroads, and because no one Railroad, nor any number that are likely to be built, will be competent to carry off the coal that is expected to be taken out, and further, that another company, now ready to commence shipping coal, has suspended operations, until further aid is granted to the River."

44. *Ibid.*, 1, 6–7.

45. "Mineral Resources of North Carolina; Description of the Oil and Iron Works of the Deep River Coal and Iron Company— Process of Obtaining Oil— Calcining— Black Band Ore— Estimate of the Quantities of Coal, Iron Ore and Oil-Bearing Slate Stone— Value of the Products and Cost of Production— Expenditures of the Company— Dissolution, &c., &c.," *The New York Times,* December 22, 1860.

46. North Carolina (1821), 30–32.

47. Edward B. Dudley, *Edward B. Dudley Letter Book, 1837–1840,* 41–45, (Raleigh: North Carolina State Archives), G.L.B. 32. .

48. Edward J. Taaffe, Richard L. Morrill, Peter R. Gould, "Transport Expansion in Underdeveloped Countries: A Comparative Analysis," *Geographical Review* 53, No. 4. (October 1963), 503–529.

49. Richard L. Morton (1917), 362, 366.

Chapter II

1. Joseph Caldwell, *The Numbers of Carlton, Addresses to the People of North Carolina, on a Central Rail-Road Through the State. The Rights of Freemen is an Open Trade* (New York: G. Long, 1828), 21–23, 41–47, UNCCH, C385 C28

2. James Mebane and Dennis Heartt, *Railroad Meeting* (Hillsborough, NC: D. Heartt, 1828), 2–8. UNCCH, Cp385 R15r.

3. John Owen. *Message of His Excellency John Owen, to the General Assembly of North Carolina,* (Raleigh: Lawrence and Lemay, 1829), 11. RSUSA N.C. D.1, Reel 1, Unit 1.

4. *Carolina Observer,* January 13, 1830, January 6, 13, March 3, 17, 1831; *Peoples Press and Wilmington Advertiser,* May 21, 1834.

5. *Carolina Observer,* May 29, June 7, 1831; David L. Swain, *Early Times in Raleigh* (Raleigh, NC: Walters, Hughes and Company, 1867), 9, 37, UNCW, F264.R1 S9, 1867.

6. John C. Cavanaugh, *Decision at Fayetteville: The North Carolina Ratification Convention and General Assembly of 1789* (Raleigh: Division of Archives and History, North Carolina Department of Cultural Resources, 1989), 4.

7. Joseph H. Schauinger, *William Gaston, Carolinian* (Milwaukee, WI: Bruce, 1949), 135–137.

8. Schauinger, 131–133; North Carolina, *Memorial of the Citizens of Orange County on the Subject of a Central Rail Road* (Raleigh, N.C.: Lawrence and Lemay, 1831). RSUSA, N.C. D.1, Reel 1, Unit 2.

9. *Carolina Observer,* June 28, August 24, December 7, 14, 21, 23, 1831, January 4, 1832; *The Peoples Press and Wilmington Advertiser,* May 1, 29, 1833; Cecil K. Brown, *A State Movement in Railroad Development* (Chapel Hill: University of North Carolina Press, 1928), 17.

10. *The Peoples Press and Wilmington Advertiser,* May 8, 13, 22, 29, 1833.

11. North Carolina, *Journal of the Senate* (Raleigh: Lawrence and Lemay, 1833), 100, North Carolina State Library (abbreviated hereafter as NHCL), Y1, 1:J86; North Carolina, *Journal of the House of Commons* (Raleigh: Lawrence and Lemay, 1833), 141, SLNC, Y1, 1:J86; *Raleigh Register,* May 7, 1833, May 14, 1833, June 11, 1833; Alan D. Watson, *Wilmington, North Carolina, to 1861* (Jefferson, NC: McFarland, 2003), 221.

12. North Carolina, *Memorial of the Convention Upon the Subject of Internal Improvements, November 1833, to the General Assembly of North Carolina* (Raleigh: Lawrence and Lemay, 1833), 4. RSUSA, N.C. D.1, Reel 1, Unit 2.

13. *Ibid.*

14. North Carolina, *Report of the Joint Select Committee of Internal Improvements,* (Raleigh: Lawrence and Lemay, 1833). RSUSA, N.C. D.1, Reel 1, Unit 2.

15. North Carolina, *Report of the Board of Internal Improvements, 1833,* (Raleigh: Lawrence and Lemay, 1833). RSUSA, N.C. D.1, Reel 1, Unit 2.

16. North Carolina, *Report of the Committee on Internal Improvements* (Lawrence and Lemay, 1833). RSUSA, N.C. D.1, Reel 1, Unit 2.

17. Charles L. Coon, *The Beginnings of Public Education in North Carolina* (Raleigh, NC: Edwards and Broughton, 1908), 641.

18. North Carolina, *Journal of the Senate* (Raleigh: North Carolina Legislature, 1834), 70, 73, 75, 81, 97, 99, 105, SLNC, Y1, 1:J86; *Raleigh Register*, November 17, 24, 1833, March 25, 1834.
19. North Carolina, *Journal of the Senate* (1833), 111, 129, 131; North Carolina, *Journal of the Senate* (1834), 114–115, SLNC, Y1, 1:J86.
20. Brown, 27.
21. North Carolina, *Journal of the Senate* (Raleigh: North Carolina Legislature, 1833), 29, SLNC, Y1, 1:J86.
22. Swain (1867), 34–37.
23. "Memoranda and Scraps from a Traveler's Note Book," *Farmers' Register*, (January 1834), 467.
24. *The Peoples Press and Wilmington Advertiser*, May 29, 1833.
25. *Raleigh Register*, June 11, 1833.
26. *Raleigh Register*, June 25, 1833; *The Peoples Press and Wilmington Advertiser*, June 26, 1833.
27. Brown, 31; James Sprunt, *Chronicles of the Cape Fear River, 1660–1916* (Raleigh, NC: Edwards and Broughton, 1916), 249–250; New Hanover County, North Carolina, *Book Y,* (Wilmington: New Hanover County Register of Deeds, 1840), 210.
28. *Raleigh Register*, July 16, 1833.
29. *Richmond Enquirer*, August 16, 1833; *Raleigh Register*, July 30, August 13, September 3, 17, December 31, 1833, January 7, 1834.
30. *The Peoples Press and Wilmington Advertiser*, May 14, 1834.
31. *Raleigh Register*, July 15, August 12, September 16, 1834.
32. North Carolina, *Report of the Board of Internal Improvements of North Carolina, Transmitted by the Governor to the General Assembly, December 10, 1834* (Raleigh: Philo White, 1834), 3–4. RSUS N.C. D.1, Reel 1, Unit 2. ; *The Peoples Press and Wilmington Advertiser*, December 17, 1834; *Raleigh Register*, January 13, 1835.
33. Brown, 27, 31–32.
34. Sprunt, 150.
35. *Wilmington Chronicle*, November 11, 1840.
36. "Letter from Charles F. Osborne to Edward B. Dudley dated January 21, 1836," *Edward C. Dudley Papers*, (1836), Raleigh: North Carolina State Archives, PC.464.1. Mr. Osborne appears to have little faith in the ability or efficiency of the Weldon Toll Bridge Company, and he questions the notion of placing a bridge at Weldon. This excerpt from the letter was transcribed for the author from a photocopy by Debra J. Justin:

Gaston is 16 miles above Weldon — a favorable point for a move across the Roanoke — costing about half as much as a move at Weldon. When, certain of business move to stand. It is doubtful whether a bridge can ever be erected at Weldon to stand the heavy freshets at Roanoke. At Gaston there is *no* draw. We shall complete the bridge at Gaston in 6 months. They have been at work at the Weldon move for more than 12 months ... 2 years now I am informed to finish it, if they ever finish it.— O.

37. "Letter from Charles F. Osborne to Edward B. Dudley dated March 1, 1836," *Edward C. Dudley Papers* (1836), Raleigh: North Carolina State Archives, PC.464.1. Mr. Osborne mentions provisions for a connection included in the amended charter of the Roanoke & Raleigh Rail Road of 1835.
38. *The Peoples Press*, March 6, 1833; *Raleigh Register*, August 13, November 17, December 24, 1833; United States, *Wilmington & W.R. Co. v. Alsbrook, Sheriff* (United States Supreme Court, December 5, 1892): 146 U.S. 279.
39. Walter Gwynn, *Report of Walter Gwynn, Esq. Engineer, to the President and Directors of the Portsmouth and Roanoke Rail Road Company,* (Norfolk, VA: T. G. Broughton, 1833), 10, UNCW, MS248/6/3.
40. "New York Farmer," *10, 7, APS Online 190,* 29 May 1837.
41. *Raleigh Register*, December 6, 29, 1835.
42. *Raleigh Register*, December 3, 1835; Brown, 45.
43. "The Raleigh and Gaston Rail Road," *Farmers' Register* (March 1836), 652.
44. "Second Annual Report of the Raleigh and Gaston Rail Road Company," *Farmers' Register* (March 1838), 740, 742; Edward A. Wyatt, "Rise of Industry in Ante-Bellum Petersburg," *William and Mary Quarterly Historical Magazine* 2.17 (January 1937), 21–22, 25n.
45. "Proceedings of the Petersburg Rail Road Company," *Farmers' Register* (April 1836), 762.
46. *Richmond Enquirer*, March 13, 1831.
47. *Raleigh Register*, January 3, 17, 1837, February 7, 14, 28, 1837.
48. *Raleigh Register*, May 2, 1837, July 31, 1837, September 4, October 23, 30, 1837; *Wilmington Advertiser*, November 10, 1837.
49. "Second Annual Report of the Raleigh and Gaston Rail Road Company," *Farmers' Register* (March 1838), 740–743.
50. *The American Farmer, and Spirit of the Agricultural Journals of the Day* (July 31, 1839), 78; Brown, 53–43; North Carolina, *Laws of the State of North Carolina Passed by the General*

Assembly at the Session 1844–45, (Raleigh: Thomas J. Lemay, 1845), 96–102, NHCL, NC 348.756 N

51. *The Farmers' Register,* March 1838, 740, 742; Charles F.M. Garnett, "Raleigh and Gaston Rail-Road," *Farmers' Register* (July 1839), 388.

52. Brown, 46, 55.

53. United States, *Railroad and Steamboat Mail Lines* (Washington, DC: Twenty-eighth Congress, Document 105, 1845), 1–7.

54. United States, *The Memorial of Many Inhabitants of the City of Charleston Praying that the Southern Mail be Carried by Way of Halifax and Wilmington* (Washington, DC: Twenty-fifth Congress, Document 184, 1838); United States, *Petition of the Citizens of Cheraw,* (Washington, DC: Twenty-fifth Congress, Document 246, 1838); United States, *Petition of the Citizens of Camden* (Washington, DC: Twenty-fifth Congress, Document 259, 1838); United States, *Memorial of John Bryce and 212 Others, Inhabitants of Columbia, S.C., and Vicinity, Remonstrating Against the Removal of the Great Southern Mail Route,* (Washington, DC: Twenty-fifth Congress, Document 271, 1838).

55. Brown, 27.

56. United States, *Memorial of the Petersburg Railroad Company, Praying the Payment of a Sum of Money Withheld from Them, Under their Contract for the Transportation of the Mail,* (Washington, DC: Twenty-fifth Congress, Document 33, 1838); United States, *In the Senate of the United States* (Washington, DC: Twenty-fifth Congress, Document 132, 1839).

57. "Extracts from the Report of Walter Gwynn, Esq., Engineer, to the President and Directors of the Wilmington and Raleigh Rail Road Company," *Farmers' Register,* (October 1836), 348.

58. *Ibid.,* 349–350.

59. Walter M. Clark, *History of the Raleigh & Gaston Railroad Company, Including All Acts of the General Assembly of North Carolina Thereto* (Raleigh, NC: The Raleigh News Steam Job Print, 1877), 28, UNCCH, Cp385.1 R16c.

Chapter III

1. *Wilmington Advertiser,* May 5, 1837.
2. James D. Dilts, *The Great Road: The Building of the Baltimore & Ohio, the Nation's First Railroad, 1828–1855* (Stanford, CA: Stanford University Press, 1993), 63–65.
3. *Raleigh Register,* October 2, 1833.
4. *Wilmington Advertiser,* April 22, May 27, 1836.
5. *Raleigh Register,* July 5, 1836.
6. "Report of Walter Gwynn, Esq., Engineer, to the President and Directors of the Wilmington and Raleigh Rail Road Company," *Farmers' Register* (October 1836), 348–349.
7. *Wilmington Advertiser,* May 18, 1838.
8. Cecil K. Brown, *A State Movement in Railroad Development* (Chapel Hill: University of North Carolina Press, 1928), 33.
9. *Raleigh Register,* November 29, 1836: "From a Report made to the meeting, it appears that about 30 miles of the Road have been located, and 25 put under contract. The contracts, so far, have fallen within the estimates of the Engineer. Six hundred tons of Iron, spikes &c., two Locomotives, and Wheels and Axles for 50 Cars, have been ordered from England deliverable in March next."
10. *Carolina Observer,* January 26, March 9, 1837; *Wilmington Advertiser,* April 17, 1837.
11. *Wilmington Advertiser,* May 5, November 10, 1837.
12. *Raleigh Register,* December 5, 1837; *Wilmington Advertiser,* January 12, March 2, 1838; Burton Alva Konkle, *John Motley Morehead and the Development of North Carolina, 1796–1866* (Philadelphia, PA: William J. Campbell, 1922), 182.
13. *Raleigh Register,* April 6, 1838.
14. *Wilmington Advertiser,* May 4, 18, October 19, December 21, 1838.
15. *Wilmington Advertiser,* December 21, 1838, January 11, February 11, March 8, 1839.
16. *Wilmington Advertiser,* May 10, May 17, May 24, August 23, October 4, 1839.
17. *Wilmington Advertiser,* September 27, October 4, October 11, November 15, 1839.
18. *Wilmington Advertiser,* January 3, 1840.
19. *Wilmington Chronicle,* April 15, 1840; James Sprunt, *Chronicles of the Cape Fear River, 1660–1916* (Raleigh, NC: Edwards and Broughton, 1916), 150; Konkle, 200n.
20. North Carolina, "Fifth Annual Report of the President and Directors of the Wilmington & Raleigh Rail Road Company," *Report of the Board of Internal Improvements to the General Assembly,* Document No. 16 (Raleigh, NC: Thomas Loring, 1840), Section A, RSUSA, N.C. D.1, Reel 1, Unit 5. The following statement of expenses was prepared by James S. Green, treasurer of the Wilmington & Raleigh Rail Road, for their annual report to the Board of Internal Improvement in 1840. The figures, current to May 1, 1840, included:

Survey and location of road, $18,879.27, Land damages, $16,262.60, Excavation and Embankment, $346,330.83, Rails, Sills and Knees,$244,330.83, Bridges and Truss work, $166,961.16, Iron, Spikes & Splicing plates, $257,145.38, Superstructure, $127,712.92, Depots, Turn Outs & Water, Stations on the Line, $22,166.17, Machine Shop & Ware Houses and Wharf at Wilmington, $56,691.51, Shop, &c. at Weldon, $2,911.06, Engines, coaches and cars, $170,815.21, Mathematical instruments, $794.61, Engineering expenses, $58,867.25, Printing, and Advertising for Instalments on Stock &c., $1,198.50, Office Expenses, (Rent, Fuel, Stationary &c.) $1,584.16, Salaries to Officers and Clerks, $18,795.84, Interest on Loans &c., $27,191.01, Discount on English loan, $36,912.91, Contingent Expenses, (Postages, Commissions, Agents, &c.) $8,930.63, Halifax & Weldon Rail Road, $54,622.14.

21. *Ibid.*, Section A.

22. R.P. Bridgens and P. Allen, *An Original Map of the City of Charleston, South Carolina* (Hayden Brother and Company, 1852); A.H. Colton, *The City of Charleston, South Carolina* (New York: A.H. Colton, 1855).

23. *Wilmington Advertiser,* May 5, 1837.

24. North Carolina, "Second Annual Report of the Wilmington and Raleigh Rail Road Company," *Report of the President and Directors of the Board of Internal Improvement to the Legislature of North Carolina* (Raleigh: Thomas Loring, Printer to the Legislature, 1838), 15–18, Section A. RSUSA, N.C. D.1, Reel 1, Unit 4; *Wilmington Advertiser,* June 14, 1839, August 23, 1839, September 27, 1839.

25. *Wilmington Advertiser,* October 19, 1838.

26. *Wilmington Advertiser,* May 10, 1839: "The non-arrival of the Steamer Vanderbilt up to yesterday morning from Charleston, (due on Sunday morning) and the North Carolina being also due yesterday morning, without making their appearance caused an intense anxiety in our community. At about 10 o'clock A.M. yesterday, the Steamer Southerner, Capt Chase, arrived from Charleston bringing the unpleasant intelligence that the Vanderbilt and North Carolina came in contact with each other on Saturday night about 11 o'clock, off Georgetown light — the former on her way to this port, the latter hence to Charleston. The Vanderbilt struck the North Carolina, on her starboard beam, near the forward gangway, cutting her down to the copper line, and otherwise damaging her to a considerable extent. The injury received by the Vanderbilt was slight, and will be repaired in a few days. Both boats made directly for Charleston, where they arrived at 6 o'clock on Sunday morning. We have heard various accounts of this unfortunate occurrence, and of causes which led to it, but forbear at present any notice of them, as we are assured that the most prompt measures are now taken by the Company's Directors, to investigate the affair thoroughly, and that such action will be had, as will strongly guard against any thing of the kind in the future."

27. *Ibid.*

28. *Wilmington Advertiser,* May 17, 1839.

29. Kemble, Frances Anne, John A. Scott, ed., *Journal of a Residence on a Georgian Plantation in 1838–1839* (Athens: University of Georgia Press, 1984), 35–36: "The afternoon was beautiful, golden, mild, and bright — the boat we were in extremely comfortable and clean, and the captain especially courteous. The whole furniture of the vessel was remarkably tasteful, as well as convenient — not forgetting the fawn-colored and blue curtains to the berths. But what a deplorable mistake it is — be-draperying up these narrow nests, so as to impede the meager mouthfuls of air which their dimensions alone necessarily limit one to. These crimson and yellow, or even fawn-colored and blue silk suffocators, are a poor compensation for free ventilation; and I always look at these elaborate adornments of sea beds as ingenious and elegant incentives to seasickness.... The captain's wife and ourselves were the only passengers; and, after a most delightful walk on deck in the afternoon, and comfortable tea, we retired for the night, and did not wake till we bumped on the Charleston bar on the morning of Christmas Day" (Tuesday, December 25, 1838).

30. T.A.R., "Locomotion: Or, Lights and Shades of Travel," *Orion, a Monthly Magazine of Literature and Art* (March/April 1843), 342–352.

31. *Wilmington Advertiser,* January 4, 1839; *Wilmington Chronicle,* November 23, 1842.

32. *Wilmington Journal,* August 31, 1849: "I wrote you a hasty letter from Charleston, yesterday, and immediately after closing it, made up my mind to come by the mail route instead of by the New York steamer, for as the weather continued blustering and threatening, I preferred the risk of twelve hours sea sickness to a delay of three days, and accordingly I was soon on board the Wilmington mail boat, the Vanderbilt, Capt. Marshall.— It has been very much the custom to decry this line of boats as inferior and unsafe, but I think without suffi-

cient cause. We have recently been accustomed to the splendid modern Ocean steamers of 1,000, 1,500 and 2000 tons, fitted up with great style and luxury, that we look with contempt upon the small, snug and comfortable boats of a few years back, when they were considered all that was necessary or desirable; and I must confess, when I drove down, and saw only the wheelhouses and the chimneys of the Vanderbilt visible above the wharf, I felt a little disappointed, and cast another look upwards towards the unquite sky and lowering clouds, but when I got on board, found every thing so snug and comfortable, even though rather on the small scale, comparatively, that I felt no regret in having selected that route. The night proved very rough, with considerable sea, but the wind was favorable, and the boat made such rapid progress, that we had to go under very low steam, so as not to reach the bar before daylight, when the buoys could be distinguished. Notwithstanding all the complaints of the boats of this line, there has been none in the United States which have run with more success; for they seldom lose a mail, and only in weather when almost any boat would do so, as they are allowed but very little margin to schedule time, and I have no recollection of any serious accident having happened to any of them in many years. The accommodations on board, are very good, as is also the fare. They have an upper saloon or cabin on deck, where the meals are given, with windows all round as in a railroad car, which makes it both light and airy. These boats are owned by the Wilmington and Weldon Railroad Company, and they are a constant drain upon them, as the expense of keeping them up is far from being covered by their earnings; on the contrary, they draw heavily on the profits of the road. This of itself is a fair reason why largest and more expensive ones are not put on the line, besides as regards size, the water on the bar of the river to Wilmington, would not admit boats of heavy draft."

33 *Wilmington Advertiser,* June 14, 1839.

34. *Wilmington Advertiser,* September 27, 1839: "Upon the delivery of the Wilmington by Watchman & Bratt, the building contractors, to the agents of the Wilmington & Raleigh Rail Road Company; it was ascertained before leaving the Chesapeake, that she was too slow for the purpose of carrying the Great Southern mail, for which she was designed. She was consequently returned to these contractors for the purpose of making the necessary alterations. Watchman & Bratt having satisfactorily ascertained that she could not generate steam as fast as she could consume it, the furnace draught was increased by adding 12 feet to the length of her smoke stack, which partially remedied the defect. She then left Baltimore for Wilmington, and arrived here on the 20th. On the 21st she made her first to Charleston and on the 24th her second. The return passage of the latter, was performed in 16 hours — and the distance from Smithville to Wilmington — 28 miles — in two hours by our editorial chronometer — ___ favourable.... The Wilmington is a new boat, just finished, and left our waters for the first time on Thursday last for Wilmington, N.C. in charge of Capt. Ivey. She is owned by the Wilmington and Raleigh Rail Road Company, for whom she was built by contract with, and under the supervision of Messrs. Watchman & Bratt, distinguished Machinists and Engine Builders of Baltimore. Mr. Langley B. Cully was the Shipwright; and competent judges who have examined, have pronounced the workmanship faithfully executed; the materials not to be surpassed in quality; and her model is certainly beautiful.— Her length is 172 feet, breath of beam 24 feet, and depth of hold 30 feet, and her admeasurements about four hundred tons. Her bucket wheels are of iron, which is a new feature in building in this country; her Engine, one of Watchman & Bratt's best, 135 horses power, and she has one of Raub's patent double self-acting safety valves, the first which has ever been introduced to operate successfully, on board of any boats on our waters.— The accommodations are ample for 100 passengers, having that number of berths by each of which depends a life preserver."

35. *Ibid.*

36. Ron Vinson, and CommunicationSolutions.ISI, "Steamboat List, 1812–1849," *North Carolina Business History,* (2006), http://www.historync.org/NCsteamboatlist1812%20-%201849.htm (accessed January 2, 2011).

37. *Wilmington Journal,* October 5, 1849: "The undersigned, passengers on the steamer Gladiator, one of the Wilmington and Charleston Line of Steamboats, recently chartered to transport Company E, 2nd Regiment of Artillery, from Fort Johnson, N.C., to Pilatka, Florida, take pleasure in testifying to her merits as a fine sea boat, where no effort is spared to contribute to the comfort of the passengers. We also avail ourselves of this opportunity to tender our grateful acknowledgments to her gentlemanly commander, Capt. Isaac B. Smith, and to the officers and crew generally, for the highly creditable manner in which the trip was performed, and the uniform kindness and attention shown us during the passage."

38. *Wilmington Journal,* November 19, 1847,

November 9, 19, 1849; Wilmington & Raleigh Rail Road Company, *Proceedings of the Wilmington & Raleigh R.R. Company, at Their Fifteenth Annual Meeting Held at Wilmington, North Carolina, November 14, 1850* (Wilmington: T. Loring, 1850), 7, WRRM; *Wilmington Herald*, November 5, 1851; Wilmington & Weldon Rail Road Company, *Proceedings of the Stockholders of the Wilmington & Weldon Rail Road Co. at their Twentieth Annual Meeting, held at Wilmington, North Carolina, November 9, 1855* (Wilmington: Thomas Loring, 1855), 15–16, NHCL, NC 385 W, 1855.

39. *Wilmington Journal*, February 3, 1854: "This morning, for, we suppose, nearly about the last time, we heard the ringing of the steamboat bell on her arrival here from Charleston, and saw her sweep along the river front of town. Hereafter, we presume, all intercourse between this place and the Queen City must be carried on by way of the Wilmington and Manchester, and the South Carolina Rail Roads. A piece of open sea navigation like that between this place and Charleston, must always occasion a break and comparative uncertainty in the operation of lines composed of Rail Road travel, so that we must have looked for grumbling so long as it existed,—no matter how prompt and faithful the service performed by the boats; and no boats have done better service, or with less loss of life or property than those belonging to the Wilmington and Raleigh Rail Road Company. Still with all the grumbling we had come to regard them as old friends. Their commanders, too we have always found exceedingly clever gentlemen, and if one *did* puke a little in rough weather, it was all for the good of his or her wholesome."

40. Wilmington & Weldon Rail Road Company (1855) 7, 15.

41. United States, *Failure of Mails — New Orleans* (Washington, DC: Twenty-fifth Congress, Document 145, 1839), 2–4; United States, *Mail: New York to New Orleans Irregularities* (Washington, DC: Twenty-sixth Congress, Document 159, 1840), 2, 6; United States, *Railroad and Steamboat Mail Lines* (Washington, DC: Twenty-eighth Congress, Document 105, 1845), 2, 9–15.

42. North Carolina, *Report of the Internal Improvement Board to the Legislature of North Carolina* (Raleigh: Seaton Gales, Printer for the State, 1848), 30, UNCCH, C380 N87i 1848.

43. *Wilmington Advertiser*, May 5, June 9, 1837, January 18, May 18, 1838, July 28, 1841; *Raleigh Register*, January 3, 1838; *Tarborough Press*, June 9, October 27, 1838.

44. *Tarborough Press*, November 17, December 22, 1838; Kemble, 27–28.

45. Kemble, 22.
46. Kemble, 19–23.
47. *Wilmington Advertiser*, October 19, 1838.
48. *Wilmington Advertiser*, August 23, 1839.
49. *Wilmington Advertiser*, October 4, 1839.
50. Jeremy F. Gilmer, *Field Map of Liet. Koener's Military Survey Between Neuse and Tar Rivers North Carolina, 1863*, (Raleigh: North Carolina State Archives, Map Collection). The Stantonsburg-Tarborough Road follows the route of modern NC 222/111, and the distance between the centers of both towns is 27.23 miles. However, several possible routes from Enfield to Tarboro on the Gilmer map approximate modern roads. There are two sets of modern roads approximating this road on the Gilmer map between western Goldsboro, the former site of Waynesborough, and present-day Tarboro. The first includes NC 581, US 117, SR 1537, NC 222/ NC 111, NC 111, SR 1006, SR 1205, US 64A, and SR 1289. The total distance is 46.96 miles. The other set of roads includes NC 581 to NC 111, SR 1543, SR 1537, NC 222/ NC 111, NC 111, SR 1006, SR 1205, US 64A, and SR 1289. Both roads are slightly over forty-eight miles, but the increase in distance is associated with the less direct modern urban block network of Goldsboro. The latter route, passing through Stony Creek and Patetown, follow the "County Road" depicted by Gilmer. In the Gilmer map, the bridge across Nahunta Swamp, and on the modern maps, this road is still known as the Seven Bridges Road. This is the only factor that recommends that set of roads as the stage route leading from Stantonsburg to Waynesborough.

51. William P. Cumming, *North Carolina in Maps* (Raleigh: Division of Archives and History, North Carolina Department of Cultural Resources, 1966), Plate X, Plate XII; Gilmer. These are Daniel's Bridge (or Wyatt's Bridge), Spear's Bridge, and Cofield's Bridge (Field's Bridge), with the most direct route between Enfield and Tarborough passing over Spear's Bridge. On a modern map, the approximate location of Spear's Bridge is the crossing of Fishing Creek on SR 1109 and the approximate location of Cofield's Bridge is the crossing of Fishing Creek on SR 1429. The routes crossing these points on Fishing Creek converge near the town of Leggett. The crossing at the former location of Daniel's Bridge follows the modern roads US 301, Speight's Chapel Road, and NC 33 that eventually passes through Leggett. The distance from Enfield to Tarborough via the supposed Cofield's Bridge site on SR 1429 is 24.60 miles, the distance by US 301 to NC 33

by the supposed site of Daniel's Bridge is 24.70 miles, and by SR 1109 to NC 33 the distance is 22.49 miles. Given the selection of the three, the direct route of 22.49 falls under twenty-four miles with 1.51 miles to spare. The other two routes are above twenty-four miles.

NC 111/NC 222 (called the Good News Church Road, Saratoga Road and Pinetops-Tarboro Road at various points between Tarboro and Stantonsburg) is the most direct route. However, it is still necessary to prove that the modern roads are built on the path of the nineteenth-century roads. The MacRae-Brazier map shows the intersection of two important roads near Toisnot Swamp. One of the roads connected Tarboro to Smithfield, with the other connecting Stantonsburg to Nashville (North Carolina). These roads remain in the *United States Coast Survey* map three decades later. In this map, the intersection now has the name of Wilson. In the modern city of Wilson, the intersection of Tarboro and Nash Streets preserve the place where the two earlier roads crossed. If Tarboro Street is traced east from Wilson, it becomes NC 42. After this highway enters Edgecombe County, NC 42 divides into NC 124 and NC 42. NC 124 intersects NC 111 at Pitt's Crossroads. If Nash Street is traced east from Wilson, it becomes NC 58/US 264 and passes through Stantonsburg on NC 58. The town of Saratoga, appearing on the *United States Coast Survey* map, also connects to Wilson. The modern NC 91 retains the curves of the road depicted on the historic map. The relationships between the modern roads and their earlier manifestations suggest that NC-111/NC-222 retains much the same path as it followed in the 1830s. The total distance of the route between Enfield and Stantonsburg using the modern road network is 49.77 miles. This route is remarkably close to the 46.69 miles of direct distance between Enfield to Stantonsburg via Tarboro.

The distance for the post route from Tarboro to Waynesborough was forty-six miles. There are two sets of modern roads approximating this road on the Gilmer map between western Goldsboro, the former site of Waynesborough, and present-day Tarboro. The first includes NC 581, US 117, SR 1537, NC 222/ NC 111, NC 111, SR 1006, SR 1205, US 64A, and SR 1289. The total distance is 46.96 miles. The other set of roads includes NC 581 to NC 111, SR 1543, SR 1537, NC 222/ NC 111, NC 111, SR 1006, SR 1205, US 64A, and SR 1289. Both roads are slightly over forty-eight miles, but the increase in distance is associated with the less direct modern urban block network of Goldsboro. The latter route, passing through Stony Creek and Patetown, follow the "County Road" depicted by Gilmer. In the Gilmer map, the bridge across Nahunta Swamp, and on the modern maps, this road is still known as the Seven Bridges Road. This is the only factor that recommends that set of roads as the stage route leading from Stantonsburg to Waynesborough.

This stage route distances mentioned in issues of the *Wilmington Advertiser* from August 23, 1839, to January 3, 1840, do not fit with the existing road network on the Gilmer map or any early map. The equivalent of present-day US 117 did exist between beyond the northern outskirts of Waynesboro. The modern roads follow the paths of the earlier roads but none run directly north. Only the railroad formed a continuous path between Waynesborough and the Tar River. The shorter distance given in the Wilmington newspapers suggests that some of the graded sections of railroad might have been used, or the writer was merely referring to the distance of the railroad that was not open. It is unclear.

There were two roads leading from Rocky Mount to Tarborough. Both paralleled the Tar River. The road on the north bank of the river proceeded east to a crossing of the river at Teat's Bridge or Bell's Bridge. After crossing the river, it joined the road on the south bank that entered Tarborough on the north side of town. The present-day roads that follow their paths are Alt US 64 and NC 97. Dunbar Road, SR 1252, crosses the Tar River near the site of Teat's Bridge.

52. Felix Grundy, and John M. Robinson, "Statistics 2 — No Title," *Niles' Weekly Register*, June 21, 1834; United States, *Post Office Department Contracts, 1830*, (Washington, DC Twenty-first Congress, Document 117, 1831), 7-8; United States, *The Report of the Postmaster General, with a Statement of the Contracts Made by that Department in the Year 1833,* (Washington, DC: Twenty-fifth Congress, Document 408, 1834), 20; United States, *Letter from the Postmaster General* (Washington, DC: Twenty-sixth Congress, Document 85, 1841), 23.

The old Stantonsburg-Tarborough Road follows the present-day NC 111/ NC 222, and remains the most direct route to Stantonsburg. This road also passes through Pitt's Crossroads. The distance from Enfield to Tarborough via the supposed Cofield's Bridge site on SR 1429 is 24.60 miles, the distance by US 301 to NC 33 by the supposed site of Daniel's Bridge is 24.70 miles, and by SR 1109 to NC 33 the distance is 22.49 miles. Given the selection of the three, the direct route of 22.49 falls under twenty-four miles with 1.51 miles to spare. The other two routes are above twenty-four miles. It is not likely that the railroad would have selected the most direct route.

53. "General Description of the Charleston and Hamburg Rail-Road," *Farmers' Register* (October 1833), 261–263.

54. James C. Burke, *North Carolina's First Railroads, a Study in Historical Geography*, (Greensboro: University of North Carolina at Greensboro, 2008), 387–404, Dissertation, NCDOCKS, *http://libres.uncg.edu/ir/uncg/listing.aspx?id=637* (accessed on December 18, 2010); Frances Anne Kemble-Butler, "A Winter's Journey to Georgia U.S," *Bentley's Miscellany* (1842:, 1–12, 113–124; The Boors of Carolina, "Revolutionary Reminiscences," *Niles' Weekly Register* (1842): 96.

Chapter IV

1. Forest G. Hill, "Government Engineering Aid to Railroads before the Civil War," *The Journal of Economic History* 11 (Summer 1951), 235–242.

2. Robert G. Angevine, "Individuals, Organizations, and Engineering: U.S. Army Officers and the American Railroads, 1827–1838," *Technology and Culture* 42.2 (April 2001), 292–318.

3. Todd Shallat, "Building Waterways, 1802–1961: Science and the United States Army in Early Public Works," *Technology and Culture* 31 (January 1990), 22–24, 28–32, 49–50.

4. Peter A. Ford, "Charles S. Storrow, Civil Engineer: A Case Study of European Training and Technological Transfer in the Antebellum Period," *Technology and Culture* 34 (April 1993), 271–276, 281, 288–292.

5. Milton Kerker, "Sadi Carnot," *The Scientific Monthly* 85 (September 1957), 143–149.

6. Milton Kerker, "Sadi Carnot and the Steam Engine Engineers," *Isis* 51 (September 1960), 267–268; Milton Kerker, "Science and the Steam Engine" *Technology and Culture* 2 (Autumn 1961), 381–390.

7. United States, *Report from the Secretary of War in Compliance with a Resolution of the Senate of 24, January 1838, with a Report of the Survey of the Charleston and Cincinnati Railroad* (Washington, DC: Twenty-fifth Congress, Senate Document Number 157, 1838), 27–32.

8. R. A. Buchanan, "The Diaspora of British Engineering," *Technology and Culture* 27 (July, 1986), 506.

9. North Carolina, *Report of Sundry Surveys, Made by Hamilton Fulton, Esq. State Engineer, Agreeably to Certain Instructions from Judge Murphey, &c. and Submitted to the General Assembly, at their Session in 1819* (Raleigh: Thomas Henderson, 1819), 22, 32.

10. Buchanan, 511.

11. *The Peoples Press and Wilmington Advertiser,* November 10, 1837.

12. Cal. Scientific Press, "Evolution of Locomotives in America," *Science* 1 (July 1880), 35.

13. Robert E. Carlson, "British Railroads and Engineers and the Beginnings of American Railroad Development," *The Business History Review* 34 (Summer 1960), 144–147.

14. William R. Siddall, "Railroad Gauges and Spatial Interaction," *Geographical Review* 59 (January 1969), 32–33.

15. Douglas J. Puffert, "The Standardization of Track Gauges on North American Railways, 1830–1890," *The Journal of Economic History* 60 (December 2000), 934–944.

16. Walter Gwynn, *Report of Walter Gwynn, Esq. Engineer, to the President and Directors of the Portsmouth and Roanoke Rail Road Company* (Norfolk, VA: T. G. Broughton, 1833), 5.

17. "General Description of the Charleston and Hamburg Rail-Road," *Farmers' Register* (October 1833), 261–263.

The Charleston & Hamburg Rail Road employed a different method of construction. It was described in the *Farmers' Register* as partially resting on the ground, but elevated five to six feet above the ground for most of its length. The 135-mile railroad ascended 510 feet to its highest point before descending into the Savannah River valley. The grade at this point was steep, and two 25 horsepower stationary engines were employed to help trains up an inclined plane.

The first of four methods used on this railroad—*Sleeper Plan No. 1*—was used on clay or gravel soil using fill, excavation, and ditching. The sills were covered with soil. The cost of the track alone cost the company $1,450 per mile. There were over five miles of track on the railroad put down with this method. Another arrangement—*Sleeper Plan No. 2*—consisted of sills oriented in the direction of the rails, buried in the soil, with a cap connecting the rail to the sill. This was the method employed on the inclined plane. There were 18 miles of this type of track, and each mile cost between $1,800 and $2,200 per mile. The other methods used on this railroad were *Pile Construction* and *Truss Construction*. Piles that were less than 7 feet in height did not require additional bracing, while some at 15 feet were braced on both sides. Piles from 7 feet to 10 feet had a single brace, and those above 10 feet had cross braces.

Pile construction cost between $1,900 and $3,000 per mile, with the average being $2,300. Truss construction, as explained earlier, was used in work over 12 feet and required a pile foundation, and assumed an upside down "W" form. The Charleston and Hamburg line contained 5 miles of truss construction averaging between $6,000 and $10,000 per mile.

18. Homer B. Vanderblue and George W. Whistler, "An Engineer Writes on Railroad Construction Standards in 1842," *Bulletin of the Business Historical Society* 13 (January 1939), 6–11.

19. United States, *Railroad-Portage Summit, Ohio, to Hudson River* (Washington, DC: Twenty-second Congress, Document Number 133, 1832), 18–19.

20. Gwynn, 6.

21. Wilmington & Raleigh Rail Road Company, *Proceedings of the Wilmington & Raleigh R. R. Company, at their Fifteenth Annual Meeting held at Wilmington, North Carolina, November 14, 1850* (Wilmington: T. Loring, 1850), 11, WRRM.

22. Gwynn, 6.

23. Raymond E. Davis, Francis S. Foote, and Joe W. Kelly, *Surveying Theory and Practice*, 5th ed., (New York: McGraw-Hill, 1966), 213–215.

24. United States, *Report from the Secretary of War, with a Resolution of the Senate 20, Inst., Transmitting the Report of the Survey of the Western and Atlantic Railroad of the State of Georgia* (Washington, DC: Twenty-fifth Congress, Document Number 57, 1837), A.

25. United States, *Rail-Road: Pensacola to Columbus. Letter from the Secretary of War Transmitting a Survey of a Rail-Road from Pensacola, to Columbus, in Georgia* (Washington, DC: Twenty-fourth Congress, Document 176, 1836), 6.

26. Gregg Turner, *A Short History of Florida Railroads* (Charleston, SC: Arcadia, 2003), 18–19.

27. *Farmers' Register* (October 1833), 261–263.

28. Gwynn, 8–9.

29. United States, *Winchester and Potomac Railroad* (Washington, DC: Twenty-fifth Congress, Document Number 465, 1838), 30–34.

30. Henri Cabannes, *General Mechanics*, translated from the second French edition by S.P. Sutera (Waltham. MA: Blaisdell, 1968), 92–93; Jack C. McCormac, *Structural Analysis*, (Scranton, PA: International Textbook, 1967), 11–12.

31. Gwynn, 6.

32. United States, *Report from the Secretary of War in Compliance with a Resolution of the Senate of 24, January 1838, with a Report of the Survey of the Charleston and Cincinnati Railroad* (Washington, DC: Twenty-fifth Congress, Senate Document Number 157, 1838), 28–30.

33. "Extracts from the Report of Walter Gwynn, Esq., Engineer, to the President and Directors of the Wilmington and Raleigh Rail Road Company," *Farmers' Register* (October 1836), 348.

34. Wilmington & Weldon Rail Road Company, *Proceedings of the Stockholders of the Wilmington & Weldon R. R. Co., at their Twenty-First Annual Meeting held at Wilmington, North Carolina, November 13, 1856; with the Reports of the President and Directors, and the Engineer and Superintendent* (Wilmington: Thomas Loring, 1856), 6, NHCL, NC 385 W

35. *Farmers' Register* (October 1836), 348.

36. R.B. Daniels, F. F. Gamble, W. H. Wheeler, and C. S. Holshey, *Carolina Geological and Atlantic Coastal Plain Geological Association, Field Trip Guidebook (the Geology of the N.C. Coastal Plain from the Sounds Near New Bern to the Piedmont of Wake County)*, (Carolina Geological Society, Guidebook for the 1972 Annual Meeting, 1972); Richard J. Councill, *The Commercial Granites of North Carolina* (Raleigh: Division of Mineral Resources, North Carolina Department of Conservation and Development, 1954), 7, 10–12, 15.

37. Councill, 7, 15.

38. Charles F.M. Garnett, "Raleigh and Gaston Rail-Road, *Farmers' Register* (July 1839), 388.

39. North Carolina Rail Road Company, *Proceedings of the General Meeting of Stockholders of the North Carolina Rail Road Company, at Greensboro,' July 10, 1851, with the By-Laws of the Company, as Revised at Said Meeting* (Greensboro, N.C.: Patriot Office, 1851), 4–6, UNCCH, C385.1 N87p.

40. William P. Cumming, *North Carolina in Maps* (Raleigh: Division of Archives and History, North Carolina Department of Cultural Resources, 1966), Plate XIV.

41. *Wilmington Journal,* May 25, 1849; July 27, 1849; October 12, 1849.

42. *Wilmington Chronicle,* May 24, 1843.

43. "Railroads of Virginia and North Carolina," *Farmers' Register* (March 1843), 165.

44. United States, *S 84* (Washington, DC: Twenty-seventh Congress, Third Session, 1843), 5.

45. *Farmers' Register* (1843), 165.

46. United States, *In Favor of Iron and Iron Machinery for Railroads Free of Duty* (Washing-

ton, DC: Twentieth Congress, First Session, Document 904, 1828), 994–996.

47. United States, *Memorial of a Number of Ironmasters at Lexington, Virginia, in Relation to an Increase of Duty of Imported Iron* (Washington, DC: Twenty-seventh Congress, Second Session, House Document 132, 1842), 5.

48. United States, *Resolutions of the Legislature of New Jersey in Favor of an Increase of the Duties on Coal, Iron, and Glass* (Washington, DC: Thirty-second Congress, First Session, Senate Miscellaneous Document 53, 1852), 1.

49. United States, *Imports and Exports of Sugar from 1821 to 1842, and Drawbacks of Duty on Railroad Iron* (Washington, DC: Twenty-seventh Congress, Second Session, House Document 265, 1842), 4–5.

50. United States, *Letter of the Secretary of the Treasury, Transmitting, in Compliance with a Resolution of the House of the 18 December 1848, Statements of the Importations, &c., of Iron Uunder the Tariff Acts of 1842 and 1846* (Washington, DC: Thirtieth Congress, Second Session, Executive Document 33, 1849), 1–16.

51. United States, *Petition of the Citizens of Pennsylvania, Praying for a Reduction of Duty on Railroad Iron Imported,* (Washington, DC: Twenty-third Congress, Second Session, House Document 167, 1835), 1–2.

52. United States, *Baltimore and Susquehannah Rail-Road Company* (Washington, DC: Twenty-fourth Congress, Second Session, House Document 224, 1837), 1–2.

53. United States, *Railroad Iron — Remission of Duties On* (Washington, DC: Twenty-eighth Congress, First Session, House Document 478, 1844), 1–2.

54. Alfred D. Chandler, Jr., "Patterns of American Railroad Finance, 1830–50," *The Business History Review* 28 (September 1954), 248–249, 251n, 253, 257, 262–263.

55. Peter L. Rousseau, "Jacksonian Monetary Policy, Specie Flow, and the Panic of 1837," *The Journal of Economic History* 62 (September 2002), 459, 484–286.

56. United States, *Letter and Memorial of Isaac K. Lippincott, on the Manufacture of Iron and the Operation of the Present Tariff Laws* (Washington, DC: Twenty-seventh Congress, First Session, House Document 24, 1841), 1–5.

57. United States, *Memorial of Inhabitants of Danville, Pa. Praying for a National Foundry at Danville, in Said State* (Washington, DC: Twenty-seventh Congress, First Session, House Document 8, 1841), 1–3.

58. United States, *National Foundry* (Washington, DC: Twenty-seventh Congress, Second Session, House Document 229, 1843), 1.

59. *Wilmington Journal,* June 22, 1849.
60. *Wilmington Journal,* September 21, 1849.
61. *Wilmington Journal,* October 5, 1849.

62. United States, *Appendix to the Congressional Globe,* (Washington, DC: Thirty-second Congress, First Session, 1852), 1056.

63. United States, *Resolutions of the Legislature of North Carolina, in Favor of the Erection of a Marine Hospital at or Near Smithville or Wilmington, in that State, and the Abolition of the Duty on Railroad Iron* (Washington, DC: Thirty-second Congress, Second Session, Senate Document 32, 1852), 1–2.

64. United States, *Memorial of the Committee of a Convention, held in Richmond, VA, December 5, 1854* (Washington, DC: Thirty-third Congress, Second Session, Senate Document 9, 1855), 5.

65. Wilmington & Raleigh Rail Road Company (1850), 8–9; James Sprunt, *Chronicles of the Cape Fear River, 1660–1916* (Raleigh: Edwards and Broughton, 1916), 152.

66. *Wilmington Journal,* November 10, 1849.

67. North Carolina, "Fifth Annual Report of the President and Directors of the Wilmington & Raleigh Rail Road Company," *Report of the Board of Internal Improvements to the General Assembly,* Document No. 16 (Raleigh: Thomas Loring, 1840), Section A, RSUSA, N.C. D.1, Reel 1, Unit 5; *Wilmington Advertiser,* November 10, 1837; Burton Alva Konkle, *John Motley Morehead and the Development of North Carolina, 1796–1866,* (Philadelphia, PA: William J. Campbell, 1922), 171.

68. *Wilmington Advertiser,* January 11, May 24, 1839.

69. North Carolina, *Report of the President and Directors of the Board of Internal Improvements* (Raleigh: Thomas Loring, 1838), 17–18, RSUSA, N.C. 1, D.1, Reel 1, Unit 4; *Wilmington Advertiser,* October 11, 1839.

70. Wilmington & Weldon Rail Road Company (1856), 20; Wilmington & Weldon Rail Road Company, *Proceedings of the Stockholders of the Wilmington & Weldon R.R. Co., at Their Twenty-third Annual Meeting held at Wilmington, North Carolina, November 11, 1858; with the Reports of the President and Directors, and the Engineer and Superintendent,* (Wilmington: Fulton and Price, 1858), 16, NHCL, NC 385 W.

71. Sprunt, 150.

72. Wilmington & Weldon Rail Road (1858), 8.

73. *Carolina Observer,* May 3, 1843.

74. *Wilmington Chronicle,* May 17, November 15, 1843.

75. *Wilmington Chronicle,* December 6, 1843.

76. *Wilmington Journal,* November 20, 1846.
77. Wilmington & Weldon Rail Road Company, *Proceedings of the Stockholders of the Wilmington & Weldon Rail Road Co. at their Twentieth Annual Meeting, held at Wilmington, North Carolina, November 9, 1855* (Wilmington: Thomas Loring, 1855), 22, NHCL, NC 385 W.
78. *Wilmington Messenger,* September 3, 1891.
79. Wilmington & Weldon Rail Road (1856), 23; Wilmington & Weldon Rail Road Company, *Annual Reports of the President and Directors, and the Chief Engineer and Superintendent of the Wilmington & Weldon R. R. Co., with the Proceedings of the General Meeting of Stockholders, November 8, 1860* (Wilmington, N.C.: Fulton and Price, 1860), 37, NHCL, NC 385 W.
80. Angus Sinclair, and John H. White, ed., *Development of the Locomotive Engine,* (Cambridge, MA: MIT Press, 1970), 643.
81. *Wilmington Journal,* November 19, 1869.
82. *Wilmington Herald,* May 21, 1851.
83. Sinclair and White, 266.
84. Wilmington & Weldon Rail Road (1856), 21.
85. Paul T. Warner, *Motive Power Development on the Pennsylvania Railroad System, 1831–1924,* (Philadelphia, PA: Baldwin Locomotives, 1924), 4–7.

Chapter V

1. Wilmington & Weldon Rail Road Company, *Proceedings of the Stockholders of the Wilmington & Weldon Rail Road Co. at their Twentieth Annual Meeting, held at Wilmington, North Carolina, November 9, 1855,* (Wilmington: Thomas Loring, 1855), 51, 53–54, NHCL, NC 385 W..
2. James Sprunt, *Chronicles of the Cape Fear River, 1660–1916* (Raleigh, NC: Edwards and Broughton, 1916), 230–231.
3. J.G. de Roulhac Hamilton, *Party Politics in North Carolina, 1835–1860* (Chapel Hill: University of North Carolina, James Sprunt Historical Publications, North Carolina Historical Society, 1916), 36; Thomas E. Jeffrey, *State Parties and National Politics: North Carolina, 1815–1961* (Athens: University of Georgia Press, 1989), 75.
4. Burton Alva Konkle, *John Motley Morehead and the Development of North Carolina, 1796–1866* (Philadelphia, PA: William J. Campbell, 1922), 144–148, 176.
5. North Carolina, *The Revised Statutes of the State of North Carolina Passed by the General Assemble at the Session of 1836-7* (Raleigh: Turner and Hughes, 1837), 346–352, NHCL, NC 348.756 N.
6. Fred E. Fiedler, "A Contingency Model of Leadership Effectiveness," in Leonard Berkowitz, ed., *Advances in Experimental Social Psychology,* (New York: Academic, 1964).
7. Sprunt, 153.
8. Wilmington & Weldon Rail Road Company (1855), 41.
9. Wilmington & Weldon Rail Road Company (1855), 30.
10. James G. Hunt, *Leadership: A New Synthesis* (Newbury Park, CA: Sage, 1996), 201–203.
11. *Raleigh Register,* January 17, 1837.
12. *Wilmington Advertiser,* March 4, 1836.
13. Sprunt, 150.
14. *Wilmington Advertiser,* April 25, 1836; North Carolina, *Laws of the State of North Carolina Passed by the General Assembly at the Session of 1836–37* (Raleigh: Thos. J. Lemay, 1837), 225, SLNC, Z2 1:1836/37.
15. *Wilmington Advertiser,* February 17, 1837.
16. *Carolina Observer,* February 9, 1837.
17. Peter Koestenbaum, *Leadership, the Inner Side of Greatness: A Philosophy for Leaders,* (San Francisco, CA: Jossey-Bass/John Wiley and Sons, 2002), 189–190.
18. North Carolina, "Fifth Annual Report of the President and Directors of the Wilmington & Raleigh Rail Road Company," *Report of the Board of Internal Improvements to the General Assembly,* Document No. 16 (Raleigh: Thomas Loring, 1840), 9, RSUSA, N.C. D.1, Reel 1, Unit 5.
19. *Wilmington Chronicle,* November 15, 1843; *Carolina Observer,* May 3, 1843.
20. North Carolina, (1837), 349–352.
21. Frank Otto Gatell, "Spoils of the Bank War: Political Bias in the Selection of Pet Banks," *The American History Review* 70 (October 1964), 54.
22. North Carolina, (1840), 7.
23. William A. Graham, *Message from His Excellency, the Governor, Relative to the State's Railroad Liabilities,* (Raleigh, NC: Seaton Gales, Printer for the State, 1848), 3–8, UNCCH, Cp385 N87g3.
24. Cecil K. Brown, *A State Movement in Railroad Development* (Chapel Hill: University of North Carolina Press, 1928), 53–58.
25. James A. Ward, "Promotional Wizardry: Rhetoric and Railroad Origins, 1820–1860," *Journal of the Early Republic* 11 (Spring 1991), 69–88.
26. Raymond Walters, "The Origins of

the Second Bank of the United States," *The Journal of Political Economy* 53 (June 1945), 115–130.
27. Bray Hammond, "Jackson, Biddle, and the Bank of the United States," *The Journal of Economic History* 7 (May 1947), 1–23.
28. Edwin J. Perkins and Andrew Jackson, "Lost Opportunities for Compromise in the Bank War: A Reassessment of Jackson's Veto Message," *The Business History Review* 61 (Winter 1987), 531–550.
29. Jacob P. Meerman, "The Climax of the Bank War: Biddle's Contraction, 1833–34," *The Journal of Political Economy* 71 (August 1963), 378–388; Bray Hammond, "The Chestnut Street Raid of Wall Street, 1839," *The Quarterly Journal of Economics* 61 (August 1947), 605–618.
30. Peter L. Rousseau, "Jacksonian Monetary Policy, Specie Flows, and the Panic of 1837," *The Journal of Economic History* 62 (June 2002), 459, 484.
31. George Macesich, "Sources of Monetary Disturbances in the United States, 1834–1845," *The Journal of Economic History* 20 (September 1960), 407–434. George Macesich advances the hypothesis that the primary source of the monetary disturbance in the United States between 1834 and 1845 was external, though he does not dismiss the influence of internal events. His examination provides an explanation of the nineteenth century international specie standard. Counties had to fix and maintain specie value, imports and exports of specie had to move freely, specie movement influenced domestic money supply, and there had to be a reasonable level of price flexibility. Macesich, using statistical methods, determined that the collapse of the banking system was an adjustment in the larger international economic structure that was dependent on the maintenance of the specie standard, not the influence of Jacksonian monetary policy alone.
32. Richard H. Timberlake, "The Specie Standard and Central Banking in the United States Before 1860," *The Journal of Economic History* 21 (September 1961), 318–341.
33. Brown, 59.
34. North Carolina, *Law for the State of North Carolina Passed by the General Assembly, at the Session 1850–51* (Raleigh: Star Office-Thomas J. Lemay, 1851), 250–258, NHCL, NC 348.756 N.
35. Brown, 40.
36. *Wilmington Journal*, February 2, 1849.
37. *Wilmington Chronicle*, November 20, 1844.
38. *Wilmington Chronicle*, November 23, 1842.
39. *Wilmington Journal*, November 28, 1846.
40. *Wilmington Journal*, November 19, 1847.
41. Ibid.
42. North Carolina, *Report of the Internal Improvement Board to the Legislature of North Carolina* (Raleigh: Seaton Gales, Printer for the State, 1848), 16–18, 20–21, UNCCH, C380 N87i 1848.
43. Ibid., 24–25.
44. Ibid.
45. Ibid., 33.
46. Brown, 50.
47. North Carolina (1848), 27–28.
48. Brown, 59.
49. North Carolina, *A Bill Concerning the Wilmington and Raleigh Rail Road Company*, (Raleigh: Seaton Gales, Printer for the State, 1848), 7–8, RSUSA, N.C. D. 1, Reel 3, Unit 1.
50. Brown, 40–43.
51. *Wilmington Journal*, November 19, 1849.
52. Wilmington & Weldon Rail Road (1856), 23; Wilmington & Weldon Rail Road Company, *Annual Reports of the President and Directors, and the Chief Engineer and Superintendent of the Wilmington & Weldon R. R. Co., with the Proceedings of the General Meeting of Stockholders, November 8, 1860* (Wilmington, N.C.: Fulton and Price, 1860), 20–21, 27, 32, 47, NHCL, NC 385 W.
53. North Carolina, *Report of the Internal Improvement Board to the Legislature of North Carolina* (1848), 25; *Wilmington Journal*, November 19, 1849; Wilmington & Weldon Rail Road Company, *Proceedings of the Stockholders of the Wilmington & Weldon R.R. Co., at their Twenty-third Annual Meeting held at Wilmington, North Carolina, November 11, 1858; With the Reports of the President and Directors, and the Engineer and Superintendent*, (Wilmington: Fulton and Price, 1858), 2, NHCL, NC 385 W.
54. Wilmington & Weldon Rail Road Company (1855), 63.
55. *Wilmington Chronicle*, November 15, 1843, August 23, 1843; North Carolina, "Second Annual Report of the Wilmington and Raleigh Rail Road Company," *Report of the President and Directors of the Board of Internal Improvement to the Legislature of North Carolina*, (Raleigh: Thomas Loring, Printer to the Legislature, 1838), Section A. RSUSA, N.C. D.1, Reel 1, Unit 4; North Carolina, "Fifth Annual Report of the President and Directors of the Wilmington & Raleigh Rail Road Company," *Report of the Board of Internal Improvements to the General Assembly*, Document No.

16, (Raleigh: Thomas Loring, 1840), 10, Section B, RSUSA, N.C. D.1, Reel 1, Unit 5; *Carolina Observer,* May 3, 1843; *Wilmington Chronicle,* May 14, 1843, December 6, 1843.
56. Brown, 38-39.
57. "Railroads of Virginia and North Carolina," *Farmers' Register* (March 1843), 165.
58. William A. Graham, *Message from His Excellency, the Governor, Relative to the State's Railroad Liabilities,* (Raleigh, NC: Seaton Gales, Printer for the State, 1848), 6-7, UNCCH, Cp385 N87g3.
59. Peter C. Stewart, "Railroads and Urban Rivalries in Antebellum Eastern Virginia," *Virginia Magazine of History and Biography* 81 (1973), 4.
60. Henderson, Archibald, *North Carolina, the Old North State and the New* (Chicago, IL: Lewis, 1941), 107.
61. Stewart, 9-14.
62. *Wilmington Chronicle,* October 28, November 11, 1840.
63. North Carolina, "Fifth Annual Report of the President and Directors of the Wilmington & Raleigh Rail Road Company," *Report of the Board of Internal Improvements to the General Assembly,* Document No. 16 (Raleigh: Thomas Loring, 1840), 10-11.
64. *Wilmington Chronicle,* December 1, 1841, May 24, 1843.
65. Editor, "Opinion of the Supreme Court of North Carolina in the Case of North Carolina v. Francis E. Rives—December Term 1844," *American Law Magazine,* (1845), 282-296.
66. *Ibid.*
67. North Carolina, *Laws of the State of North Carolina Passed by the General Assembly at the Session 1844-45* (Raleigh: Thomas J. Lemay, 1845), 107.
68. *Ibid,* 108-111, 119.
69. North Carolina, *Law for the State of North Carolina Passed by the General Assembly, at the Session 1850-51* (Raleigh: Star Office—Thomas J. Lemay, 1851), 282, 284-302.
70. Thomas C. Parramore, Peter C. Stewart, and Tommy L. Bogger, *Norfolk, the First Four Centuries* (Charlottesville and London: University Press of Virginia, 1994), 162-163, 172-175.
71. Walter M. Clark, *History of the Raleigh & Gaston Railroad Company, Including All Acts of the General Assembly of North Carolina Thereto* (Raleigh, NC: The Raleigh News Steam Job Print, 1877), 137-138, UNCCH, Cp385.1 R16c.
72. Charles L. Coon, *The Beginnings of Public Education in North Carolina,* (Raleigh, NC: Edwards and Broughton, 1908), 988-991, 1012, 1024-1026, 1033-1037, 1039, 1044.
73. North Carolina, *Report of the President and Directors of the Literary Fund, to the Legislature of North Carolina* (Raleigh: Lawrence and Lemay, 1842), Statement A, Statement D, UNCCH, C328.4 D63.
74. Coon, 802.
75. North Carolina (1845), 99.
76. Brown, 69.
77. James E. Vance, *The North American Railroad, Its Origins, Evolution, and Geography* (Baltimore and London: Johns Hopkins University Press, 1955), 22-25.

Chapter VI

1. Cecil K. Brown, *A State Movement in Railroad Development* (Chapel Hill: University of North Carolina Press, 1928), 41n.
2. *Wilmington Tri-weekly Commercial,* March 20, 1847.
3. *Wilmington Journal,* November 20, 1846.
4. *Peoples Press and Wilmington Advertiser,* October 15, 1834, May 17, 1839.
5. *Wilmington Daily Journal,* November 13, 1868.
6. *Wilmington Daily Journal,* November 8, 1868.
7. *Wilmington Journal,* September 22, 1854.
8. *Wilmington Journal,* January 12, February 2, 23, 1849.
9. *Wilmington Journal,* February 3, March 10, 1854.
10. North Carolina, "Fifth Annual Report of the President and Directors of the Wilmington & Raleigh Rail Road Company," *Report of the Board of Internal Improvements to the General Assembly,* Document No. 16, (Raleigh: Thomas Loring, 1840), Section B, RSUSA, N.C. D.1, Reel 1, Unit 5.
11. *Ibid.* 8-9.
12. North Carolina, *Report of the Internal Improvement Board to the Legislature of North Carolina,* (Raleigh: Seaton Gales, Printer for the State, 1848), 18, UNCCH, C380 N87i 1848; Wilmington & Weldon Rail Road Company, *Proceedings of the Stockholders of the Wilmington & Weldon Rail Road Co. at their Twentieth Annual Meeting, held at Wilmington, North Carolina, November 9, 1855,* (Wilmington: Thomas Loring, 1855), 22, 26, NHCL, NC 385 W, 1855; Wilmington & Weldon Rail Road Company, *Annual Reports of the President and Directors, and the Chief Engineer and Superin-*

tendent of the Wilmington & Weldon R. R. Co., with the Proceedings of the General Meeting of Stockholders, November 8, 1860 (Wilmington: Fulton and Price, 1860), 33, NHCL, NC 385 W.

13. *Wilmington Journal,* September 18, 1854.

14. Wilmington & Weldon Rail Road Company, *Proceedings of the Stockholders of the Wilmington & Weldon R. R. Co., at their Twenty-First Annual Meeting held at Wilmington, North Carolina, November 13, 1856; with the Reports of the President and Directors, and the Engineer and Superintendent* (Wilmington: Thomas Loring, 1856), 13–14, NHCL, NC 385 W.

15. Wilmington & Weldon Rail Road Company (1860), 39.

16. *Ibid.,* 3–4.

17. Charles W. Calomiris, Larry Schweikart, "The Panic of 1857: Origins, Transmission, and Containment," *The Journal of Economic History* 51, No. 4 (December 1991), 808–815.

18. *Ibid.,* 831–832.

19. *Ibid.,* 813, 815–816.

20. Wilmington & Weldon Rail Road Company (1860), 33.

21. Charles L. Coon, *The Beginnings of Public Education in North Carolina* (Raleigh, NC: Edwards and Broughton, 1908), 622–623.

22. United States, *The Seventh Census of the United States: 1850,* (Washington, DC: Robert Armstrong, Public Printer, 1853), 318–319.

23. United States, *Agriculture of the United States in 1860; Compiled for the Original Returns of the Eighth Census, under the Direction of the Secretary of the Interior, by Joseph C. G. Kennedy,* (Washington, DC: Government Printing Office, 1864), 104, 108.

24. Wilmington & Weldon Rail Road Company (1855), 39–40.

25. *Wilmington Advertiser,* October 19, 1838.

26. William P. Cumming, *North Carolina in Maps* (Raleigh: Division of Archives and History, North Carolina Department of Cultural Resources, 1966), Plate X.

27. Wilmington & Weldon Rail Road Company, *Proceedings of the Stockholders of the Wilmington & Weldon R.R. Co., at their Twenty-third Annual Meeting held at Wilmington, North Carolina, November 11, 1858; with the Reports of the President and Directors, and the Engineer and Superintendent* (Wilmington: Fulton and Price, 1858), 9, NHCL, NC 385 W.

28. Cumming, Plate XIII.

29. Peter Saunders, *Capitalism* (Minneapolis: University of Minnesota Press, 1995), 9–12.

30. James Sprunt, *Chronicles of the Cape Fear River, 1660–1916* (Raleigh: Edwards and Broughton, 1916), 153.

31. *Wilmington Journal,* November 16, 1849.

32. *Wilmington Journal,* January 5, 1849.

33. Robert C. Black, *The Railroads of the Confederacy* (Chapel Hill: University of North Carolina Press, 1952), xxii–xxiv, 274.

34. Virginia, *Proceeding and Debates of the Virginia-State Convention of 1829–30 ... to which are Subjoined, the New Constitution of Virginia, and the Votes of the People,* (Richmond, VA.: Samuel Shepherd and Co. for Ritchie and Cook, 1830), 76.

35. *Ibid.,* 72–77.

36. William A. Graham, *Message of His Excellency, Gov. Graham, to the Legislature of North Carolina, at the Session of 1846–'47* (Raleigh, NC: W.R. Gales, Printer to the Legislature, 1846), 17, RSUSA, N.C. D.1, Reel 2, Unit 2.

Appendix A

1. "Extracts from the Report of Walter Gwynn, Esq., Engineer, to the President and Directors of the Wilmington and Raleigh Rail Road Company," *Farmers' Register* (October 1836), 348.

2. James Sprunt, *Chronicles of the Cape Fear River, 1660–1916* (Raleigh, N.C.: Edwards and Broughton, 1916), 160–162, 169.

3. *Farmers' Register* (October 1836).

4. Sprunt, 162, 169.

5. Sprunt, 72.

6. *Farmers' Register* (October 1836).

7. New Hanover County, *Book Y* (Wilmington, NC: New Hanover County Register of Deeds, 1840), 208–215.

8. New Hanover County, *Book 86* (Wilmington, NC: New Hanover County Register of Deeds, 1915), 15.

9. Sprunt, 57.

10. Sprunt, 160.

11. *Carolina Observer,* January 26, 1837

12. A town block was 330 feet by 330 feet and four of them together would have made ten acres, i.e., a square that is 40 poles on each side not including avenues dividing them. Five acres would consist of two town blocks; and an additional 43,560 square feet (132 feet by 300 feet) would make six acres.

13. *Wilmington Advertiser,* November 10, 1837; November 23, 1842

14. Nickolas Schenk, *Diary* (Wilmington, NC: UNC–Wilmington, Randall Library Special Collections, 1905), 119.

15. *Wilmington Advertiser,* September 27, 1839.

16. Wilmington & Weldon Rail Road Company, *Annual Reports of the President and Directors, and the Chief Engineer and Superintendent of the Wilmington & Weldon R. R. Co., with the Proceedings of the General Meeting of Stockholders, November 8, 1860* (Wilmington, NC: Fulton and Price, 1860), 17, 35, NHCL, NC 385 W.

17. Wilmington & Weldon Rail Road Company, *Proceedings of the Stockholders of the Wilmington & Weldon Rail Road Co. at their Twentieth Annual Meeting, held at Wilmington, North Carolina, November 9, 1855,* (Wilmington: Thomas Loring, 1855), 15–17, NHCL, NC 385 W, 1855.

18. Sprunt, 160, 162.

19. Walter Gwynn, *Report of Walter Gwynn, Esq. Engineer, to the President and Directors of the Portsmouth and Roanoke Rail Road Company* (Norfolk, VA: T. G. Broughton, 1833), 7, UNCW, MS248/6/3.

Appendix B

1. Wilmington & Weldon Rail Road Company, *Annual Reports of the President and Directors, and the Chief Engineer and Superintendent of the Wilmington & Weldon R. R. Co., with the Proceedings of the General Meeting of Stockholders, November 8th, 1860* (Wilmington, NC: Fulton and Price, 1860), 4–11, 15–16, 23.

2. Wilmington & Weldon Rail Road Company (1860), 22–24; Wilmington & Weldon Rail Road Company, *Proceedings of the Stockholders of the Wilmington & Weldon Rail Road Co. at their Twentieth Annual Meeting, held at Wilmington, North Carolina, November 9, 1855* (Wilmington, NC: Thomas Loring, 1855), 14.

3. *Wilmington Journal,* November 13, 1854.

4. Wilmington & Weldon Rail Road Company, *Proceedings of the Stockholders of the Wilmington & Weldon Rail Road Co. at their Twentieth Annual Meeting, held at Wilmington, North Carolina, November 9th. 1855* (Wilmington: Thomas Loring, 1855), 11–12, 16, 25.

5. *Wilmington Journal,* March 10, April 7, 1856.

6. *Wilmington Chronicle,* May 17, 1843.

7. *Wilmington Star,* May 1, 1868, New Hanover County Library, Bill Reeves Collection, Wilmington & Weldon Railroad Folder (hereafter abbreviated as NHCL-R).

8. *Wilmington Star,* April 4, 1871. NHCL-R.

9. *Wilmington Star,* December 15, 1875. NHCL-R: "The old freight warehouse of the W. & W. road, at the end of Front street, is being razed and the adjoin lots on Nutt street trenched with an activity that would seem to indicate building operations of magnitude in the near future."

10. *Wilmington Star,* January 28, 1876, NHCL-R: "Going west from Boney Bridge the work of improvement and change is visible on all sides. One of the tracks leading to the Weldon shops has been removed of the earth and consequent lowering of the general grade. A new track is being run close under the embankment on the right, to make room for which considerable fallen earth has to be removed, resulting in the bringing to light of some long-buried relics of the early road. This earth, as well as that taken from the widening of the cut at Boney Bridge, is being used to fill up the old, unsightly, miasma-breeding marsh at the foot of the hill on the left, near the crossing of Front Street. To the left of the old tracks at this point the ground has been sufficiently graded to admit of the laying of a new broad-gauge track for the Wilmington, Columbia & Augusta Road, and this has been extended through the lot to the north of the Co-operative Store, laying bare and cutting through the massive foundations of the warehouse which formerly occupied the ground, thence crossing Nutt street, and reaching, almost to the water's edge at the old Cotton Press. Still to the left of this track and east of the bridge another track will branch off and cross the marsh, bearing toward the centre of the Co-operative Store, necessitating the demolition of a portion of that building and the making of another cut through the hill under the same, to the south of the present bridge, as we understand."

11. Wilmington & Weldon Rail Road Company (1860), 22, 24; *Wilmington Star,* January 28, 1876, NHCL-R. The same article also notes extensive expansion of the railroad cut from bridge at Fourth Street, and a overall lowering of the grade. In the process of grading and excavation, "long buried relic of the early days of the road" (presumably rails) were unearthed, and excavated earth was being used to fill the marshy area near the bridge at Front Street.

12. *Carolina Observer,* May 3, 1843; *Wilmington Chronicle,* May 17, 1843.

13. Wilmington & Weldon Rail Road Company (1860), 22.

14. William J. Twining, "Map of Wilmington," Mark A. Moore, *The Wilmington Campaign and the Battles for Fort Fisher* (Cambridge, MA, and New York: Da Capo, 1999), North Carolina Historic Sites, North Carolina De-

partment of Cultural Resources, Office of Archives and History, (2010), (accessed on December 24, 2010), *http://www.nchistoricsites.org/fisher/map_wilmington2.htm*.

15. As a topic unto itself, the morphology of the depot site at Wilmington can best be described as successive periods where the natural landscape of what appears on the Wilmington block plan as blocks 230, 231, 245, 246, 248, and parts of 249 and 250 are graded and filled to accommodate additional track, buildings that suit the primary function of the facility at a given time, and the create new land at the edge of the Cape Fear River. A geomorphologist might take a stochastic approach, based upon the archival maps and existing nearby landforms, and envision the land as the railroad obtained it from Marsden Campbell as similar to that which can be observed today at undeveloped Old Brunswick Town on the Cape Fear, with a bluff descending steeply to marsh at the water's edge. The stream that cut through the bluff at the boundary of Wilmington (at Front and Campbell streets) was a modest stream of low competency draining from the highest above Fifth Street as with the other natural streams that once cut through old Wil-mington. The excavation of the four hundred yard inclined plane after the Great Fire of 1843 in the ravine cut by the stream was the first significant alteration of the natural topography.

16. Wilmington & Weldon Rail Road Company, *Annual Reports of the President and Directors, and the Chief Engineer and Superintendent of the Wilmington & Weldon R.R. Co., with the Proceedings of the General Meeting of Stockholders, November 16th, 1870,* (Wilmington, NC: Engelhard & Price, Steam Power Press Printers, Journal Buildings, 1870), 6, 9, -10, UNCCH, Cp385.1 W78a1.

17. Wilmington, Columbia & Augusta and the Wilmington & Weldon Rail Road Companies, *Annual Reports of the President and Directors and the General Superintendents of the Wilmington, Columbia & Augusta and the Wilmington & Weldon Rail Road Companies, with the Proceedings of the General Meeting of Stockholders, November 21st, 1876,* (Wilmington, NC: The Morning Star Steam Power-Presses, 1876), 10, 19, UNCCH, C385.1 W78.

18. Wilmington & Weldon Rail Road Company, *Annual Reports of the President and Directors and the General Superintendent of the Wilmington & Weldon Rail Road Company, with the Proceedings of the General Meeting of Stockholders, November 10th, 1880,* (Wilmington, NC: The Morning Star Steam-Power Presses, 1880), 9, UNCCH, Cp385.1 W78a2.

Bibliography

The American Farmer, and Spirit of the Agricultural Journals of the Day. July 31, 1839, 78.

Angevine, Robert G. "Individuals, Organizations, and Engineering: U.S. Army Officers and the American Railroads, 1827–1838." *Technology and Culture* 42.2 (April 2001): 292–320.

Black, Robert C. *The Railroads of the Confederacy.* Chapel Hill: University of North Carolina Press, 1998.

The Boors of Carolina. "Revolutionsry Reminiscences." *Niles' Weekly Register,* 1842: 96.

Bridgens, R.P., and P. Allen. *An Original Map of the City of Charleston, South Carolina.* Hayden Brother and Company, 1852.

Brown, Cecil K. *A State Movement in Railroad Development.* Chapel Hill: University of North Carolina Press, 1928.

Buchanan, R.A. "The Diaspora of British Engineering." *Technology and Culture* 27 (July 1986): 501–524.

Burke, James C. "Antebellum Plans for Reopening Roanoke Inlet." *The North Carolina Geographer* 17 (2009–2010): 17–25.

_____. *North Carolina's First Railroads: A Study in Historical Geography.* Greensboro: University of North Carolina at Greensboro, 2008, Dissertation, NCDOCKS, *http://libres.uncg.edu/ir/uncg/listing.aspx?id=637* (accessed on December 18, 2010).

Cabannes, Henri. *General Mechanics Translated from the Second French Edition by S.P. Sutera.* Waltham, MA: Blaisdell, 1968.

Cal. Scientific Press. "Evolution of Locomotives in America." *Science* 1 (July 1880): 35.

Caldwell, Joseph. *The Numbers of Carlton, Addressed to the People of North Carolina, on a Central Rail-Road Through the State. The Rights of Freemen is an Open Trade.* New York: G. Long, 1828.

Calomiris, Charles, and Larry Schweikart. "The Panic of 1857: Origins, Transmission, and Containment." *Journal of Economic History* 51, No. 4 (December 1991): 807–834.

Carlson, Robert E. "British Railroads and Engineers and the Beginnings of American Railroad Development." *The Business History Review* 34 (Summer 1960), 137–149.

Carolina Observer and Fayetteville Gazette. Microfilm; Raleigh: North Carolina Department of Archives and History, Divisions of Archives and Manuscripts.

Cavanaugh, John C. *Decision at Fayetteville: The North Carolina Ratification Convention and General Assembly of 1789.* Raleigh: Division of Archives and History, North Carolina Department of Cultural Resources, 1989.

Chandler, Alfred D. "Patterns of American Railroad Finance, 1830–50." *The Business History Review* 28 (September 1954): 248–263.

Clark, Walter M. *History of the Raleigh & Gaston Railroad Company, Including All the Acts of the General Assembly of North Carolina Thereto.* Raleigh: The Raleigh News Steam Job Print, 1877.

Colton, A.H. *The City of Charleston, South Carolina.* New York: A.H. Colton, 1855.

Conner, Robert D.W. *Ante-Bellum Builders of North Carolina.* Greensboro: North Carolina College for Women, 1930.

Coon, Charles L. *The Beginnings of Public Education in North Carolina.* Raleigh, NC: Edwards and Broughton, 1908.

Councill, Richard J. *The Commercial Granites of North Carolina.* Raleigh: Division of Mineral Resources, North Carolina Department of Conservation and Development, 1954.

Cumming, William P. *North Carolina in Maps.* Raleigh: Division of Archives and History, North Carolina Department of Cultural Resources, 1966.

Daniels, R.B., E.E. Gamble, W.H. Wheeler, and C.S. Holzhey. "Carolina Geological and Atlantic Coastal Plain Geological Association, Field Trip Guidebook (The Geology of the NC Coastal Plain from the Sounds Near New Bern to the Piedmont of Wake County)." *Carolina Geological Society, Guidebook for the 1972 Annual Meeting,* 1972: 1–33.

Davis, Raymond E., Francis S. Foote, and Joe W. Kelly. *Surveying Theory and Practice,* 5th ed. New York: McGraw-Hill, 1966.

"Desultory Remarks on Rail Roads, and Other Public Improvements." *Farmers' Register,* March 1836, 684–685.

Dilts, James D. *The Great Road: The Building of the Baltimore & Ohio, the Nation's First Railroad, 1828–1855.* Stanford, CA: Stanford University Press, 1993.

Dodd, William E. *The Life of Nathaniel Macon.* Raleigh, NC: Edwards and Broughton, 1903.

Dudley, Edward B. *Edward B. Dudley Letter Book, 1837–1840.* 1840. Raleigh: North Carolina State Archives, G.L.B. 32.

Editor. "Opinion of the Supreme Court of North Carolina in the Case of the State of North Carolina v. Francis E. Rives — December Term, 1844." *American Law Magazine,* 1845: 282–296.

"Extracts from the Report of Walter Gwynn, Esq., Engineer, to the President and Directors of the Wilmington and Raleigh Rail Road Company." *Farmers' Register,* October 1836, 348–351.

Fiedler, Fred E. "A Contingency Model of Leadership Effectiveness." In Leonard Berkowitz, ed., *Advances in Experimental Social Psychology,* New York: Academic, 1964.

Ford, Peter A. "Charles S. Storrow, Civil Engineer: A Case Study of European Training and Technological Transfer in the Antebellum Period." *Technology and Culture* 34, (April 1993): 271–299.

Garnett, Charles F.M. "Raleigh and Gaston Rail-Road." *Farmers' Register,* July 1839, 388.

Gatell, Frank Otto. "Spoils of the Bank War: Political Bias in the Selection of Pet Banks." *The American History Review* 70 (October 1964): 35–58.

"General Description of the Charleston and Hamburg Rail-Road." *Farmers' Register,* October 1833, 261–163.

Gilmer, Jeremy Francis. *Field Map of Liet.*

Koener's Military Survey Between Neuse and Tar Rivers North Carolina. Raleigh: North Carolina State Archives, Map Collection, 1863.

Graham, William A. *Message of His Excellency, Gov. Graham, to the Legislature of North Carolina, at the Session of 1846–'47.* Raleigh: W.R. Gales, Printer to the Legislature, 1846.

_____. *Message from His Excellency, the Governor, Relative to the State's Railroad Liabilities.* Raleigh, NC: Seaton Gales, Printer for the State, 1848.

Grundy, Felix, and John M. Robinson. "Statistics 2 — No Title." *Niles' Weekly Register,* June 21, 1834.

Gwynn, Walter. *Report of Walter Gwynn, Esq. Engineer, to the President and Directors of the Portsmouth and Roanoke Rail Road Company.* Norfolk, VA: T.G. Broughton, 1833.

Hamilton, J.G. de Roulhac. *Party Politics in North Carolina, 1835–1860.* Chapel Hill: University of North Carolina, James Sprunt Historical Publications, North Carolina Historical Society, 1916.

Hammond, Bray. "The Chestnut Street Raid on Wall Street, 1839." *The Quarterly Journal of Economics* 61 (August 1947): 605–618.

_____. "Jackson, Biddle, and the Bank of the United States." *The Journal of Economic History* 7 (May 1947): 1–23.

Henderson, Archibald. *North Carolina: The Old North State and the New.* Chicago, IL: Lewis, 1941.

Hill, Forest G. "Government Engineering Aid to Railroads Before the Civil War." *The Journal of Economic History* 11 (Summer 1951): 235–246.

Hunt, James G. *Leadership, A New Synthesis.* Newbury Park, CA: Sage, 1996.

"Internal Improvements of North Carolina." *North American Review and Miscellaneous Journal* (1821): 16–37.

Jeffrey, Thomas E. "Internal Improvements and Political Parties in Antebellum North Carolina." *North Carolina Historical Review* 55, No. 2 (April 1978): 114.

_____. *State Parties and National Politics: North Carolina, 1815–1861.* Athens: University of Georgia Press, 1989.

Kemble, Frances Anne. *Journal of a Residence on a Georgian Plantation in 1838–1839.* Athens: University of Georgia Press, 1984.

Kemble-Butler, Frances Anne. "A Winter's Journey to Georgia U.S." *Bentley's Miscellany,* 1842: 1–12, 113–124.

Kerker, Milton. "Sadi Carnot." *The Scientific Monthly* 85 (September 1957): 143–149.

_____. "Sadi Carnot and the Steam Engine

Engineers." *Isis* 51 (September 1960): 257–270.

____. "Science and the Steam Engine." *Technology and Culture* 2 (Autumn 1961): 381–390.

Koestenbaum, Peter. *Leadership, the Inner Side of Greatness: A Philosophy for Leaders.* San Francisco, CA: Jossey-Bass/John Wiley and Sons, 2002.

Konkle, Burton Alva. *John Motley Morehead and the Development of North Carolina, 1796–1866.* Philadelphia, PA: William J. Campbell, 1922.

Macesich, George. "Sources of Monetary Disturbances in the United States, 1834–1845." *The Journal of Economic History* 20 (September 1960): 407–434.

McCormac, Jack C. *Structural Analysis.* Scranton, PA: International Textbook, 1967.

Mebane, James, and Dennis Heartt. *Rail-Road Meeting.* Hillsborough, NC: D. Heartt, 1828.

Meerman, Jacob P. "The Climax of the Bank War: Biddle's Contraction, 1833–34." *The Journal of Political Economy* 71 (August 1963): 378–388.

"Memoranda and Scraps from a Traveler's Note Book." *Farmers' Register,* January 1834, 467–470.

Merrens, Harry R. *Colonial North Carolina in the Eighteenth Century: A Study in Historical Geography.* Chapel Hill: University of North Carolina Press, 1964.

Morton, Richard L. "The Virginia State Debt and Internal Improvements, 1820–38." *Journal of Political Economy* 25, No. 4 (April 1917): 339–373.

Murphey, Archibald D. *Memoir of the Internal Improvements Contemplated by the Legislature of North Carolina and on the Resources and Finances of the State.* Raleigh, NC: J. Gales, 1819.

New-Hampshire Gazette. In *America's Historic Newspapers, 2004.* NewsBank and/or the American Antiquarian Society.

New Hanover County. *Book 86.* Wilmington, NC: New Hanover County Register of Deeds, 1915.

New Hanover County. *Book Y.* Wilmington, NC: New Hanover County Register of Deeds, 1915.

New York Farmer. Vol. 10, No. 7, APS Online 190, May 29, 1837.

New York Times. In ProQuest Historical Newspapers.

Newport Mercury. In *America's Historic Newspapers, 2004.* NewsBank and/or the American Antiquarian Society.

North Carolina. *Annual Report of the Board for Int'l Improvements, November 28, 1829.* Raleigh: Lawrence & Lemay, 1829.

____. *Annual Report of the Board of Public Improvements of North-Carolina to the General Assembly, November 27, 1820; Together with Mr. Fulton's Reports to the Board, on the Public Works Projected and Carrying on Throughout the State During the Present Year.* Raleigh: J. Gales, 1820.

____. *Annual Report of the Board of Public Improvements of North-Carolina, to the General Assembly, November 26, 1821; Together with Mr. Fulton's Reports to the Board, and Other Papers in Relation to the Improvement of the State.* Raleigh: J. Gales, 1821.

____. *A Bill Concerning the Wilmington and Raleigh Rail Road Company.* Raleigh: Seaton Gales, Printer for the State, 1848.

____. *A Bill to Incorporate the Raleigh and Gaston Rail Road Company.* Raleigh: Thomas J. Lemay, 1850.

____. "Fifth Annual Report of the President and Directors of the Wilmington & Raleigh Rail Road Company, Annual Report of the Board of Internal Improvement, 1840." *Report of the Board of Internal Improvements to the General Assembly,* Document No. 16, Raleigh: Thomas Loring, 1840.

____. *Journal of the Senate and House of Commons of the General Assembly of the State of North Carolina at the Session 1833–34.* Raleigh: Lawrence and Lemay, 1831/34. North Carolina State Library, Yl, 1:J86 1831/34.

____. *Laws of the State of North Carolina Passed by the General Assembly at the Session of 1836–37.* Raleigh: Thomas J. Lemay, 1837.

____. *Laws of the State of North Carolina Passed by the General Assembly, at the Session of 1844–45.* Raleigh: Thomas J. Lemay, 1845.

____. *Laws of the State of North Carolina Passed by the General Assembly, at the Session 1850–51.* Raleigh: Star Office—Thomas J. Lemay, 1851.

____. *Memorial of the Citizens of Orange County on the Subject of a Central Rail Road.* Raleigh: Lawrence and Lemay, 1831.

____. *Memorial of the Convention upon the Subject of Internal Improvements held in Raleigh, November 1833, to the General Assembly of North Carolina.* Raleigh: Lawrence and Lemay, 1833.

____. *Mr. Murphey's Report to the Legislature of North-Carolina on Inland Navigation, December 1816.* Raleigh: Thomas Henderson, 1818.

____. *Report of the Board of Internal Improvements, 1833.* Raleigh: Lawrence and Lemay, 1833.

____. *Report of the Board of Internal Improve-

ments of North Carolina, Transmitted by the Governor to the General Assembly, December 10th, 1834. Raleigh: Philo White, 1834.

———. *Report of the Committee on Inland Navigation, Submitted to the Legislature of North Carolina, November 30, by Archibald D. Murphey, Their Chairman*. Raleigh: Thomas Henderson, 1815.

———. *Report of the Committee on Internal Improvements*. Raleigh: Lawrence and Lemay, 1833.

———. *The Report of the Committee on Int. Improvements on the Cape Fear and Deep River Navigation Company*. Raleigh: W.W. Holden, Printer to the State, 1855.

———. *Report of the Internal Improvement Board to the Legislature of North Carolina*. Raleigh: Seaton. Gales, Printer for the State, 1848.

———. *Report of the Joint Select Committee on Internal Improvements*. Raleigh: Lawrence and Lemay, 1833.

———. *Report of the President and Directors of the Board of Internal Improvements*. Raleigh: Thomas Loring, 1838.

———. *Report of the President and Directors of the Literary Fund, to the Legislature of North Carolina*. Raleigh: Thomas J. Lemay, 1842.

———. *Report of Sundry Surveys, made by Hamilton Fulton Esq. State Engineer, Agreeably to Certain Instructions from Judge Murphey, Chairman &c. and Submitted to the General Assembly, at their Session in 1819*. Raleigh: Thomas Henderson, 1819.

———. *The Revised Statutes of the State of North Carolina Passed by the General Assembly at the Session of 1836-7*. Raleigh: Turner and Hughes, 1837.

———. "Second Annual Report of the Wilmington and Raleigh Rail Road Company." *Report of the President and Directors of the Board of Internal Improvement to the Legislature of North Carolina*. Raleigh: Thomas Loring, Printer to the Legislature, 1838.

North Carolina Rail Road Company. *Proceedings of the General Meeting of Stockholders of the North Carolina Rail Road Company, at Greensboro.' July 10, 1851, with the By-Laws of the Company, as Revised at Said Meeting*. Greenboro: Patriot Office, 1851.

Olmsted, Frederick Law. *A Journey in the Seaboard Slave States with Remarks on Their Economy*. New York: Mason Brothers, 1861.

"On the Rail Roads of North Carolina, and the South Generally." *Farmers' Register*, July 1836, 140–141.

"On the Rail-Roads of North Carolina, and the South Generally." *Farmers' Register*, October 1836, 342–343.

"On the Schemes for Rail Roads in North Carolina." *Farmers' Register*, April 1836, 766–767.

Osborne, Charles F. "Letter from Charles F. Osborne to Edward B. Dudley dated January 21, 1836." *Edward C. Dudley Papers* (1836), Raleigh: North Carolina State Archives, PC.464.1.

———. "Letter from Charles F. Osborne to Edward B. Dudley dated March 1, 1836," *Edward C. Dudley Papers* (1836), Raleigh: North Carolina State Archives, PC.464.1.

Owen, John. *Message of His Excellency John Owen, to the General Assembly of North Carolina*. Raleigh, NC: Lawrence and Lemay, 1829.

Parramore, Thomas C., Peter C. Stewart, and Tommy L. Bogger. *Norfolk: The First Four Centuries*. Charlottesville and London: University Press of Virginia, 1994.

People's Press and Wilmington Advertiser. Microfilm, Raleigh: North Carolina Department of Archives and History, Division of Archives and Manuscripts.

Perkins, Edwin J., and Andrew Jackson. "Lost Opportunities for Compromise in the Bank War: A Reassessment of Jackson's Veto Message." *The Business History Review* 61 (Winter 1987): 531–550.

Price, William S. "Nathaniel Macon, Antifederalist." *North Carolina Historical Review* 81, No. 3 (July 2004): 288–312.

———. "Nathaniel Macon, Planter." *North Carolina Historical Review* 78, No. 2 (April 2001): 187–214.

"Proceedings of the Petersburg Rail Road Company." *Farmers' Register*, April 1836, 762–767.

"Progress and Conditions of the Petersburg and Roanoke Rail Road." *Farmers' Register*, May 1834, 758.

Puffert, Douglas J. "The Standardization of Track Gauge on North American Railways, 1830–1890." *The Journal of Economic History* 60 (December 2000): 933–960.

"Rail Road in North Carolina." *Farmers' Register*, May 1836, 35–38.

"Railroads of Virginia and North Carolina." *Farmers' Register*, March 1843, 165–166.

"The Raleigh and Gaston Rail Road." *Farmers' Register*, March 1836, 652–653.

Richmond Enquirer. In *America's Historic Newspapers*, 2004. NewsBank and/or the American Antiquarian Society.

Roanoke Navigation Company. *Report on the Progress and Present Condition of the Affairs of the Roanoke Navigation Company*. Raleigh, NC: Lawrence and Lemay, 1831.

Rousseau, Peter L. "Jacksonian Monetary Policy, Specie Flows, and the Panic of 1837."

The Journal of Economic History 62 (September 2002): 457–488.

Saunders, Peter. *Capitalism*. Minneapolis: University of Minnesota Press, 1995.

Schauinger, Joseph H. *William Gaston, Carolinian*. Milwaukee: Bruce, 1949.

Schenk, Nickolas. *Diary*. Wilmington: University of North Carolina at Wilmington, Randall Library Special Collections, 1905.

"Second Annual Report of the Raleigh and Gaston Rail Road Company." *Farmers' Register,* March 1838, 740–743.

Shallat, Todd. "Building Waterways, 1802–1861: Science and the United States Army in Early Public Works." *Technology and Culture* 31 (January 1990): 18–50.

Siddall, William R. "Railroad Gauges and Spatial Interaction." *Geographical Review* 59 (January 1969): 29–57.

Sinclair, Angus, and John H. White, eds. *Development of the Locomotive Engine*. Cambridge, MA: MIT Press, 1970.

Sprunt, James. *Chronicles of the Cape Fear River, 1660–1916*. Raleigh, NC: Edwards and Broughton, 1916.

_____. *Tales and Traditions of the Lower Cape Fear, 1661–1896*. Wilmington, NC: LeGwin Brothers, 1896.

Swain, David L. *Early Times in Raleigh*. Raleigh, NC: Walters, Hughes and Company, 1867.

_____. *Letter Book of Governor David L. Swain, 1834*. Raleigh: North Carolina State Archives, G.L.B. 30.

Taaffe, Edward J., Richand L. Morrill, and Peter R. Gould. "Transport Expansion in Underdeveloped Countries: A Comparative Analysis." *Geographical Review* 53, No. 4 (October 1963): 503–529.

T.A.R. "Locomotion: Or, Lights and Shades of Travel." *Orion, a Monthly Magazine of Literature and Art* (MarchApril 1843): 342–352.

Tarborough Press. Microfilm, Raleigh: North Carolina Department of Archives and History, Division of Archives and Manuscripts.

Timberlake, Richard H. "The Specie Standard and Central Banking in the United States Before 1860." *The Journal of Economic History* (1961): 318–341.

"To the Stockholders of the Petersburg Rail Road Company." *Farmers' Register,* May 1834, 758–759.

Turner, Gregg. *A Short History of Florida Railroads*. Charleston, SC: Arcadia, 2003.

Turner, Herbert S. *The Dreamer, Archibald DeBow Murphey, 1777–1832*. Verona, VA: McClure, 1971.

United States. *Agriculture of the United States in 1860; Compiled from the Original Returns of the Eighth Census, under the Direction of the Secretary of the Interior, by Joseph C.G. Kennedy*. Washington, DC: Government Printing Office, 1864.

_____. *Appendix to the Congressional Globe*. Washington, DC: 32nd Congress, 1852.

_____. *Baltimore and Susquehannah Rail-Road Company*. Washington, DC: 24th Congress, 1837.

_____. *A Bill for Relief of the Petersburg Railroad Company, S 84*. Washington, DC: 27th Congress, 1843.

_____. *Compendium of the Sixth Census*. Washington, DC: Thomas Allen, 1841.

_____. *Failure of Mails—New Orleans*. Washington, DC: 25th Congress, Document 145, 1839.

_____. *Imports and Exports of Sugar from 1821 to 1842, and Drawbacks of Duty on Railroad Iron*. Washington, DC: 27th Congress, 1842.

_____. *In Favor of Iron and Iron Machinery for Railroads Free of Duty*. Washington, DC: 20th Congress, 1828, 904: 994–996.

_____. *In the Senate of the Unites States*. Washington, DC: 25th Congress, Document 132, 1839.

_____. *Letter and Memorial of Isaac K. Lippincott, on the Manufacture of Iron and the Operation of the Present Tariff Laws*. Washington, DC: 27th Congress, 1841.

_____. *Letter from the Postmaster General*. Washington, NC: Twenty-sixth Congress, 85, 1841.

_____. *Letter of the Secretary of the Treasury, Transmitting, in Compliance with a Resolution of the House of the 18th December 1848, Statements of the Importations, &c., of Iron Under the Tariff Acts of 1842 and 1846*. Washington, DC: 30th Congress, 1849.

_____. *Mail: New York to New Orleans—Irregularities*. Washington, DC: 26th Congress, Document 159, 1840.

_____. *Memorial of a Number of Ironmasters of Lexington, Virginia, in Relation to an Increase of Duty on Imported Iron*. Washington, DC: 27th Congress, 1842.

_____. *Memorial of Inhabitants of Danville, PA Praying for a National Foundry at Danville, in Said State*. Washington, DC: 27th Congress, 1841.

_____. *Memorial of John Bryce and 212 Others, Inhabitants of Columbia, S.C., and Vicinity, Remonstrating Against the Removal of the great Southern Mail Route*. Washington, DC: 25th Congress, Document 271, 1838c.

_____. *The Memorial of Many Inhabitants of the City of Charleston Praying that the South-*

_____. *ern Mail be Carried by Way of Halifax and Wilmington.* Washington, DC: 25th Congress, Document 184, 1838.

_____. *Memorial of the Committee of a Convention Held in Richmond, VA, December 4, 1854.* Washington, DC: 33rd Congress, 1855.

_____. *Memorial of the Petersburg Railroad Company, Praying the Payment of a Sum of Money Withheld from Them, Under Their Contract for the Transportation of the Mail.* Washington, DC: 25th Congress, Document 33, 1838.

_____. *National Foundry.* Washington, DC: 27th Congress, 1843.

_____. *Petition of the Citizens of Camden.* Washington, DC: 25th Congress, Document 259, 1838.

_____. *Petition of the Citizens of Cheraw.* Washington, DC: 25th Congress, Document 246, 1838.

_____. *Petition of the Citizens of Pennsylvania, Praying for a Reduction of Duty on Railroad Iron Imported.* Washington, DC: 23rd Congress, 1835.

_____. *Post Office Department Contracts, 1830.* Washington, DC: 21st Congress, Document 117, 1831a.

_____. *Rail-Road: Pensacola to Columbus. Letter from the Secretary of War Transmitting a Survey of a Rail-Road from Pensacola, to Columbus, in Georgia.* Washington, DC: 24th Congress, Document 176, 1836.

_____. *Railroad and Steamboat Mail Lines.* Washington, DC: 28th Congress, Document 105, 1845.

_____. *Railroad Iron — Remission of Duties On.* Washington, DC: 28th Congress, 1844.

_____. *Railroad-Portage Summit, Ohio, to Hudson River.* Washington, DC: 22nd Congress, Document 133, 1832.

_____. *Railroads: Atlantic to the Mississippi.* Washington, DC: 23th Congress, 1835.

_____. *Report of the Postmaster General.* Washington, DC: 28th Congress, Document 87, 1845.

_____. *Report from The Secretary of War in Compliance with a Resolution of the Senate of 24th January 1838, with a Report of the Survey of the Charleston and Cincinnati Railroad.* Washington, DC: 25th Congress, Senate Document Number 157, 1838.

_____. *Report from the Secretary of War, with a Resolution of the Senate 20th. inst., Transmitting the Report of the Survey of the Western and Atlantic Railroad of the State of Georgia.* Washington, DC: 25th Congress, Document 57, 1837.

_____. *Resolutions of the Legislature of New Jersey in Favor of an Increase of the Duties on Coal, Iron, and Glass.* Washington, DC: 32nd Congress, 1852.

_____. *Resolutions of the Legislature of North Carolina, in Favor of the Erection of a Marine Hospital at or Near Smithville or Wilmington, in that State, and the Abolition of the Duty on Railroad Iron.* Washington, DC: 32rd Congress, 1853.

_____. *The Report of the Postmaster General, with a Statement of the Contracts Made by that Department in the Year 1833.* Washington, DC: 23rd Congress, Document 408, 1834.

_____. *S 84.* Washington, DC: 27th Congress, Third Session, 1843.

_____. *The Seventh Census of the United States: 1850.* Washington: Robert Armstrong, Public Printer, 1853.

_____. *Wilmington & W.R. Co. v. Alsbrook, Sheriff.* United States Supreme Court, December 5, 1892: 146 U.S. 279.

_____. *Winchester and Potomac Railroad.* Washington, DC: 25th Congress, Document 465, 1838e.

Vance, James E. *The North American Railroad: Its Origin, Evolution, and Geography.* Baltimore and London: John Hopkins University Press, 1995.

Vanderblue, Homer B., and George W. Whistler. "An Engineer Writes on Railroad Construction Standards in 1842." *Bulletin of the Business Historical Society* 13 (January 1939): 6–11.

Vinson, Ron, and CommunicationSolutions/ ISI. "Steamboat List, 1812–1849." *North Carolina Business History,* 2006. http://historync.org/NCsteamboats1812%20-%2018 49.htm (accessed January 2, 2011).

Virginia. *Proceeding and Debates of the Virginia-State Convention of 1829–30 ... to Which are Subjoined, the New Constitution of Virginia, and the Votes of the People.* Richmond: Samuel Shepherd & Co. for Ritchie & Cook, 1830.

Walters, Raymond. "The Origins of the Second Bank of the United States." *The Journal of Political Economy* 53 (June 1945): 115–131.

Ward, James A. "Promotional Wizardry: Rhetoric and Railroad Origins, 1820–1860." *Journal of the Early Republic* 11 (Spring 1991): 69–88.

Warner, Paul T. *Motive Power Development on the Pennsylvania Railroad System, 1831–1924.* Philadelphia, PA: Baldwin Locomotives, 1924.

Watson, Alan D. *Internal Improvements in Antebellum North Carolina.* Raleigh: Office of Archives and History, North Carolina Department of Cultural Resources, 2002, 81–85.

_____. *Wilmington, North Carolina, to 1861.* Jefferson, NC: McFarland, 2003.

Wilmington & Raleigh Rail Road Company. *Proceedings of the Wilmington & Raleigh R. R. Company, at their Fifteenth Annual Meeting held at Wilmington, North Carolina, November 14th, 1850.* Wilmington: T. Loring, 1850.

Wilmington & Weldon Rail Road Company. *Annual Reports of the President and Directors, and the Chief Engineer and Superintendent of the Wilmington & Weldon R. R. Co., with the Proceedings of the General Meeting of Stockholders, November 8th, 1860.* Wilmington: Fulton and Price, 1860.

_____. *Annual Reports of the President and Directors, and the Chief Engineer and Superintendent of the Wilmington & Weldon R.R. Co., with the Proceedings of the General Meeting of Stockholders, November 16th, 1870.* Wilmington: Engelhard and Price, Steam Power Press Printers, Journal Buildings, 1870

_____. *Annual Reports of the President and Directors and the General Superintendent of the Wilmington & Weldon Rail Road Company, with the Proceedings of the General Meeting of Stockholders, November 10th, 1880.* Wilmington: The Morning Star Steam-Power Presses, 1880.

_____. *Proceedings of the Stockholders of the Wilmington & Weldon R. R. Co., at their Twenty-First Annual Meeting held at Wilmington, North Carolina, November 13th 1856; with the Reports of the President and Directors, and the Engineer and Superintendent.* Wilmington: Thomas Loring, 1856.

_____. *Proceedings of the Stockholders of the Wilmington & Weldon R.R. Co., at their Twenty-third Annual Meeting held at Wilmington, North Carolina, November 11, 1858; with the Reports of the President and Directors, and the Engineer and Superintendent.* Wilmington: Fulton and Price, 1858.

_____. *Proceedings of the Stockholders of the Wilmington & Weldon Rail Road Co. at their Twentieth Annual Meeting, held at Wilmington, North Carolina, November 9th, 1855.* Wilmington: Thomas Loring, 1855.

Wilmington Chronicle. Microfilm; Raleigh: North Carolina Department of Archives and History, Division of Archives and Manuscripts.

Wilmington, Columbia & Augusta and the Wilmington & Weldon Rail Road Companies. *Annual Reports of the President and Directors and the General Superintendents of the Wilmington, Columbia & Augusta and the Wilmington & Weldon Rail Road Companies, with the Proceedings of the General Meeting of Stockholders, November 21st, 1876.* Wilmington, NC: The Morning Star Steam Power-Presses, 1876

Wilmington Herald. Microfilm; Raleigh: North Carolina Department of Archives and History, Division of Archives and Manuscripts.

Wilmington Journal. Microfilm; Raleigh: North Carolina Department of Archives and History, Division of Archives and Manuscripts.

Wilmington Messenger. Microfilm; Raleigh: North Carolina Department of Archives and History, Division of Archives and Manuscripts.

Wilmington Tri-weekly Commercial. Microfilm; Raleigh: North Carolina Department of Archives and History, Division of Archives and Manuscripts.

Wyatt, Edward A. "Rise of Industry in Ante-Bellum Petersburg." *William and Mary Quarterly Historical Magazine* 2.17 (January 1937): 1–29.

Index

A & J Ralston Company 52
Adams, William 34
Adamson, James 88
Albemarle Sound 12, 15–16, 18, 21, 133, 161
Albright, William 33
Allen, Horatio 82
Anderson, Alexander 69, 102
Anderson, Walker 35
Armstrong, William 171
Armstrong's farm 65
Army of Northern Virginia 159
Ashe, William S. 7–8
Atlantic Coastline Railroad 167, 177, 178; freight office at Wilmington 184
Augusta, GA 54

bacon 66
Baltimore, MD 23, 70
Baltimore & Ohio Rail Road 32, 61, 79, 82, 101
Bank of the Cape Fear 44, 138
bank stock 39
Barnes, John 169
Battle, James S. 112
Battle's Depot (Battleboro, N.C.) 67, 179
Beaufort, N.C. 9, 19–20, 35, 39–40, 42, 47, 110
Beauregard, Pierre G.T. 159
Becton, J.L. 173
Bell, John 34
Betts, Pusey & Harlan Company (Wilmington, Del.) 102
Black Creek 91
Blakeley, N.C. 11, 13, 23–24, 50, 56–57, 59, 132, 134, 162
Bollman Truss 142
Boney Bridge 182
Boston & Lowell Railroad 81
British Great Western Railway 83
Brogden, N.C. 91
Burgaw (Burgaw Swamp), N.C. 65, 89

Caldwell, Joseph 32–33, 111; *The Numbers of Carlton* 32–33; president of the University of North Carolina 32
Camden, S.C. 13, 55–56, 142
Camden County, N.C. 16
Cameron, Duncan 38, 55
Campbell, Marsden 170, 173
Campbellton (Fayetteville, N.C.) 33–34, 47
canals 9, 27–28, 30
Cape Fear & Deep River Navigation Company 27, 193
Cape Fear & Western Rail Road 110
Cape Fear & Yadkin Rail Road 30, 35–39, 42–43, 47, 62, 93–94, 131; Cape Fear & Yadkin Valley Railroad (late 1800s) 62–63, 93; subscriptions to stock 36–38; survey 36–37
Cape Fear Canal and Rail Road Company 40
Cape Fear Coal and Iron Company 28
Cape Fear Community College 184–187
Cape Fear Navigation Company 22, 28, 39
Cape Fear River 18, 26–27, 30, 33, 35, 44, 63, 142, 170–171, 175, 179; Branson's Mill 28; Buckhorn Falls 27–28; Jones Falls 27; Parker's Creek 28; Pullen's Falls 27; Smiley's Falls 27
capitalization of railroads 34, 118, 160
Capitol Fire (Raleigh, N.C.) 35, 43–44
Cardiff, Wales 95
Carolina Central Railroad 93
Carolina Observer 37
Carthage, N.C. 54
Cass, Lewis 14
Catawba Navigation Company 22
Catawba River 18
Central Rail Road 8, 33, 35, 37, 39, 44, 58
Charleston, S.C. 5, 9, 54–56, 58, 60, 67, 69–71, 127, 141, 165; Chamber of Commerce 55
Charleston & Cincinnati Rail Road 60, 81
Charleston & Hamburg Rail Road 9, 32, 34,

57, 79, 82; construction techniques 83, 87, 90, 200–201
Charleston Mercury 141, 143
Charlotte, N.C. 26–27, 93, 149
Charlotte & Columbia Rail Road 158
Charlotte & South Carolina Railroad 158
Cheraw, S.C. 26, 40, 55–56, 93
Cherokee 110
Clarendon Plantation 173; *see also* Campbell, Marsden
Clark, Walter McKenzie 137–138
Clingman, Thomas 99, 115
Clinton, N.C. 43, 46
Clubfoot & Harlowe Creek Canal 18–20, 22, 39; company 22
coal 25–28, 94, 192; Cumnock 27; Egypt coalfields (Chatham County, N.C.) 25–27
coastal navigation 22
Columbia, S.C. 9, 13, 40, 50, 54–56, 164
Commonwealth of Virginia 2, 6–7, 11–13, 15–17, 20–21, 23–24, 30–31, 41, 47; Board of Public Works 17; Legislature 24, 41, 165; public debt 17
Conoconnara Creek 63
Contentnea Creek 63, 91
corn 23, 192
cotton 9, 22–23, 51, 149–151, 153–156, 192
Cotton Plant (steamboat) 70
Cowan, Hugh 171, 174
Cowan, Robert H. 109, 111, 115, 129
Crimean War 118, 150
Crozet, Claudius 80, 86

Dan River 21–22
Danville, Va. 60, 158
Danville & Charlotte Railroad 158
Darlington, S.C. 14–15, 142
Davidson County, N.C. 37
Deep River 27–28
Deep River Coal and Iron Company 28; coal oil 28
Delaware & Hudson Canal Company 82
DeRosset, Armand J. 94, 99–100
Devine, John F. 182
Dickinson, P.K. 42, 171, 175; *see also* experimental railroads
Dismal Swamp Canal 12, 15–17, 20, 30, 38, 131–133, 139, 161
double track 37
Dudley, Edward B. 7, 28, 47–49, 51–52, 64, 140–141, 157, 163–164, 194; political career 110, 138; president of the Wilmington & Raleigh Rail Road Company 109–115, 129, 142
Dudley, N.C. 66, 77, 90, 91
Duplin Courthouse 65

early railroad technology 1–2, 6, 8
Ecole Polytechnique 80–81

economic "stream piracy" 7, 163
E.D. McNair (steamboat) 66
Edenton, N.C. 38
Edwards Bridge 63–64
Elizabeth River 16
Elm City, N.C. 188
Elzey, A. (U.S. Army) 70
embankments 86, 88–89, 200–201
Emerson, Arthur 137
Enfield, N.C. 56, 62, 65–66, 73, 74, 76, 77
England 7, 51, 52, 82–83, 150; Bank of England 119; banking 53, 100–101, 119, 122; bonds 122; collieries 8; engineering tradition 32
Erwin, N.C. 27
Experimental Rail Road Company 43–44, 46
experimental railroads 8, 29, 32–34; New England 42; Swift Creek 14; *see also* Fulton, Hamilton

Fair Bluff, N.C. 142
Faison's Depot (Faison, N.C.) 64, 66, 89, 91
farm values (N.C. counties) 154
Fayetteville, N.C. 13–14, 25–27, 29, 31, 33, 35–37, 42–43, 47, 50, 52, 54–55, 62, 94, 110, 192; Great Fire of 1831 34–35; old State House 34
Fayetteville & Campbellton Rail Road 41
Fayetteville & Western Railroad 26–27, 30, 118
Fayetteville Canal 18
Fayetteville Rail Road 8–9, 29, 34, 52; capitalization 34; charter 34
Fiedler Contingency Model 111
Fisher, Charles 35
Fishlow, Albert 118
Flemming, L.J. 143
Foster, Rastrick & Company 82
Fowler, Joseph 45
Fredericksburg, Va. 23, 56
Fredericksburg & Potomac Railroad Company 17
Freemont, S.L. 182
French Broad River 18, 40
Fulton, Hamilton 14, 18–19, 28, 81

Garnett, Charles F. M. 92–93
Garysburg, N.C. 136–137
Gaston, N.C. (Old Gaston, Wilkes' Ferry) 13, 40, 49–50, 53, 57, 59, 165, 192
Gaston, William 35, 36, 44
General Survey Act of 1824 79–80, 84
geographic analysis 12, 29–30, 57, 139–140, 156–157, 160–168
geology 92
geomorphology and physiographic regions 15, 26 31, 89–93, 108, 160–162
Georgetown, S.C. 69

Gilmer, Jeremy Francis 76
Gleason's Pictorial Drawing-Room Companion 179–181
Goldsboro, N.C. *see* Waynesboro (Goldsboro), N.C.
Governor Dudley (steamboat) 69–71; *see also* Kemble, Frances Anne
Graham, James D. 86
Graham, William A. 52, 110, 112, 131, 137, 158, 165–166
Green, James 69
Greensboro 27, 60, 94
Greensville & Roanoke Rail Road 13, 15, 40–42, 48–51, 54–55, 59, 93, 163–165
Guyonneau, François Marie (le Comte de Pambour) 81, 88
Gwynn, Walter 50, 58, 61–64, 79, 80, 83, 85–89, 91, 93–94, 108, 113–114, 133, 143, 159, 169, 174–175, 177

Halifax, N.C. 11, 13–14, 36, 38, 42, 46–49, 51–52, 55–56, 58, 61–65, 73, 77, 113
Halifax & Weldon Rail Road 24, 40–42, 46, 48, 50, 52, 57, 65, 114, 140, 162–163
Halifax Rail Road Bridge Company 40, 50
Halsey, B.F. 73
Hause, C.W. 73
Haw River 35
Haywood, N.C. 27–28, 35–36
Haywood, William H. 45
Hicksford (Emporia, Va.) 50
historical significance 1, 160
Hogg, Gavin 46–47, 54, 113, 164
Holliday, James 113
horse path 85
Hort, William P. 37

Internal Improvements Convention at Greensboro 157–158
Internal Improvements Conventions of 1833 (Raleigh) 6, 9, 38–40, 44, 46, 50, 58, 163
Iredell, James, Jr. 33
iron 7, 27–28, 43, 66, 83, 84, 85, 117, 123, 125–126, 131; American iron 52, 99; British iron 25, 30, 52, 94–101; duties 7, 95–100; Endor Iron Works 27; H-rail 84; heavy iron rail 117; strap-iron 7, 117, 121–123, 166, 186–187; T-rail 7, 84, 95, 105
Ivey, Charles 70

Jacksonian Era (Andrew Jackson) 8; Deposit Act of 1836 98, 119–120; federal surplus 52, 116, 120, 138; monetary policy 52, 116, 119, 137, 150, 204; Second Bank of the United States 116, 119–120, 150; Specie Circular 119; *see also* Panic of 1837
James River 17
James River & Kanawha Company 17

James River Company 17
Johnson, Albert 103
Johnston County, N.C. 24
Jones, John D. 44, 171
Joyner, Andrew 112, 137

Kemble (Butler), Frances Anne 69, 73–74, 76–78, 90–91, 196; *see also Governor Dudley* (steamboat); Wilmington & Raleigh Rail Road stagecoach line; Wilmington & Raleigh Rail Road steamboat line
Kidder, Edwin 171, 175
Kidder, William Calder Frederick 171, 175
Kyle, James 34

land values (N.C. counties) 151–153
Latrobe, Benjamin H. 18, 81
Liverpool & Manchester Railway 32, 81–82
locomotives 34, 50, 66, 88, 94; Baldwin locomotives 102–107; Burr & Sampson 103; Burr, Pea & Sampson 102, 106; Company shops 106; D.J. Burr & Company 102; Manchester Locomotive Works 104–106; Norris locomotives 67, 102–106; Rogers 107; Stephenson locomotives 65, 81, 101; *see also* Robert Stephenson and Company; *S.D. Wallace* (locomotive)
Long, Colonel S.L. 14–15, 86, 88, 164
Long Creek 170
Louisburg, N.C. 35–36
Lumber River 40
Lumberton, N.C. 25
Lynches Creek 143

Mackenzie, D. 24
MacLaurin, John 169
Macon, Nathaniel 20
MacRae (McRae), Alexander 8, 112, 170, 173
Mahan, Dennis Hart 80–81
Manchester Junction, S.C. 143
Manly, Charles 110
Margarettsville, N.C. 87, 117
Marshall, N.C. 40
Martin's farm 65
Mason, John M. 34
Maury, Latham and Company 52
Mazell, Pompy 170
McCombs, Robert S. 170, 174
McCoy, Elijah 104
McNeill, William George 28, 79, 88
Meherrin River 87
Metropolitan Route 9, 39, 160, 162, 164
Mexican War 118
Miller, James T. 71
Montague, N.C. 62–63
Moore, Thomas 18
Moore's Creek 62–63, 170
Mordecai, George W. 51, 53, 138

Mordecai, Samuel 51
Morehead, John M. 110, 158
Morganton, N.C. 8, 25, 36
Mosley, William D. 112
Mt. Olive, N.C. 91
multimodal transportation 5, 160
Murphey, Archibald D. 15–16, 18–20, 111

Nahunta Swamp 91
Neuse Navigation Company 22
Neuse River 18–20, 43, 45, 50, 61–63, 66, 89, 91–92
New Bern, N.C. 8, 19, 35, 39, 43–46, 50–51, 66
New Hanover County, N.C. 41, 44, 170; public library 173; Register of Deeds 173; *see also* Wilmington, N.C.
New York 49
Newport River 19
Norfolk, Va. 7, 12, 22, 25, 29, 47, 51–52, 55, 131–133, 137, 139–140, 161–162, 164, 179
Norfolk Herald 23, 29
North Carolina *see* State of North Carolina
North Carolina Central Railroad 30, 35, 110, 118
North Carolina Centre & Seaport Rail Road 42
North Carolina Railroad 2, 8, 26–27, 93, 141, 148–150, 157–158, 166
Northeast Cape Fear River 44, 52–53, 61–63, 65, 89–91, 169–170; Bear Swamp 62–63, 89, 169–170; bridge construction 65, 89; Brooks Branch (Brooks Swamp) 62, 89–91; Goshen Swamp 61, 90; Long Creek 61–63; Prince George Creek 169; Reedy Branch 89; Rockfish Creek 62–63, 65, 89, 170; Rockfish Creek bridge 179; Smith Creek 61, 169–171; Stewart Creek 62, 89, 170; Turkey Creek 170; Yellow Marsh 62
Nottoway River 87

Oberlin (ship) 66
Olmsted, Denison 18
Olmsted, Fredrick L. 27, 29, 192
Orange County, N.C. 35
Osborne, Charles F. 48–49, 51, 57, 163, 194
Owen, James 68, 113, 115–116, 138, 146
Owen, John 33, 190
Oxford, N.C. 52

Palmer, John J. 136
Panic of 1837 7, 52, 53, 98, 118, 120, 140, 150, 160
Panic of 1857 118, 149
Paradise Plantation 174; *see also* Cowan, Hugh
Pasquotank River 16
Pearson, John 35
Pee Dee River 13, 33, 143

Peoples Press 36
Petersburg, Va. 7, 23, 25, 28–30, 47–49, 51, 58, 111, 131–133, 137, 139–140, 149, 153, 161, 164, 179
Petersburg Rail Road 9, 11, 13, 15, 17–18, 21, 23–24, 26, 29–31, 40–42, 48–52, 55, 57–59, 61, 93, 117, 131, 133–134, 136, 146, 162–163, 166
Piedmont Railroad 60
Pierce, E.E. 171
Pitts Crossroads 77
Pittsboro, N.C. 54
plank roads 26–28
Polk, Sarah 43
Portsmouth, Va. 16, 66, 139, 149, 179
Portsmouth & Roanoke Rail Road 9, 11, 13, 15, 17, 21, 24, 30–31, 38, 41, 48–50, 56, 58–59, 61, 74, 85–89, 117, 131–137, 139, 146, 162, 165–166, 177
Post Office Department 5, 55–57, 70, 73, 146, 165, 199; Second Class routes 55; Southern Great Mail 5, 9, 54–57, 72, 165, 189
Pottsville, PA 28
public-private partnership 2, 160

Quankey Creek 64

rail construction techniques 37, 43
Raleigh, N.C. 5, 8, 13, 14–15, 24–26, 29, 35, 38–46, 48–52, 54, 58, 111, 140, 164
Raleigh & Augusta Air Line Railroad 93–94
Raleigh & Columbia Rail Road 52–56, 93, 118, 162, 164
Raleigh & Gaston Rail Road 8–9, 11, 14–15, 26, 40–41, 49, 51–59, 93, 120, 126, 131, 139, 140–141, 153–154, 158, 160, 163–165, 192; bonds 53, 114, 116–118, 120, 126; bridge 50–53, 59, 165, 194; mortgage and foreclosure 11, 53, 138; new charter 120; smallpox 52; survey 49
Raleigh Register 13, 37, 42–44, 46
Rawle, William 37
Richmond, V.A. 23
Richmond & Danville Railroad 158
Richmond Enquirer 25
Rives, Francis 133–135, 137, 139, 165
roads 12, 22, 62; Buncombe Turnpike 39; Swannanoa Turnpike 39; Tennessee Turnpike Company 39; turnpikes 9, 30, 42–44
Roanoke & Raleigh Rail Road 40–41, 48, 137, 165
Roanoke & Yadkin Rail Road 24, 41
Roanoke Canal 12–13, 15, 17–22, 24, 132, 161–162; bateau(x) 21, 24; Chockoyotte Creek 18; steamboats 22
Roanoke Inlet 12, 18–20, 133, 161
Roanoke Navigation Company 18, 20, 22, 23, 39, 132

Roanoke Rapids, N.C. 21
Roanoke River 5, 7–9, 11, 13, 21, 23–24, 38–41, 43, 46–48, 50, 53, 142, 162–163; basin 12, 17, 21, 23, 31, 132–133, 161; Great Falls of the Roanoke 12, 18, 132, 161, 163
Roanoke Valley Railroad Company 136–138; militia 137
Robert Stephenson and Company 81–82
Rockford Bridge (Rockfort, N.C.) 61–64
Rockingham, N.C. 54
Rocky Mount, N.C. 64, 73, 76, 179
Rogers, Allen 45
Roles Store 45
Rowan County, N.C. 25
Ruffin, Edmund 11, 13, 43, 61

S.D. Wallace (locomotive) 107
Sadi Carnot, Nicholas Leonard 81
Salisbury, N.C. 25, 27–28, 35
Sanborn Fire Insurance Maps 185
Saunders, Romulus M. 116
Schenk, Nicholas 176
Schuffleton, N.C. 63
Scotland Neck, N.C. 64
Seaboard & Roanoke Rail Road 133, 136, 149
Seaboard Coastline Railroad 64
slaves 9, 20, 65, 74, 122, 125, 128–130, 159
Slocomb, Ezekiel 77
Smallwood, Samuel 47
Smith, J.S. 35
Smithville (Southport, N.C.) 70
South Carolina *see* State of South Carolina
South Carolina Railroad 60
South Washington 43–44, 46, 56, 75, 170
Speed, N.C. 64
Sprunt, James 25, 48, 102, 109, 111, 113, 174
stagecoaches 2, 5, 26–27, 54, 65–66, 72–75, 78, 198–200
Stantonsburg, N.C. 73–74, 76
State of North Carolina 2, 5, 8, 13, 15, 20–22, 31, 114, 126–127, 129, 131, 133–135, 137–138, 160, 164–165; *An Act to Aid Internal Improvements of the State* 116; Board of Internal Improvements (North Carolina) 28, 39, 69, 102, 116, 143; Board of Public Improvements of North Carolina 12, 18–19, 28, 37, 39, 47; canal and navigation company stock 19, 22–23; General Assembly (Legislature) 6, 7, 9, 14, 24, 27, 30, 33–36, 38–41, 43, 44–48, 50–53, 56, 99, 110–112, 116, 127, 131, 134–138, 141, 163; Literary Board (Fund) 110, 122, 128–129, 136, 138; political regions 34–35, 50; state bank 53, 116; supreme court 134–135, 165–166; *see also* two-fifths investment policy
State of South Carolina 7–8, 12, 15, 23, 31, 38–39, 43, 46–47, 68, 122, 142–144; Legislature 56

Staunton River 21–22
staves 23
Stephenson, George 32, 82; *see also* locomotives; Robert Stephenson and Company
Stockton & Darlington Railway 32, 82
Storrow, Charles S. 80
Sumterville (Sumter, S.C.) 142–143
surveys 21, 36–37, 49, 61–64, 81, 85–89
Swain, David L. 24, 34, 43, 45, 111

Tar Navigation Company 22
Tar River 64, 67, 77, 91, 93, 179
Tarborough (Tarboro) 61, 63–64, 73–74, 76–77
Tennessee 9, 33, 38
tobacco 18, 22–23
trestlework 83–84, 89–90, 200–201
Trevithick, Richard 32
Troublefield Creek 137
turpentine 66, 150–151
Twining, William J. 182
two-fifths investment policy (North Carolina and Virginia) 6, 15, 17, 30, 38, 40, 47, 52, 55, 110, 116, 120

United States 17, 94
United States Congress 7, 55–57, 81, 87, 94–100, 110, 112, 119–120
United States Topographical Engineers (Bureau) 6, 13–14, 20, 40, 61, 79, 84
University of North Carolina 18, 32
Upshur, Abel 159

Virginia & North Carolina Transportation Company 22
Virginia State Lottery 17

W.W. Harllee (steamboat) 179
Wadesboro, N.C. 54
Wake County, N.C. 34, 45
Wanett, A.A. 171, 175–176
War of 1812 39
Warren County, N.C. 53
Washington, D.C. 23
Wateree River 143
Waynesborough (Goldsboro, N.C.) 7–8, 13–14, 24, 44–46, 49–51, 56, 61–64, 66, 73–75, 92–93, 114, 149, 156, 166
Weldon, N.C. 2, 5, 11–13, 15, 21–23, 26, 29–31, 36, 41–42, 46, 48–50, 55–56, 58–60, 64, 74, 142, 149, 162–163, 165, 192
Weldon Toll Bridge (Company) 11, 13, 21, 24, 30, 41, 48–50, 52–53, 56, 117, 132–134, 136–137, 140, 162–163, 194
West Point 61, 79–80, 84, 108, 118
Western & Atlantic Railroad 93
wheat 18, 23, 150–151
Whig governors of North Carolina 7

Whistler, George W. 79, 84
White, Leonard 143
Williams, W.G. 88
Wilmington, N.C. 2–3, 5, 8, 11, 13–14, 24–27, 29, 31, 36, 38–39, 42–45, 51, 53–54, 56, 58, 71, 169, 206; Burgwyn 169; Campbell Street 169, 176–177; Castle Haynes 169; Coastline Convention Center 184; Dry Pond 61, 64, 169, 174; Eagle(s) Island 63; Great Fire of 1843 102, 110, 115, 117, 129, 182; harbor 179–181; Love Grove Plantation 169, 171, 176; Marsden Campbell plot 170–174, 173, 180, 208; McKay 173; Nutt Street 180, 181, 183, 185, 188; Point Peter 62, 181; Wilmington Committee 45, 47, 113
Wilmington & Manchester Railroad 2, 7, 60, 67, 71–72, 122–123, 127, 141–143, 148, 166, 179, 188
Wilmington & Raleigh Rail Road stagecoach line 72–78; *see also* Kemble (Butler) Frances Anne; stagecoaches
Wilmington & Raleigh Rail Road steamboat line 2, 5, 9, 54–55, 58, 60, 67–72, 121, 124–125, 130, 143, 148, 161, 163, 166, 167, 187–188, 196–198; captains 71; collision between the North Carolina and the C. Vanderbilt 69; crews 71; Cully, Langley B. (builder of the *Wilmington*) 70; names of steamboats 68; T. Morris & Son 70; Watchman & Bratt 69; *see also* Ivey, Charles; Miller, James T.
Wilmington & Raleigh Rail Road 1–3, 6, 30, 32, 48, 55–58, 118, 141, 160–167; bonds and mortgage 7, 114, 117, 121–122, 127–129, 138, 146; Charleston docks 67; charter 11, 31, 41, 52, 111–113, 156; consolidated deed for Wilmington depot 170–173, 176; construction 52, 65–68, 75, 78; construction costs 67, 195–196; depots 64, 66–67, 128, 156; financial reports 121–130, 143–150; freight 146, 150; locomotives and rolling stock 66–67, 101–108, 129; passenger station at Wilmington 179–188, 207–208; passengers 124–125, 144–145, 147–148; photograph of 1880s Wilmington depot 184; route 42, 58; shares 45, 99, 112–113, 116; shops 65, 70–71, 101–102, 104, 106, 108, 125, 129, 174, 176, 181–183; survey 61–64; wages 130; Wilmington & Weldon Railroad 2, 6, 106–107, 109, 148–149, 167; *see also* Great Fire of 1843; Halifax & Weldon Rail Road; iron
Wilmington, Charlotte & Rutherford Railroad 25, 27
Wilmington, Columbia & Augusta Railroad 177, 182, 188
Wilmington Railroad Museum 186–187; Koenig, Mark 186–187
Winchester & Potomac Railroad Company 17, 92
Winston, P.H. 35
Winston-Salem, N.C. 26
Wyche, James 28, 37

Yadkin Navigation Company 22
Yadkin River 8, 25, 29, 31, 37, 41, 51, 110; Flat swamp Creek 37; Narrow of the Yadkin 29, 35–37, 94; valley 26
yellow fever 69

www.ingramcontent.com/pod-product-compliance
Ingram Content Group UK Ltd.
Pitfield, Milton Keynes, MK11 3LW, UK
UKHW041950140426
5217IPUK00014B/733